LEARN to LISTEN
LISTEN to LEARN

Academic Listening and Note-Taking

Second Edition

Teacher's Manual

Roni S. Lebauer

Learn to Listen; Listen to Learn
Second Edition
Teacher's Manual

Copyright © 2001, 1991 by Prentice Hall Regents.
Addison Wesley Longman, Inc.
A Pearson Education Company.
All rights reserved.
No part of this publication may be reproduced,
stored in a retrieval system, or transmitted
in any form or by any means, electronic, mechanical,
photocopying, recording, or otherwise,
without the prior permission of the publisher.

Pearson Education, 10 Bank Street, White Plains, NY 10606

Vice president, director of publishing: Allen Ascher
Editorial director: Louisa B. Hellegers
Vice president, director of design and production: Rhea Banker
Development editor: Lise Minovitz
Executive managing editor: Linda Moser
Production manager: Ray Keating
Production editor: Noël Vreeland Carter
Director of manufacturing: Patrice Fraccio
Manufacturing manager: Edith Pullman
Cover design: Carey Davies
Interior design: F. C. Pusterla
Text composition: Rainbow Graphics
Credits: See page vii.

ISBN: 0-13-919440-1

8 9 10 - OPM - 07

CONTENTS

Introduction v

Text Credits vii

Unit 1   Pre-Coursework Evaluation 1

Unit 2   Looking at Lecture Transcripts 6

Unit 3   Note-Taking Basics 7

Unit 4   Noting Numbers and Statistics 11

Unit 5   Listening for Organization in Lectures 22

Unit 6   Lecture Comprehension and Note-Taking Practice 35

Unit 7   Post-Coursework Evaluation 87

INTRODUCTION

The materials in this manual are offered so that you, the teacher, can adapt this text to your needs. Included are teaching suggestions, lecture presentation options, lecture outlines, lecture and exercise audioscripts, and answers to exercises.

Lecture Presentation
One of the key features of *Learn to Listen; Listen to Learn, 2nd edition* is that it allows teachers the option of delivering lectures live, using prerecorded lectures from the companion audioprogram, or both. Teachers who choose to deliver lectures live can use the lecture outlines, which provide the core information of the lecture. It is up to the teacher, as the lecturer, to paraphrase, summarize, repeat, go off on tangents, etc. in order to create a realistic-sounding lecture. Lecture outlines are included in this manual. Audioscripts of the lectures from the audioprogram are also included. (In order to best express the natural speech pattern of the lecturer, these scripts use ellipses to indicate pauses.) Please note, however, that these tapescripts should not be read aloud to the class, as this would create very artificial, awkward lectures. Rather, these audioscripts are included as a resource.

Activities for Vocabulary Development
In *Learn to Listen; Listen to Learn, 2nd edition,* there are numerous opportunities for vocabulary development. This is particularly so in Units 6 and 7, which focus on lecture comprehension and note-taking practice. Each lecture in these units has a section on Vocabulary Related to the Topic. During the Pre-Lecture Discussions, the teacher can present relevant vocabulary in context as needed by paraphrasing students' ideas. Exercises in Defining Vocabulary, Using Vocabulary, and Retaining Vocabulary provide additional practice. Defining Vocabulary exercises typically require students to listen to words in context and guess their meanings. Audioscripts for these exercises are included in this manual. Teachers, of course, are encouraged to paraphrase or add information, as they deem necessary. In addition, teachers are encouraged to ask students to try to recall how each word was used in the lecture. Using Vocabulary exercises provide further practice in recognizing and using relevant vocabulary by intertwining vocabulary development and listening comprehension. Finally, in Retaining Vocabulary exercises, students select five to ten words from the lecture that they want to focus on (since in most lectures, more vocabulary is presented than can be retained and some specialized vocabulary need not be retained by all students). This selection process allows students to choose the words that have the most meaning for them and take the initiative to learn them. The success of this activity depends on the teacher's encouragement and use of this selection process. For example, teachers might give quizzes in which students are only held responsible for the words they have chosen.

Multiskill Development through Topic Exploration and Discussion
Though this book focuses on listening and note-taking, during the process of learning and practicing these skills, students can improve their speaking and reading skills through Pre-Lecture Discussions. Many of these sections involve reading, critiquing, and responding to related newspaper, magazine, and journal articles. In addition, each unit ends with a Speaking and Listening or Writing Activity related to the lecture.

Feedback on Notes
The Note-Taking Feedback Form on pages 5–6 of the textbook lists common teacher comments. You may want to use this form (or an adaptation) when evaluating your students' notes. For detailed information about what criteria to look for when evaluating notes, see Eight DOs and DON'Ts for Improving Lecture Comprehension and Note-Taking on pages 10–11 of this manual. Examples of good and poor student notes are also in this section.

TEXT CREDITS

Unit 2, Lecture 2: J. Greenberg, "Mental Health of Working Women," *Science News*, 117 (April 26, 1980), p. 266. **Unit 4, Lecture 3:** Christopher Caggiano, "What Do Workers Want?" *Inc.* (November 1992), pp. 101–102. **Unit 4, Lecture 4:** *American Heritage Dictionary Second College Edition*, Houghton Mifflin Company, Boston, MA, 1982; *The Universal Almanac, 1997*, John W. Wright (Ed.), Andrews and McMeel, A Universal Press Syndicate Co., Kansas City, MO, 1996, pp. 591–593. **Unit 5:** Ellen Broidy, UC Irvine Research Librarian; Andrew Harper, "Academic Listening Comprehension: Does the Sum of the Parts Make Up the Whole?" Occasional Paper #7. Dept. of ESL. University of Hawaii at Manoa (1985); Michael Rost "On-line Summaries as Representations of Lecture Understanding" (1994), in John Flowerdew (Ed.) *Academic Listening: Research Perspectives*, Cambridge University Press, Cambridge, England: pp. 93–127. **Unit 6, Lecture 6:** Tom Greening and Dick Hobson, *Instant Relief: The Encyclopedia of Self-Help*, Simon and Schuster Pub., New York, 1979, pp. 329–352. **Unit 6, Lecture 7:** E. J. Kormandy, *Concepts of Ecology, 3rd Ed.*, Prentice Hall Inc., Englewood Cliffs, NJ, 1984, pp. 274–277; Bernard J. Nebel and Richard T. Wright, *The Way the World Works: Environmental Science, 5th ed.*, Prentice Hall Inc., Upper Saddle River, NJ, 1996, pp. 382–385; 400–408. **Unit 6, Lecture 8:** Dina Ingber, "New Tools Unearth the Past," *Science Digest* (Nov.–Dec. 1980), pp. 99–101. **Unit 6, Lecture 10:** H. H. Shorey, *Animal Communication by Pheromones*, Academic Press, New York, NY, 1976. **Unit 6, Lecture 11:** Susan Carpenter, "Gearing Up for the New Race to Space," *Los Angeles Times* (June 23, 1998), pp. E1, E5; K. C. Cole, "Water Possibly Found on Moon," *Los Angeles Times* (March 6, 1998), pp. A1, A18; Robert T. Dixon, *Dynamic Astronomy*, Prentice Hall Inc., Englewood Cliffs, NJ, 1984, pp. 151–160. **Unit 6, Lecture 12:** Suzanne Hamlin, "Science May Help Green Tea Get Steeped in U.S. Culture," *The OC Register* (June 30, 1994), p. 9; "Can Green Tea Help Prevent Cancer?" *University of California at Berkeley Wellness Letter*, 14:3 (Dec. 1997), pp. 1–2. **Unit 6, Lecture 13:** James MacGregor Burns, J.W. Peltason, and Thomas E. Cronin, *Government by the People, 12th alt. ed.*, Prentice Hall Inc., Englewood Cliffs, NJ, 1985, pp. 195–199. **Unit 6, Lecture 14:** Philip Yenawine, *How to Look at Modern Art*, Harry N. Abrams Inc. Pub., New York, 1991, pp. 143–144. **Unit 6, Lecture 15:** David R. Olmos, "Is There a Robot in the House?" *Los Angeles Times* (July 14, 1997), p. D1. **Unit 6, Lecture 16:** Frederick K. Lutgens and Edward J. Tarbuck, *Foundations of Earth Science*, Prentice Hall, Upper Saddle River, NJ, 1996; Terry R. West, *Geology Applied to Engineering*, Prentice Hall, NJ, 1994. **Unit 6, Lecture 17:** Elizabeth Hall, "How Cultures Collide," *Psychology Today* (July 1976), pp. 66–74. **Unit 7, Lecture 18:** Judith Crosher, *Ancient Egypt*, Penguin Group, New York, 1993; Anne Millard, *Pyramids*. Larousse Kingfisher Chambers Inc., New York, 1996. **Unit 7, Lecture 19:** David Bruns, "The Perfectionist's Script for Self-defeat," *Psychology Today* (November 1980), pp. 34–52.

UNIT 1 PRE-COURSEWORK EVALUATION

Unit Summary: In this unit, teachers evaluate students' listening comprehension and note-taking abilities at the beginning of the course. In addition, students reflect on their own strengths and weaknesses as listeners and note-takers. The lecture content in the unit provides information about the linguistic and paralinguistic challenges of listening and note-taking.

Lecture 1: The Process of Lecture Comprehension

Lecture Outline: Part 1, page 2
Use this outline if you'd like to deliver the lecture yourself.

INTRODUCTION: At the university, students are called on to perform many types of listening tasks: listening in a group discussion, listening to a teacher on a one-on-one basis, listening to recordings or films, listening to academic lectures. For many students, listening to an academic lecture is one of the hardest listening tasks. For this reason, what I will talk about today is how listening to academic lectures differs from other types of listening situations. Later on, I'll talk about what a listener needs to be able to do in order to comprehend an academic lecture efficiently.

  I. How does listening to an academic lecture differ from listening in other situations?
   A. Language may be different from language used in everyday listening situations.
      1. It may be more formal, although not necessarily.
         a. e.g., "on the contrary," "nevertheless," instead of "but"
      2. It may have more subject-specific vocabulary (jargon).
   B. Interaction between speaker and listener in an academic lecture situation is different from interaction in everyday listening situations.
      1. The communication is completely unidirectional (information is transferred in one direction only), whereas in everyday listening situations, the participants take turns or, at minimum, one participant indicates comprehension and encourages the other to continue.
      2. The listeners in an academic lecture situation have no control over the direction of the lecture, whereas the listener in an everyday situation can ask for clarification or repetition.
      3. The speaker in an academic lecture situation gets little feedback from the audience, whereas the speaker in an everyday situation can see if a listener looks puzzled or wants to ask a question.
         a. In an academic lecture situation, a speaker might get some feedback from drooping heads, people leaving, etc., but this is very different from the subtle feedback a speaker might get face-to-face with a listener.
      4. The speaker in an academic lecture situation often "holds the floor" (takes his/her turn) for a long time (fifteen minutes to, perhaps, two hours), whereas in an everyday situation, the participants either take turns or the speaker provides openings for the listener to speak.
   C. Expectations in an academic lecture situation are different from expectations in everyday listening situations.
      1. In an academic lecture situation, the listeners are often expected to take notes, whereas in an everyday situation, this would be inappropriate.
      2. In an academic lecture situation, the listeners need to retain information for later use, whereas in an everyday situation, an immediate response is more necessary.

CONCLUSION: As you can see, listening to a lecture is quite different from listening for everyday purposes. Later I'll talk about what a listener needs to do in order to comprehend a lecture efficiently.

Lecture Audioscript: Part 1, page 2
This audioscript shows one speaker's delivery of the lecture, as recorded in the audio program. Use it as a resource.

OK . . . what I'm going to talk about is a very relevant subject probably to many of you . . . and that is listening to lectures . . . listening to academic lectures . . . and for many students listening to lectures is one of the hardest listening skills . . . much harder than your everyday conversational skills . . . and that's for many reasons . . . so . . . what I'm going to look at in this lecture . . . are the ways that listening to a lecture differ . . . from listening in other types of situations . . . everyday conversations, for instance, and then later . . . in the second part of this lecture . . . talk about what listeners need to do when they listen to lectures . . . and take notes . . .

OK . . . so first . . . how does listening to a lecture differ from listening in other situations? . . . now let's think about it . . . first of all the language , , , you know that the language is sometimes very different in a lecture . . . as compared to . . . for instance, talking to friends . . . talking to people on the street . . . there's an academic language that we may use . . . OK? . . . we may use words like "on the contrary" . . . "nevertheless" instead of simpler words like "but" . . . now this is not to say that lecturers never use the word "but" . . . but some lecturers may use a more formal level of the language . . . also in lectures . . . one would expect to hear more subject specific language . . . or jargon . . . of a field . . . words that would rarely be found in everyday conversation . . . but are necessary to talk about a discipline . . . so language is one thing that differs between lectures and everyday listening . . .

another thing that's different between the lecture situation and the everyday situation is the *interaction* between the speaker and the listener . . . for example in a lecture situation . . . the interaction is all unidirectional . . . meaning that it goes in one direction . . . all the interaction goes from the lecturer to the listener . . . the listener has very little role to play . . . maybe the listener nods his or her head but really there's no interaction between the two . . . in an everyday situation . . . the participants take turns . . . or at least one participant indicates comprehension . . . and the other . . . continues . . . it goes in two directions . . . bidirectional interaction . . . OK . . . also in a lecture the listener has no control . . . whereas in everyday speaking situations if you don't understand you can ask the speaker to repeat . . . but in a lecture . . . a listener can't say "repeat things" . . . they can't say "I don't understand" . . . the listener has no control in a lecture situation . . . and finally in a lecture situation the speaker often talks continuously for a long, long time whereas in an everyday situation . . . usually there are breaks . . . people take turns . . . or people react . . . OK? . . .

now the last difference between a lecture situation and the everyday listening situation is the expectation . . . now in a lecture situation you are expected to keep the information for later use . . . maybe take notes . . . you're supposed to remember what you hear . . . in an everyday listening situation you need to react right at that moment . . . you don't need to take notes . . . you don't need to think about it later . . . you need to react right then . . . so in a lecture you need to write down things so you can remember them for later use . . . in an everyday situation you need to react . . . right at the moment . . . so as you can see listening to a lecture is quite different from listening in an everyday situation for everyday purposes . . . now uh . . . I uh I'll stop here and later I'll talk about what a listener needs to do in order to comprehend a lecture efficiently.

Possible Answers, Part 2, page 2

	Lecture	Everyday Language
Language	—may be more formal, but not necessarily so —may use subject-specific vocab.	—more informal

Interaction	—unidirectional
	—listeners—no control
	—speaker—no feedback
	—speaker "holds the floor" continuously
		—two-way communication
		—listener has some control
		  e.g., can ask for repetition, clarification
		—speaker can see or hear if listener confused
		—speakers take turns or give others
		  opportunity to speak

Expectations	—take notes; retain info. for later use	—must respond immediately

Lecture Outline: Part 2, page 3
Use this outline if you'd like to deliver the lecture yourself.

INTRODUCTION: Previously, I talked about how listening to a lecture differed from listening in an everyday situation. However, the important thing for you is not necessarily to learn how they differ but rather to learn how to listen to a lecture efficiently.

I. What does a listener need to do in order to comprehend a lecture efficiently? There are four tasks.
    A. Task no. 1: The listener must be aware of all of the carriers of meaning.
        1. Words, obviously, carry meaning.
        2. Other features carry meaning.
            a. Stress: "**I** went to the bar." (no special stress) vs. "**I** went to the bar." (not someone else)
            b. Intonation: "He came." vs. "He came?" (One is a statement; one is a question.)
            c. Rhythm: "Can you **see**, Karen?" vs. "Can you see **Karen**?" (One means that I am asking Karen if she can use her eyes to see; the other means that I am asking someone if he/she can see a person named Karen.)
            d. Body language: "the first thing" (pointing one finger)

    B. Task no. 2: The listener must be able to add information that the lecturer expects the audience to add.
        1. Listeners are not tape recorders; they do not take the lecturer's words and retain them word for word.

2. Rather, they "reinterpret" the words they hear, and one of the ways they do this is by adding information.
    a. Their ability to add information stems from two sources: knowledge of subject matter and world experience.
        (1) Example of using subject-matter knowledge: If a speaker says "The temperature in the region never falls below 32 degrees Fahrenheit, so the residents do not have to worry about protecting their pipes," the speaker is assuming that his/her audience has the knowledge that water freezes at 32 degrees Fahrenheit and that water freezing in pipes can damage the pipes. The listener must add this information in order to make sense of the lecturer's statement.
        (2) Example of using world knowledge: If a speaker says "John and Jane were ready to walk down the aisle, but then they realized that they didn't have the ring," Americans listening to this would be able to add the nonspoken information—based on their cultural knowledge—that this takes place at a wedding ("walk down the aisle") and that the reason they are nervous is that a wedding ring is often an essential part of the ceremony. Without adding this information, the lecturer's statement would make little sense.
3. Listening is not a matter of absorbing the speaker's words, word for word; it would be impossible to remember. Rather, listening involves listening to the speaker's words and reinterpreting them. ("The meaning is not in the word; it is in the person who uses it or responds to it.")

C. Task no. 3: The listener needs to predict appropriately while listening.
  1. Reason no. 1: Prediction helps overcome "noise." Noise (which includes anything that interferes with hearing—mechanical failure, language unclearness, outside noise, inattentiveness, etc.) often makes words and ideas unclear.
  2. Reason no. 2: Prediction helps save time for processing information and taking notes.
  3. There are two types of predictions: predictions of content and predictions of organization.
      a. Example of predicting content: If you hear "Because he loves to cook, his favorite room is the . . .", you might guess that the next word would be "kitchen." You can make this guess because of your world knowledge that one cooks in a kitchen. You might also guess this because your knowledge of English tells you that after the word "the," you can expect a noun or noun phrase.
      b. Examples of predicting organization: If someone is going to tell a story, we expect them to begin with some sort of setting for the story. If someone gives some examples, we expect them to make some generalization to tie the examples together.

D. Task no. 4: The listener must constantly evaluate while listening (that is, decide how important or unimportant something is or how it relates to another idea).
  1. Reason no. 1: Evaluating helps the listener figure out what to note because he/she cannot note everything.
  2. Reason no. 2: Evaluating helps the listener retain information.
      a. More information is retained when information is related to other pieces of information or known information. By evaluating incoming information, listeners figure out the interrelationship between pieces of information.
      b. Isolated and unrelated information is less likely to be retained.

CONCLUSION: Clearly, a lot is involved in listening to a lecture. Notice that I primarily talked about what all people do when they listen to lectures (native speakers and nonnative speakers). Based on what you have heard in this lecture, I will leave it to you to imagine and discuss what problems would particularly affect nonnative speakers and why they would have these problems.

Lecture Audioscript: Part 2, page 3
This audioscript shows one speaker's delivery of the lecture, as recorded in the audio program. Use it as a resource.

OK . . . what do you need to do in order to understand the lecture? . . . and that's probably the important question for you . . . now there are four things that I'm going to talk about . . . the first thing is that you need to be aware of all of the parts of the language that carry meaning . . . now you all know that words carry meaning . . . so words are obvious . . . you've got to be aware of the vocabulary of the language . . . the words . . . but there are other features of the language that you need to be aware of . . . for one thing you need to be aware of stress . . . OK? I'll give you an example . . . "I went to the bar" . . . "I went to the bar" . . . it makes a difference . . . in the second example . . . I'm stressing the fact that it was me and not someone else . . . "I went to the bar" . . . so that this means stress has some meaning . . . now the next thing that you might want to listen for is intonation . . . so for example if I say "He came." . . . "He came?" . . . there are two different meanings . . . one is a statement . . . the other one is a question . . . and another thing you need to listen for is rhythm . . . for example "Can you see, Karen?" versus "Can you see Karen?" da da Da da da . . . da da da DA da . . . those two mean something different "Can you see, Karen?" "Can you see Karen?" one says "can you see?" and they're talking directly to Karen . . . the other one says "Can you see Karen . . . over there?" . . . OK . . . so rhythm has something to do with understanding . . . and finally body language . . . if you watch me speak . . . sometimes you can see what I'm doing . . . I'll say "the first thing" and point a finger . . . "on the other hand" . . . and change my body position . . . so I use my body . . . to give you meaning . . . or emphasize my meaning . . . so when you listen you need to understand all the carriers of meaning . . . in language . . .

OK . . . the next thing you must do when you listen is when you listen you need to add information that the lecturer expects you to add . . . all lecturers assume that they share some information with their audience and that their audience does not need them to spell out every word . . . and listeners have an ability to add this information due to two sources of information . . . their knowledge of a particular subject and their knowledge or experience of the world . . . so for example . . . let's take an example which requires subject-matter knowledge . . . if you heard a speaker say "The temperature in the region never falls below 32 degrees Fahrenheit so the residents don't have to worry about protecting their pipes" . . . the lecturer is assuming that you . . . the listener . . . can add the information that water freezes below 32 degrees Fahrenheit . . . and this could be dangerous to pipes . . . the lecturer does not need to say all this because he or she assumes that the audience can add this information based on its basic knowledge of the subject matter . . . now here's another example . . . this time requiring adding information based on world experience . . . that is, knowledge of the world . . . if I say something like . . . "John and Jane were ready to walk down the aisle but then they realized that they didn't have the ring" . . . if Americans heard that . . . they'd probably automatically assume that it was a wedding . . . because they think of walking down the aisle . . . and exchanging rings . . . as essential parts of the American wedding ceremony . . . but if you didn't know that that was the culture . . . you'd have a harder time understanding my sentence . . . because you didn't add the needed information . . . the information that I . . . as the speaker . . . expected you to be able to add . . . OK so remember . . . listening is not a matter of just absorbing the speaker's words . . . the listener has to do more than that . . . the listener is not a tape recorder . . . absorbing the speaker's words and putting them into his or her brain . . . rather listening involves hearing the speaker's words and reinterpreting them . . . adding information if necessary . . . so the meaning is not in the word alone . . . rather it is in the person who uses it or responds to it . . . so that's the second thing that a listener must do . . . add information that the lecturer assumes that they share . . .

OK the third thing that a listener needs to do . . . and this is to me the most important thing of all . . . and that's to predict as you listen . . . now let me um let me give you two reasons why you have to predict . . . for one thing . . . if you predict it helps you overcome noise . . . what do I mean by noise? . . . maybe there's noise outside and you can't hear me . . . maybe you're in the back of the room and you can't hear all that well . . . maybe someone's talking next to you . . . maybe the microphone doesn't work . . . maybe there's noise inside your head . . . by that I mean maybe you're thinking of something else . . . and then all of a sudden . . . you'll remember . . . oh! . . . I've got to listen! . . . by being able to predict during the lecture . . . you can just keep listening to the lecture and not lose the idea of what's going on . . . so predicting is important to help you overcome outside noise and inside noise . . . OK? . . . and another reason that predicting is important is because it saves you time . . . now when you listen you need time to . . . think about the information . . . relate it to old ideas . . . take notes . . . and if you're only keeping up with what I'm saying or what the lecturer's saying . . . you have no time to do that . . . and I'll bet a lot of you are having that problem right now because it's so hard just to follow everything I'm saying . . . that you don't have time to note down ideas . . . so predicting saves you time . . . if you can guess what I'm going to say . . . you're able to take notes . . . you're able to think . . . you have more time . . . OK? . . . and there are two types of predictions that you can make . . . predictions of *content* and predictions of *organization* . . . let me give you an example . . . in terms of content . . . if you hear the words "because he loved to cook . . . his favorite room was the . . ." . . . what would you expect? anyone? . . . "kitchen . . ." you can guess this because you know people cook in the kitchen . . . also you can guess this because you know that after the word "the" you expect a noun phrase . . . so you can predict words . . . content . . . OK? . . . and you can also predict organization . . . so if I gave you some examples . . . you'd probably expect me to tie the examples together . . . make a generalization to tie the examples together . . . if I was going to tell you a story . . . you'd expect me to tell you why the story is important . . . give you a setting for the story . . . so you have expectations of what the speaker is going to talk about . . . and how the speaker will organize his or her words . . .

now the last thing that a listener must do . . . the listener must evaluate . . . as he or she is listening . . . decide what's important . . . what's not . . . decide how something relates to something else . . . OK? . . . and there are again two reasons for this . . . the first one is evaluating helps you to decide what to take notes about . . . you can't . . . again . . . you're, you're not a tape recorder . . . so you can't get down every word . . . if you evaluate . . . you think . . . what's important to write down? . . . what's not important to write down? . . . and the second reason is that evaluating helps you to retain . . . or keep . . . information . . . OK? . . . and studies have shown that we retain more information . . . if ideas are connected to one another . . . rather than just individually remembered . . . so for example if I give you five ideas that are not related to one another . . . that's much more difficult to remember than five ideas that are related . . . right? . . . so evaluating helps you remember information better because it connects ideas . . . to one another . . .

clearly there's a lot involved in listening to lectures . . . and notice that I primarily talked about what all people do . . . when they listen to lectures . . . this was not just for nonnative speakers . . . this was for native speakers and nonnative speakers . . . and what I'd like you to do is think about or imagine what problems would particularly affect nonnative speakers . . . why would a nonnative speaker have more problems than native speakers . . . based on some of the things that we've talked about?

Example Notes, Part 2, page 3
The following is an example of student notes for Lecture 1, Part 2.

What does listener need to do to comprehend efficiently?

    A. must be aware of all carriers of meaning—words, stress, intonation, rhythm, body lang.

    B. must add information that lecturer expects
        —impossible to be tape recorder
        —2 sources for adding info.
            —knowledge of subject matter
            —knowledge of world
        —listening involves "reinterpreting" lecturer's words

    C. must predict while listening
        Why?
            —to overcome "noise" (external & internal) which makes listener miss words or ideas
            —to gain time to process info. & take notes
        2 types of prediction:
            —predict content
            —predict organization

    D. must evaluate while listening—decide how ideas relate and what is important/not imp.
        Why?
            —to figure out what to note
            —to relate ideas to one another & make it easier to remember
                —isolated info. harder to retain

This is for all listeners—native/nonnative

Answers, Part 2, page 3

1. be aware of all the carriers of meaning; add information that the lecturer expects; predict; evaluate   **2.** stress, intonation, rhythm, body language   **3.** it helps the listener overcome noise (internal and external); it saves time that can be better used processing information and taking notes   **4.** predictions about content; predictions about orga-nization   **5.** subject-matter knowledge; world knowledge   **6.** it helps them decide what to note; it helps them retain information (because related information is easier to remember than isolated information).

Post-Lecture Discussion, page 4
    Answers:

1. Answers will vary. This question can begin a discussion about the problems (which go beyond language) that nonnative speakers might have when listening to lectures. Some possible answers include: **a.** Native speakers are less aware of all the carriers of meaning, even if they understand the vocabulary (e.g., stress, intonation, body language).   **b.** Intonation and body language may mean different things in different languages and cultures and may therefore lead nonnative speakers in the wrong direction.   **c.** It may be harder for nonnative speakers to add information that the lecturer expects the audience to have. Nonnative speakers do not always share the same world knowledge with the lecturer. The lecturer may take it for granted that the audience knows something (e.g., what happens at a wedding in the United States), but students from different cultures may have different concepts of the same event.   **d.** Nonnative speakers may have a harder time predicting. For one thing, they may have different expectations about the organization of lectures. Also, they may not be as aware of the cues that help listeners predict.   **2.** Answers will vary.

Dictation of Numbers, Audioscript, page 4
Students will listen to the statements and write the numbers they hear. Read or play each item only once.

    1. Michelangelo, the artist, was born in 1475.
    2. Georgia O'Keeffe, the artist, was born in 1887 and died in 1986.
    3. A cup of raisins has 580 calories.
    4. One slice of white bread has 70 calories.
    5. The zipper was invented in 1891.
    6. The piano was invented in 1709.
    7. The microscope was invented in 1590.
    8. The Missouri River is 2,533 miles long. That's 2,533 miles long.
    9. The earth's diameter is 7,920 miles. 7,920 miles.
    10. Mount Everest is 29,028 feet high. Again, 29,028 feet high.
    11. The Sahara Desert is 3,500,000 square miles.

12. The earth is 93 million miles away from the sun.
13. Pluto, the planet farthest from the sun, is 3 billion, 670 million miles away from the sun. Amazing! 3 billion, 670 million miles away.
14. Tokyo is projected to have 28,700,000 people in the year 2015.
15. One pound equals 453.59 grams. One pound equals 453.59 grams.
16. An earthquake occurred in Iran on June 20, 1990.
17. This earthquake measured 7.7 on the Richter scale and caused more than 50,000 deaths and more than 60,000 injuries.
18. The length of the board was 4⅜ feet; the width was 5½ inches and the depth was ⅛ inch.

Note-Taking Feedback Form, pages 5–6
For detailed information about what criteria to look for when evaluating notes, see Eight DOs and DON'Ts for Improving Lecture Comprehension and Note-Taking on pages 10–11 of this manual.

UNIT 2 LOOKING AT LECTURE TRANSCRIPTS

Unit Summary: Unit 2 provides information and exercises that increase students' awareness of how lectures are formatted and that enable them to better predict lecture content and organizational direction while listening. Transcripts of actual lectures are used to demonstrate discourse features that are unique to lectures.

Unit 2 allows students to talk about and learn some basics about lecture discourse. It is not meant to be an in-depth analysis of lecture discourse. Rather, this unit should provide students with an overview and general understanding about some basic concepts regarding the language of lectures. Basically, the student should understand the following:

- There is much repetition and paraphrase in lectures. This repetition and paraphrase allows the listener time to absorb ideas and take notes. In addition, it may serve to emphasize important ideas.

- Speakers use cues to let the listener know what is happening and what will happen in the lecture. Specific cues introduce a topic, the organization that follows, or a conclusion. These cues can help students predict, plan, or get back into a lecture if they get lost.

Much of Unit 2 can be assigned for homework and then compared and discussed in class. The goal of this unit is discussion and increased awareness; therefore, different answers are acceptable as long as students are able to explain their choices.

Avoid spending too much time on this unit, since it is just an introduction. (See example syllabi on pages viii–x of the textbook for suggested time allotments.)

Exercise, page 8
Possible Answers:

Lecture Excerpt	Magazine Paragraph
There are more words.	There are fewer words.
The sentences seem to go on and on.	There are clear beginnings and endings to sentences.
The speaker uses words like "all right" and "hmmmm."	Words like "all right" and "hmmmm" aren't used.
There is more repetition.	The ideas are presented more succinctly.
There's no punctuation.	There is punctuation.
The speaker sometimes goes off the topic.	The speaker stays on the topic.
It seems more informal.	It seems more formal.

Exercise, pages 14–15
Possible Answers:

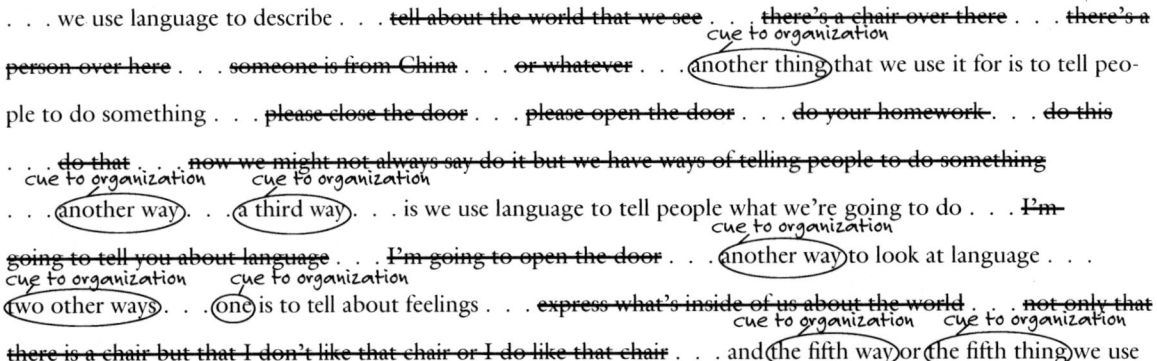

is to change the world . . . ~~certain things that you say change the world~~ . . . ~~if I say you fail this course~~ . . . ~~that language changes the world~~ . . . ~~just my four words make you unhappy and hate me~~ . . . ~~something has changed because of my words and nothing else except those words~~ . . . (so) we can change the world with language . . .
cue to conclusion
(now) since we have (all these different purposes) and you probably can think of other purposes with which we want to
cue to conclusion   *cue to conclusion*
use language to win or accomplish what we want inside . . . (so) it's kind of like a game that way.
cue to conclusion

Exercise, pages 16–18
This is a good group activity.

Answers, page 18:
1. The "players" change.   2. You're out to win something.   3. Everybody has his or her own style.   4. You can change your style.   5. There are rules.

Exercise, pages 18–20
This is a discussion activity. Have students cover each unit of the lecture until they are ready to read it. After each unit, allow a few minutes to discuss what content might come next and what organization students expect. Have students explain their reasons for their predictions. Rather than correcting students, allow students to confirm or refute their hypotheses by themselves when reading the next unit. Discuss why certain hypotheses were unlikely expectations. Make sure students realize that guessing does not have to be correct, but should be a likely choice.

UNIT 3   NOTE-TAKING BASICS

Unit Summary: Unit 3 introduces and provides practice exercises for the basics of note-taking: choosing key words to note, judging the relative importance of information, and visually representing the relationship between pieces of information. The unit ends with eight "DOs and DON'Ts" for successful note-taking.

Exercise, page 23
Have three students take notes at the board while others take notes from their seats. After each exercise, discuss and compare the different note-taking examples on the board. In particular, point out where symbols and note-taking conventions are especially useful and point out which words are essential and which are not. After three or four exercises, invite another group of three to the board. Read or play each excerpt once for listening and a second time for note-taking. Use your judgment as to the need to read or replay the excerpt additional times.

Audioscript, page 23

1. I'd like to tell you about a famous American painter . . . named Georgia O'Keeffe. That's O-apostrophe-K-E-E-F-F-E . . . Georgia O'Keeffe . . . now Ms. O'Keeffe is one of the major artists of the 20th century.
2. Do you know where the Sahara Desert is? . . . Well . . . the Sahara Desert, that's S-A-H-A-R-A . . . the Sahara Desert is located in North Africa . . . and it extends for approximately 3½ million square miles . . . quite big . . . very big!
3. Each day we see more and more people using computers . . . at work . . . at home . . . on planes . . . in the U.S., in 1993, there were about 300 computers for every 1,000 people . . . 300 computers for every 1,000 people. I'd be curious what the statistics are now. Does anyone know?
4. Are people smoking less? more? what do you think? Actually, on the average, worldwide, smoking is increasing at a rate of 2% per year . . . and this is mostly because of increases in developing countries . . . where people are smoking more now than they did in the past.
5. Smoking rates in the U.S. . . . on the other hand . . . have gone down. Fewer people are smoking each year. Why is this? There are many reasons . . . but public education about the dangers of smoking is clearly one of the important ones . . . I'm sure you can think of other reasons.
6. I'm going to talk about earthquakes. Have you ever experienced one? Even if you haven't, you've all certainly seen the effects through news reports on TV . . . now the, the strength of an earthquake is measured by a scale called the Richter scale . . . that's R-I-C-H-T-E-R . . . and the Richter scale is a scale that measures a quake's strength by assigning it a number . . . a 1 or 2 on the Richter scale shows an earthquake that is hardly noticeable . . . it's usually not felt by people.
7. Television . . . TV . . . how much do you watch? Do you think it's too much? Do you wish you had time to watch more? In 1994, a study showed that the television was on . . . in the average American house . . . more than six hours a day . . . that's quite a bit . . . more than six hours a day!
8. I'm going to talk a little bit about the planets in our solar system . . . let me start with Mercury . . . now as you may know . . . Mercury is the nearest planet to the sun . . . now something that you may not know is that it is also the second-smallest of the nine planets known to be orbiting the sun.
9. One of the most exciting events of the 20th century was the day man first walked on the moon. That first

moonwalk took place in 1969 . . . July 1969 to be exact . . . and many of you were not even born yet . . . but anyway . . . the astronaut was Neil Armstrong . . . Armstrong? . . . A-R-M-S-T-R-O-N-G . . . How much time do you think Mr. Armstrong spent outside of the spacecraft . . . time actually spent on the moon? . . . two minutes and thirty-two seconds . . . but those two minutes and thirty-two seconds surely changed our world.

10. There is a species of whale called the blue whale. Has anyone seen a picture of it? It's a huge animal . . . one of the biggest in the world . . . Well, this blue whale once had a population of approximately 210,000 . . . but now, there are only estimated to be about 11,000 blue whales in the whole world . . . a drastic reduction . . . generally this reduction is due to hunting . . . uncontrolled hunting.

Example Notes, page 23

1. Georgia O'Keeffe—one of major artists 20th c.
2. Sahara Desert—N. Africa—3,500,000 sq. mi.
3. U.S. 1993: 300 computers/1,000 people
   Now: ?
4. Smoking worldwide ↑ 2%/yr.
   Why? ↑ in developing countries
5. Smoking U.S.: ↓
   Why? public ed. about danger
6. Richter scale—measures earthquake strength w/ #
   e.g., 1 or 2—not felt
7. 1994—study—TV on in average U.S. household: 6+ hrs./day
8. Mercury—nearest planet to sun
   2nd-smallest of 9 planets
9. First moonwalk—July 1969—astronaut Neil Armstrong:
   2 min. 32 sec. time on moon
10. Blue whale
    ← pop. 210,000
    now ↓ ~11,000
    ∴ hunting

Exercise, pages 25–26

Have three students take notes at the chalkboard while others take notes from their seats. After each exercise, discuss and compare the different note-taking samples on the board. In particular, point out where symbols and note-taking conventions are especially useful and point out which words are essential and which are not. Point out how different people arranged information (e.g., indentation) to show how ideas are related. After three or four exercises, invite another group of three to the board. Read or play each excerpt once for listening and a second time for note-taking. Use your own judgment as to the need for rereading or replaying the excerpt additional times.

Exercise Audioscript, pages 25–26

1. I want to tell you about the official languages in the country Switzerland . . . Switzerland has four official languages and those are German . . . French . . . Italian . . . and a language called Romansch . . . let me spell that for you . . . R-O-M-A-N-S-C-H . . . now German is spoken by the majority of the total population . . . by about 65% . . . French by 18% . . . Italian by 12% . . . and Romansch is the lowest . . . or the least frequently spoken . . . and that's spoken by only about 1%.
2. Nowadays, many women take the right to vote for granted. But actually . . . it is only slightly more than a century since women first got the right to vote . . . speaking globally . . . the first country where this happened . . . the first country which gave women the right to vote was New Zealand . . . in 1893 . . . Australia was next when women got the right to vote there in 1901 . . . in the U.S. women, by the way, did not get the right to vote until 1920 . . . 1920.
3. The average American household size has gone down considerably over the years . . . in 1970, there were 3.14 people in every household . . . in 1980 . . . this went all the way down to 2.76 people per household . . . in 1990 . . . this declined even further to 2.63 people per household . . . what could have contributed to this decline? . . . what do you think? well some factors might have been a relatively low birth rate and a low marriage rate . . . a high level of separation and divorce . . . and a great increase in the number of people living alone.
4. I want to tell you . . . I'm going to talk a little bit about astronomy . . . and in particular I want to tell you about the two planets that are closer to the sun than the Earth . . . and those two planets are called Mercury . . . and Venus . . . Mercury orbits the sun . . . that is . . . completes its circuit around the sun in 88 days . . . Venus on the other hand takes longer . . . it takes 225 days.
5. Have you ever heard of the expression in English . . . "once in a blue moon" . . . maybe you heard people say something like "oh . . . I see them once in a blue moon" or "oh . . . I write letters once in a blue moon" . . . it means "rarely" . . . "very infrequently" . . . "I watch TV once in a blue moon" means . . . "I hardly ever watch TV" . . . where do you think this expression came from? What is a blue moon? Well . . . a "blue moon" is actually the term used to describe the second full moon in a particular month

. . . of course this happens very rarely . . . only when the first full moon is right at the beginning of the month . . . only then can there be a second full moon falling right at the end of the month . . . this only occurs on the average every 2.7 years . . . so . . . now not only do you know the expression "once in a blue moon" . . . but you also know where it came from!

6. I want to tell you about Diego Rivera . . . that's Diego, D-I-E-G-O . . . Rivera . . . R-I-V-E-R-A . . . now Diego Rivera is a well-known Mexican painter who painted in the 20th century . . . Rivera . . . was one of the principal artists in the mural art movement in Mexico . . . mural art . . . as you may know . . . is a type of art that involves painting on public buildings and walls . . . in fact . . . if you go to many public buildings in Mexico, you can see wonderful examples of art created during the height of this movement.

7. I'm going to talk a little bit about twins. As many of you might know, there are two types of twins . . . there are identical twins . . . and these twins come from one fertilized egg . . . these are the kind of twins that are hard to tell apart . . . they're always of the same sex . . . and blood type . . . and are genetically the same . . . now the other kind . . . fraternal twins . . . that's F-R-A-T-E-R-N-A-L . . . differ in that they come from two eggs which are fertilized by two sperm at approximately the same time . . . now . . . these twins are genetically not the same . . . and they do not have to be the same sex and they don't have to have the same blood type . . . in fact they may look nothing like each other!

8. The family in American life has not always been the same as it is today . . . prior to the 19th century . . . in the United States . . . the family was self-sufficient and took care of itself . . . work and family life were combined . . . work was done at home . . . but during the 19th century . . . the 1800s . . . there were many changes that occurred and most of these changes occurred because of industrialization . . . the Industrial Revolution . . . at that time the women began devoting themselves to raising children while men went outside of the family to work . . . so the sex roles became much more pronounced . . . the division between outside work and home work became more well-defined.

9. Many of you have been around for elections in this country and you probably know that the two major parties in the U.S. are the Democrats and the Republicans . . . but are you aware of the differences between the parties? . . . who supports the different parties? . . . well generally . . . and of course there are always exceptions . . . the Democrats are generally supported more by lower-income people . . . city dwellers . . . blacks . . . Catholics . . . and Jews . . . and union members . . . and it's generally considered the more liberal party . . . the Republicans on the other hand are generally supported by businesspeople . . . people with higher incomes . . . suburbanites . . . that is people who live in the suburbs of cities . . . farmers with large farms . . . people over 45 . . . and they're considered the more conservative party . . . now of course these are just generalizations.

10. Well what is the difference between these two parties? for one thing . . . and again I'm talking very generally . . . the Democrats and Republicans have very different ideas about the role of government . . . Democrats feel that it is the government's job to make sure that social services are provided and that wealth is . . . somewhat shared . . . and they do this through higher taxes and social programs . . . on the other hand . . . Republicans feel that social services should be provided at state and city levels . . . and that the government should concern itself with national affairs like foreign policy and defense . . . and they should leave state and local affairs to state and local governments . . . one other difference is that Democrats feel that it is the government's job to regulate business . . . and Republicans feel that business should be allowed to function without strict government controls.

11. I'm going to talk about a term called "balance of payments" . . . and the term "balance of payments" means the difference between all payments made to foreign countries and all payments coming in from abroad . . . over a set period of time . . . therefore a favorable balance of payments occurs when more payments are coming in than going out . . . an unfavorable balance of course exists when the opposite is true . . . when more payments are going out than are coming in.

12. Does anyone here know first aid . . . or emergency medicine? OK . . . if you found someone with a burn . . . from a fire for example . . . what would you do? . . . would you know what to do? . . . Well . . . let me tell you . . . doctors say that if the burn is mild . . . so it's not too severe . . . and there's no broken skin . . . what you should do is put the burn into ice water . . . submerge it in ice water . . . now if the burn is severe . . . you should call a doctor . . . and keep the patient quiet and warm . . . until the doctor arrives.

Example Notes, pages 25–26

1. Switzerland—4 official langs.
    1. German—spoken by 65% of total pop.
    2. French—   "   " 18% "   "   "
    3. Italian—   "   " 12% "   "   "
    4. Romansch— "   "   1% "   "   "
2. ♀—right to vote received
    1st: New Zealand—1893
    2nd: Australia—1901
    . . .
    U.S.—1920

3. avg. U.S. household size ↓
    1970—3.14 people
    1980—2.76 ″
    1990—2.63 ″
    Why ↓?
        low birth & marriage rate?
        high level—separation, divorce
        ↑ # people living alone

4. 2 planets closer to sun than Earth
    Mercury: orbits sun 88 days
    Venus: ″ ″ 225 days

5. "once in a blue moon"—means "rarely"
    Where from?
        —blue moon: 2nd full moon in a month
        —occurs every ~2.7 yrs.

6. Diego Rivera—Mex. painter 20th c.
    —one of princ. artists—mural art movement (i.e., painting on public bldg.)

7. twins—2 types
    identical—fr. 1 fertilized egg
        —always same sex
          ″ blood type
          ″ genes
    fraternal—fr. 2 eggs & 2 sperm fert. ~ same time
        —genet. not same
        —not nec same sex/blood

8. family in U.S. diff. before
    prior 19th c.—self-sufficient; work/family combined
    19th c. → change
        Why? industrialization
        ♀ raised children, ♂ worked outside
        sex roles more defined

9. 2 major parties in U.S.

Democrats	Republicans
—supported by lower income	—supported by business
blacks	higher inc.
Catholics	suburbanites
Jews	large farmers
union	age 45+
—considered liberal	—more conservative

    JUST GENERALIZATIONS

10. diff. betw.   Dem.   &   Repub.?
    diff. ideas re: govt.: Govt. job—provide soc.   govt.—involved w/ natl. affairs
                              service   soc. service provided by state
                          —share $
                          ↑ tax & soc. prog.   —business w/o govt. controls
                          ∴—govt. regulate business

11. balance of payments—diff. betw. payments to foreign countries and $ coming in

12. What to do if burned?
        —if mild—(no broken skin)—put in ice H_2O
        —if severe—call Dr.—keep patient warm

Lecture 2: Women and Work

Note-Taking Practice Exercise, page 28
Use the lecture excerpt on pages 18–20 of the textbook as a resource if you'd like to deliver the lecture yourself.

Eight DOs and DON'Ts for Improving Lecture Comprehension and Note-Taking, page 29
Key points about note-taking to emphasize:

- Good note-takers note key words, not every word.

- Good note-takers use symbols and abbreviations they will understand even when the ideas are no longer fresh in their mind.

- Good note-takers use the space on the page to visually represent the relationship of ideas. Examples of poor and good notes for Lecture 1 follow.

    <u>Poor notes</u>
    To comprehend efficiently, listeners must be aware of all carriers of meaning, add info., predict, evaluate
    <u>Good notes</u>
    To comprehend efficiently, listeners must
    —be aware of carriers of meaning
    —add info.
    —predict
    —evaluate

<u>Poor notes</u>	<u>Good notes</u>
Diff. betw. lect. & everyday listen.	Diff. betw. lect. & everyday listen.
—language	—language
—amount of jargon	—amount of jargon
—interaction	—interaction
—expectations	—expectations

- Good note-takers use headings to organize and group ideas. Examples of good and poor notes for Lecture 1 follow.

<u>Poor notes</u>	<u>Good notes</u>
—language	Diff. betw. lect. & everyday listen
—interaction	—lang.
—expectations	—interaction
	—expectations

<u>Poor notes</u>	<u>Good notes</u>
Efficient listeners predict	Efficient listeners predict
—overcome noise	Why?
—save time	—overcome noise
	—save time
—subject matter knowl.	Sources of predict?
—world knowl.	—subj. matter knowl.
	—world knowl.

- Good note-takers listen for the larger picture. They know that it is easier to retain and remember details if they have the overall ideas and general concepts than to re-create the main points from details.
- Good note-takers develop their own style. Some students write occasional words in their native language; others don't. Some people write neat notes; others take very messy notes but still understand what they have written.
- Good note-takers take time as soon as possible after listening to a lecture to rewrite or add to their notes. They add information that they remember but did not have time to note, and they reorganize information to best reflect the importance of ideas and the relationship between them.

UNIT 4 NOTING NUMBERS AND STATISTICS

Unit Summary: Often even advanced students have problems noting numbers and statistics. Unit 4 provides tips and practice exercises to enable students to better comprehend and note numbers, including fractions, decimals, and years. The three lectures in this unit provide practice with these numbers in meaningful contexts.

Exercises, page 31
Read or play each number once. Use judgment as to the need for reading or replaying numbers a second time.

Answers:
Exercise A: **1.** 13 **2.** 14 **3.** 15 **4.** 60 **5.** 7 **6.** 18 **7.** 9 **8.** 40 **9.** 16 **10.** 8
Exercise B: **1.** 17 **2.** 70 **3.** 19 **4.** 9 **5.** 50

Exercise, page 31
Read or play each number once. When the students have finished, have them read all the years.

Answers:
1. 1605 **2.** 1827 **3.** 2014 **4.** 1920 **5.** 1850 **6.** 1502 **7.** 1589 **8.** 1870 **9.** 1808 **10.** 2001

Exercises, page 32
Read or play each number twice. When the students have finished, have them read all the numbers.

Answers:
Exercise A: 1. 102   2. 150   3. 1,020   4. 1,250   5. 3,056   6. 53,000   7. 407,000   8. 1,213,000
9. 5,020,000   10. 16,010,001
Exercise B: 1. 14,569   2. 67,440   3. 15,515   4. 2,000,001   5. 2,000,100   6. 202,202,000
7. 95,825,000   8. 95,925,000,000   9. 175,240,150   10. 12,000,565,000

Exercises, page 33
Read or play each number once. Use judgment as to the need for reading or replaying numbers a second time.

Answers:
Exercise A: 1. ½   2. 2⅛   3. 2.5   4. 1½   5. 106   6. 3.4   7. 78   8. ⅔   9. 35   10. 2.6
Exercise B: 1. ⅛   2. 1.5   3. 1⅛   4. ⅞   5. 8½   6. 206   7. 98.6   8. 2.6   9. ¼   10. 3.14

Lecture 3: American Attitudes toward Work

Lecture Outline for Listen and Note, pages 34–35
Use this outline if you'd like to deliver the lecture yourself.

INTRODUCTION: Work is a fact of life—whether we work in an office, a hospital, a school, a factory, on a farm, or at home; whether we receive a regular salary or earn income based on the profits of our own business; or whether we are part of a family economy, such as unpaid work done by housewives. Most of us spend the majority of our lives working.

For many people in the world, there are few elements of choice in the selection of work. In traditional societies, men have their roles and women have theirs. In poor societies or in countries where education is limited, many people do the work that is available or that is needed. People follow in the footsteps of their own parents, learning the trades that they did. However, more and more—with greater mobility, allowing people to relocate to find the jobs they want; with greater opportunities for higher education and training, allowing people to choose the fields that interest them—there is choice in career and work.

Still, whether or not workers choose their jobs, they can and do have opinions about what makes one job—for them—better than another job. Sometimes these same workers have the power and opportunity to change jobs to make their preferences into reality; sometimes they don't.

I'd like to look at two polls, both done in the 1990s, whose purposes were to find out what issues or job characteristics were important to American workers.

Some people might guess that the answer is obvious—people want higher salaries, more money. Is that true? Let's take a look and see.

I. The first poll (1990)
   A. Asked respondents to choose what job characteristic was most important to them among five items
      1. The five items were: important and meaningful work, high income, chances for advancement, job security, and shorter work hours.
      2. The results (for 1990) showed that 50% considered "important and meaningful work" most important.
      3. 24% said high income was the most important characteristic.
      4. 16% said chances for advancement was the most important characteristic.
      5. 6% said job security was most important.
      6. 4% said short work hours was most important.
   B. What is striking about the results is how—by far—workers valued "important and meaningful work" as more important than any of the other characteristics, including salary.

II. The second poll (1991)
   A. Asked respondents to reflect on how important certain job characteristics are in their work
   B. This was a different type of poll from the previous one. In the previous poll there was only one question—what is most important to you? In this poll, respondents were given an opportunity to rank each characteristic as not important, somewhat important, important, or very important.
      1. Good health insurance and other benefits: 81% of the respondents ranked this as very important.
         a. This is probably a result of the increasing costs of health care in the U.S.

b. This is a monetary issue, but it is not an issue of salary. It's an issue of benefits—health, retirement, education, etc.
2. Interesting work: 78% of the respondents ranked this as very important.
   a. This is a key point—one often sees people working for less if they enjoy their work and feel as if they're being treated fairly.
   b. This doesn't mean that people will be satisfied if they're receiving less than a fair wage, but it does show that interesting work may be more important to people than receiving a top salary.
3. Job security: 78% of the respondents ranked this as very important.
   a. Again, this is not a salary issue.
   b. With increases in layoffs, people are looking for security, the sense of knowing that they can keep their jobs as long as they want.
4. Opportunity to learn new skills: 68% of the respondents ranked this as very important.
   a. This goes back again to the ideas of interest level and personal satisfaction.
   b. People want their work to be meaningful.
5. Having a week or more of vacation: 66% of the respondents ranked this as very important.
   a. This is a benefits issue.
   b. This also shows the differences in expectations regarding vacation time around the world. In some European countries, for example, five or six weeks of vacation is the norm. However, in the U.S., the typical job offers two weeks of vacation per year, increasing the longer a worker is at the company.
6. Being able to work independently: 64% of the respondents ranked this as very important.
   a. This relates to working conditions.
7. Recognition from coworkers: 62% of the respondents ranked this as very important.
   a. Recognition can be considered a psychological benefit. (There is no monetary reward, but there is a psychological reward in terms of appreciation.)
8. Regular hours (no weekends, no nights): 58% of the respondents ranked this as very important.
9. Having a job in which you can help others: 58% of the respondents ranked this as very important.
10. Limited job stress: 58% of the respondents ranked this as very important.
11. High income: 56% of the respondents ranked this as very important.
    a. High income is far from the top of this list.
    b. Yet more than half of workers still think this is very important.
12. Working close to home: 55% of the respondents ranked this as very important.
13. Work that is important to society: 53% of the respondents ranked this as very important.
14. Chances for promotion: 53% of the respondents ranked this as very important.
    a. This seems to go along with both high income and recognition; there is a psychological reward to a promotion as well as a monetary reward.
15. Contact with a lot of people: 52% of the respondents ranked this as very important.
16. Flexible hours: 49% of the respondents ranked this as very important.

CONCLUSION: Overall, these results show that salary is not the most important issue for American workers. Interesting, isn't it? Now, a note of caution here—these are averages. Researchers have also found out that pay increases in importance as education decreases. That is probably because workers at this level are already receiving lower salaries to begin with. Still, it seems that it would be a good idea for employers to become more aware of polls like these—they might be able to keep their workers satisfied in ways that they hadn't thought of, ways that are not necessarily monetary.

Lecture Audioscript for Listen and Note, pages 34–35
This audioscript shows one speaker's delivery of the lecture, as recorded in the audio program. Use it as a resource.

OK . . . we all work . . . or very few people can get away with not working . . . work is a fact of life when we're adults . . . whether we're working in an office . . . a hospital . . . a school . . . a factory . . . a farm . . . at home . . . whether we receive a regular salary . . . or we earn an income based on the profits of our own business . . . or whether we're part of a family economy . . . the unpaid work that's done by housewives . . . but which is still part of the economy of the family . . . anyway most of us spend the majority of our lives working . . . and for many people in the world . . . there aren't very many . . . the . . . there's not a lot of choice in the selection of work . . . in traditional societies for example . . . men have their roles . . . women have theirs . . . in poorer societies or in countries where education is limited . . . many people just do the work that's available . . . the work that is needed . . . people often follow in the footsteps of their own parents . . . they learn the trades that they did . . . however more and more . . . with greater mobility . . . at least that's offered for example in this society . . . the mobility that is offered when people can relocate to find the jobs they want for example

. . . the mobility that is offered when people have greater opportunities for higher education or training . . . adult training . . . anyway more and more people are able to choose the fields that interest them . . . there's choice for them in career and work . . . *still* whether workers choose the work or not . . . they can and do have opinions about what makes one job for them better than another job . . . and sometimes workers have the ability . . . or opportunity to change jobs . . . and make their preferences into a reality . . . and sometimes they don't . . . still workers have preferences . . .

anyway . . . what I want to look at . . . is . . . what do people want from their jobs? . . . what are workers' opinions about what makes one job better than another? . . . and what I'm going to look at are two polls . . . two surveys . . . they were both done in the 1990s . . . and the purposes were to find out what issues . . . or job characteristics . . . were especially important to American workers . . . so we're not going to go into the idea today of choice . . . mobility . . . although those are important issues . . . but more . . . we're going to look at . . . given the choice . . . what are important job characteristics or issues for American workers? . . . and some of you might guess that the answer is obvious . . . you might say . . . "oh . . . people just want higher salaries . . . more money" . . . but let's see if that's true . . . let's take a look . . .

now the first poll . . . and the first poll was taken in 1990 . . . and this poll asks respondents to choose what was most important to them among five items . . . so this was a limited poll . . . the surveyors gave a list of five items to the respondents . . . and said . . . here . . . here are these items . . . you tell me what's most important to you out of these five . . . and they were only allowed to choose one out of the five . . . and the five items were "important and meaningful work" . . . that was the first item "important and meaningful work" . . . the second item was "high income" . . . the third item was "chances for advancement" . . . promotion . . . and so on . . . the fourth item was "job security" and the fifth item was "shorter work hours" . . . OK? . . . so "important and meaningful work" . . . "high income" . . . "chances for advancement" . . . "job security" . . . and "shorter work hours" . . .

now the results that they found showed that 50% considered "important and meaningful work" the most important characteristic of a job . . . that's the item they chose out of these five when asked to choose only one item . . . to say which was the most important to them of these five items . . . they chose "important and meaningful work" . . . they didn't choose "high income" . . . interesting . . . anyway . . . 24% did say "high income" was the most important characteristic of a job . . . so we can see that about half considered "important and meaningful work" as the most important characteristic . . . and almost a quarter said "high income" was the most important characteristic . . . of the remaining . . . 16% said "chances for advancement" was the most important characteristic for a job . . . maybe these were younger workers . . . starting out on a career . . . 6% said "job security" was most important . . . and finally . . . 4% said "short work hours" was most important . . . and as you can see these add up to 100% because the respondents could only choose one out of the five . . .

I think what's striking about the results is that . . . by far . . . workers valued important and meaningful work . . . as more important than *any* of the other characteristics . . . and that included salary . . . so half of the respondents said that meaningful work . . . important work . . . was the most important characteristic for them . . .

OK . . . I'm going to tell you about *another* poll . . . and this poll was taken a year later . . . in 1991 . . . and it asked respondents to reflect on how important certain job characteristics were in their work . . . and this is a different type of poll . . . because . . . whereas in the first poll . . . respondents had to choose only one out of five . . . in this case they wanted the respondents to react to *each* item separately . . . and they wanted the respondents to rank each item as "not important" . . . "somewhat important" . . . "important" . . . or "very important" . . . so they had four choices for each one . . . and so instead of choosing only one item out of all and having to choose the *most* important of all . . . here they had a chance to say "well yeah this is important . . . uh . . . this is very important . . ." and they could really give a response to each one . . .

let me give you an example of this . . . the first item they asked about was "good health insurance and other benefits" . . . they said to them "well . . . how would you rank this . . . good health insurance and other benefits? . . . is it not important to you? . . . is it somewhat important to you? . . . is it important to you? . . . is it very important to you?" . . . and I'm not going to tell you everything about the poll but I'm just going to tell you what percentage of respondents said that this item . . . or any item I mention . . . is "very important" . . . for the first one . . . good health insurance and other benefits . . . 81% of the respondents ranked this as very important . . . what can . . . what does this tell you? . . . I think it tells you a bit about the increasing costs of health care in the U.S. and people's fears about not being able to pay for their own health care . . . and we can look at this as a monetary issue . . . it's not an issue of salary . . . but it is an issue of benefits . . . health benefits . . . retirement benefits . . . education benefits . . . and people are realizing that benefits do have a significant monetary value . . . and in this case . . . "health insurance and other benefits" is considered very important by 81% of the respondents . . . a very very high number . . .

the second item they asked about is "interesting work" . . . they asked "how important is interesting work to you?" . . . and again . . . I'm just going to tell you about how many people said it was very important . . . in this case . . . 78% of the respondents ranked this as very important to them . . . this is a key point I think . . . one often sees people working for a lot less if they enjoy their work . . . and feel that they're being treated fairly . . . and it doesn't mean that Americans are going to be satisfied when they're receiving less than a fair wage . . . but it does show that doing interesting work can be more important to people than receiving a top salary . . .

OK . . . the third item is "job security" . . . how important is job security to you? . . . and in this case 78% of the respondents . . . again . . . ranked this as very important . . . again it's not a salary issue . . . but perhaps in our society with increases in layoffs . . . the idea that we don't have jobs for life . . . people are looking for security . . . the sense of knowing that they can keep their jobs as long as they want . . .

the fourth item they asked about was "opportunity to learn new skills" . . . how important is that to you? . . . how important is it to learn new skills? . . . 68% of the respondents ranked this as very important . . . and I think that goes again to the idea of interest level . . . personal satisfaction . . . and the idea that people want their work to be meaningful . . .

the fifth item was "having a week or more of vacation" . . . how important is that to you? . . . and 66% of the respondents . . . two-thirds . . . said that that was very important to them . . . again . . . this is a benefits issue . . . and I think this is interesting because it shows the differences in expectations regarding vacation time around the world . . . as you may know . . . in some European countries, for example . . . five or six weeks of vacation is the norm . . . however . . . in the U.S. the average vacation is two weeks of vacation per year . . . and that might increase the longer a worker is at a company . . . but you can see . . . for two-thirds of the respondents having a week or more of vacation is very important . . . I'm actually surprised that that's not higher . . .

the sixth item was "being able to work independently" . . . 64% of the respondents ranked this as very important . . . people want to work . . . or at least this group of respondents wanted to work independently . . . and this relates to working conditions . . .

the seventh item . . . "recognition from coworkers" . . . 62% of the respondents said that this was very important . . . it was important to them to be recognized . . . to be respected and acknowledged for the work that they'd done . . . and I see recognition as a psychological benefit . . . there's no monetary reward necessarily attached to it . . . although sometimes there could be . . . but more . . . people are looking at the psychological reward . . . in terms of appreciation . . .

OK . . . the eighth item was "regular hours" . . . so not working weekends . . . not working nights . . . how many people ranked this as very important? 58% of the respondents said that this was very important to them . . .

the ninth item . . . "having a job in which you can help others" . . . so being involved in a helping profession . . . again . . . 58% of the respondents said that this was very important to them . . . and we see a lot of these items have to do with the job itself . . . how meaningful the job is . . . the satisfaction people get from the job . . . and not necessarily money . . .

the tenth item was "limited job stress" . . . and here 58% of the respondents ranked this as very important . . . "limited job stress" . . .

number eleven? . . . "high income" . . . so here we're really seeing how important the salary is to you . . . 56% of the respondents ranked this as very important . . . so people do think that this is important . . . as you can see in the first poll when they had to prioritize . . . when they had to say which is the most important to them . . . high income didn't always have the first priority . . . but when asked just to talk about high income and to talk about how important it is in general . . . 56% said that it is very important to them . . . now as you can see, it's *far* from the top of *this* list . . . but still more than half of the workers think it's important . . .

OK the remaining items . . . number twelve . . . "working close to home" . . . 55% of the respondents thought that this was very important to them . . . to work close to home . . . to not have a long commute . . .

number thirteen . . . "to do work that is important to society" . . . again that idea of meaningful work . . . 53% of the respondents said that this was very important to them . . . to do work that's important to society . . . I think that's kind of similar to where people talk about helping others . . .

number fourteen was "chances for promotion" . . . 53% of the respondents said that this was very important to them . . . it was important to them to have opportunities for advancement . . . chances for promotion . . . and I think this goes along with high income and recognition . . . there's both a psychological reward to promotion as well as a monetary reward . . .

fifteen is "contact with a lot of people" . . . some people are very people-oriented . . . and 52% of respondents said that this was very important to them . . . they wanted to have contact with a number of people . . .

and finally the last item was "flexible hours" . . . 49% of the respondents ranked this as very important to them . . . to be able to have hours that weren't set in stone we might say . . . that were more flexible . . .

so as you can see . . . workers have a lot of things that are very important to them . . . but you can also see the variation in numbers . . . so going all the way from the first item that was mentioned . . . which was ranked as "very important" by 81% all the way down to the 49% who ranked the last item as "very important" . . . so if you were a business owner . . . if you had a number of workers working for you . . . this kind of list might give you an idea of how to make your working environment more attractive to workers . . . let's say . . . if you couldn't offer high salaries . . .

anyway . . . overall these results show that salary is not the most important issue for American workers . . . it's important . . . but certainly not the most important issue . . . interesting, I think . . . now a note of caution here . . . these are averages . . . and polls talk about averages . . . researchers have also found out that pay increases in importance as education decreases . . . and that's probably because workers at lower levels are already receiving lower salaries to begin with . . . and so they may care less about job satisfaction or job interest . . . and really are concerned about the money they're making . . . but still . . . I think it's important for employers and business owners to become more aware of polls like these . . . because it might allow them to keep their workers satisfied . . . in ways that maybe they hadn't thought of before . . . ways that are not necessarily monetary.

Example Notes, pages 34–35

2 Polls: Purpose: find out what job characteristics most important to U.S. workers

Poll #1 (1990): asked respondents to choose which of five items was most important to them

Item:	% saying item was most important
1. important & meaningful work	50%
2. high income	24%
3. chances for advancement	16%
4. job security	6%
5. short work hours	4%

Poll #2 (1991): asked respondents to rank importance of each job characteristic

Characteristic	% ranking as very important
1. good health insurance & other benefits	81%
2. interesting work	78%
3. job security	78%
4. opportun. to learn new skills	68%
5. have a wk. or + vacation	66%
6. being able to work independently	64%
7. recognition fr. coworkers	62%
8. reg. work hrs. (e.g., no nights)	58%
9. have job where help others	58%
10. ltd. job stress	58%
11. high income	56%
12. work close to home	55%
13. work important to society	53%
14. chances for promotion	53%
15. contact w/ many people	52%
16. flexible hrs.	49%

Conclusions: salary not most important issue
 caution—these are averages (pay ↑ in importance as education ↓)
  still—employers should look at polls (maybe keep workers satisfied in non-$ ways)

Using Your Notes, page 36

Answers:
a. F b. T c. F d. F e. F f. T g. F

Post-Lecture Discussion, page 36

Answers:
1. Answers will vary. 2. Answers will vary. 3. The first and third quotes emphasize the importance of work. The second and fourth quotes emphasize the importance of leisure.

Using Vocabulary, page 37

Answers:
1. polls 2. income 3. value 4. meaningful 5. rank 6. monetary 7. satisfaction

Lecture 4: Milestones in Technology

Pre-Lecture Reading and Discussion, page 38

Answers:
1. Answers will vary. 2. Answers will vary. 3. The three listed are (a) being open to serendipity and providing time for workers to pursue their own ideas without having to worry about accountability or reporting (at 3M, scientists and engineers can spend up to 5% of company time on their own projects, without even telling managers what they're up to, and at Du Pont, researchers may pursue blue-sky ideas one day a week), (b) bringing together a variety of specialists (e.g., Bell Labs threw together physicists with metallurgists and chemists to develop the transistor), and (c) taking monetary risks.

Lecture Outline for Listen and Note, pages 38–39

Use this outline if you'd like to deliver the lecture yourself.

  INTRODUCTION: Discuss definition of "technology" as written in handout.

   technology: 1a. The application of science, esp. to industrial or commercial objectives. 1b. The entire body of methods and materials used to achieve such objectives. *Anthropol.* the body of knowledge available to a civilization that is of use in fashioning implements, practicing manual arts and skills, and extracting or collecting materials.

The goal of the lecture is to give an introductory talk on technology, an overview of millions of years. Talk about the major discoveries in the history of technology.

2,400,000 B.C.	First stone tools were made.
1,000,000 B.C.	Our ancestors (not *Homo sapiens* yet) began to control fire.
90,000 B.C.	People in Africa first started making bone points for hunting, chipping bones to make a sharp point.
25,000 B.C.	People began weaving cloth, using natural fibers to make clothes and material.
23,000 B.C.	The bow and arrow is being used.
10,000 B.C.	We find the first known pottery in Japan.
5000 B.C.	Egyptians start mining copper.
3500 B.C.	The first wheeled vehicles appear in Syria.
2000 B.C.	The first interior bathrooms are built in palaces in Greece.
1500 B.C.	We find the earliest glass vessels from Egypt.
140 B.C.	The Chinese start making paper.
100 B.C.	In Eastern Europe, water is being used to power mills.
	Cultures are learning to harness natural energy so that they can achieve goals that wouldn't be possible or easily done relying solely on human strength.
A.D. 600	The first windmills are built in what is now Iran.
	Again, cultures are learning to harness the energy of the wind to power tools.
A.D. 1040	The Chinese develop gunpowder.
	Technology necessary for warfare, protection.
A.D. 1041	A Chinese inventor develops movable type for printing, a forerunner for later printing presses.
A.D. 1608	The first telescope is developed in Holland.

We're well into the Industrial Revolution.

We see mechanical technology now proceeding at an incredible speed (machines for creating clothing, for mining, for farming, for communicating, etc.). It's impossible to talk about all the new technology. Here are some of the ones that are especially relevant to students.

A.D. 1876	Alexander Graham Bell invents the telephone.
A.D. 1879	Edison discovers how to make a practical electric light.
A.D. 1903	The Wright brothers fly the first successful airplane.
A.D. 1908	Henry Ford introduces the Model T, the first affordable automobile.
A.D. 1926	Television is invented.
A.D. 1937	An American invents the first method of photocopying.
A.D. 1963	Audiocassettes are introduced.
A.D. 1975	The first personal computer is marketed—in build-it-yourself kit form.
A.D. 1982	CD (compact disc) players are introduced.

CONCLUSION: No mention of rockets going into space or computer advances or robots or medical technology. It would all be impossible in a short lecture. Each one of those has its own sequence of discovery. We've come a long way from stone tools.

Lecture Audioscript for Listen and Note, pages 38–39
This audioscript shows one speaker's delivery of the lecture, as recorded in the audio program. Use it as a resource.

TEACHER: what is technology? does anyone here want to give me a definition? what comes to your mind when I say the word "technology"?
STUDENT: inventions?
STUDENT: mechanical . . . devices?
TEACHER: OK . . . so something to do with mechanics . . . inventing something . . . well . . . if you look at your handout, I've written a full definition of the word . . . let's take a look . . . technology . . . 1 . . . a . . . the application of science . . . especially to industrial or commercial objectives . . . 1b . . . the entire body of methods and materials . . . used to achieve such objectives . . . 2 . . . an anthropological use of the term . . . the body of knowledge . . . available to a civilization . . . that is of use in fashioning implements . . . practicing manual arts and skills . . . and extracting or collecting materials . . . so what else do you notice about technology here?

STUDENT: uh it has to do with science? . . . a . . . as it relates to business and industry . . .
TEACHER: uh-huh . . .
STUDENT: or *commerce* and industry . . .
TEACHER: uh-huh . . . just science?
STUDENT: well . . . that's in the first part of the definition . . . uh . . . but then the second part says it's "the *entire* body . . . uh . . . of methods and materials used to achieve" those goals . . .
TEACHER: right . . . so one definition . . . one very broad definition is 1b—*everything*—science . . . tools . . . machinery . . . not just science . . . that is used to achieve industrial or commercial goals . . . and the second definition . . . this one is more specific to the field of anthropology . . . and here technology refers to the whole body of knowledge that any civilization uses to create tools . . . to make things . . . to collect things . . . . um . . . so let's see . . . would a wheel be technology? what do you think?
STUDENTS: yeah . . .
TEACHER: yeah sure . . . in primitive cultures, the wheel was a turning point in technology . . . pun intended . . . allowing people to gather and move objects with greater ease than ever before . . .

OK . . . what I'd like to do then is give a little introductory talk on technology . . . kind of an overview of millions of years . . . talk about some milestones in the history of technology . . . and as you'll see, in some cases, our definition of technology is going to be closer to that of the anthropological one . . . but at other times . . . it's closer to the most specific definition . . . the definition in 1a . . . so . . . probably we should start back with the first tools . . . made of?
STUDENTS: stone . . .
TEACHER: right . . . stone . . . and that occurred more than 2 million years ago . . . we estimate that that began about 2,400,000 B.C. . . . 2,400,000 B.C. . . .

now I'm going to make broad jumps here . . . because I can't possibly cover every discovery over the years . . . but anyway . . . let's jump to 1,000,000 B.C. . . . what happened then? . . . our ancestors . . . at that time our present human form *Homo sapiens* . . . didn't exist yet . . . but the ancestors of *Homo sapiens* began to control fire . . . that is . . . fire existed before then . . . it's a natural phenomenon . . . but now . . . our ancestors learned to use it . . . to make it . . . to limit it . . .

OK moving on . . . we've got millions of years to cover remember . . . in 90,000 B.C. people in Africa first started making bone points . . . for what? . . . probably for hunting . . . so they chipped and chipped and chipped at an animal bone to give it a sharp point . . . what did they use to do this chipping? . . . stones probably . . . a major technological advance for civilization . . .

OK . . . 25,000 B.C. . . . in 25,000 B.C. . . . people began weaving cloth . . . using natural fibers . . . from plants . . . trees . . . to make clothes and material . . . is this technology? . . . of course . . .

only 2,000 years later, in 23,000 B.C. . . . we find that the bow and arrow is being used . . . now before that people threw the arrow . . . but in 23,000 B.C., they learned to increase the speed and power of each arrow toss by using a tool . . . and that tool is the bow . . . again a great advance in technology . . .

moving along to 10,000 B.C. . . . we find the first known pottery in Japan . . . so people are using clay to make pots . . . certainly an advance in technology . . . people can now hold liquids without depending on natural vessels . . .

um OK 5000 B.C. . . . in 5000 B.C. Egyptians started mining copper . . . and this is just one of a long line of technological advances that involve the discovery and use of metal . . . whether iron or bronze or steel . . . but in this case . . . in 5000 B.C. we're talking about the mining of copper . . .

OK 3500 B.C. . . . in 3500 B.C. we find the first wheeled vehicles in Syria . . . imagine the change that this discovery made . . . items could be transported in vehicles that have wheels . . . we've come a long way to the car haven't we . . .

OK . . . moving ahead 2000 B.C. . . . and obviously we're not going to be touching on every single major discovery . . . and this next one is really not on the level of the ones I've mentioned before . . . but still . . . it certainly has touched our lives . . . so anyway . . . this next one . . . in 2000 B.C. was . . . the first interior bathrooms . . . the first interior bathrooms were built in palaces in Greece . . . technology? . . . absolutely!

OK . . . let's move a bit more quickly . . . 1500 B.C. . . . we find the earliest glass vessels from Egypt . . . so we start seeing the use of glass . . .

140 B.C. . . . the Chinese start making paper . . .

100 B.C. . . . in Eastern Europe . . . water is used to power mills . . . so cultures are learning to harness the natural energy of water . . . so that they can achieve goals that wouldn't be possible or easily done relying solely on human strength . . .

in 600 A.D. the first windmills are built in what is now Iran . . . so again cultures are learning to harness natural energy . . . in this case the energy of the wind to power tools . . . so in 100 B.C. it was water that was first used . . . and in 600 A.D. it was wind . . .

in 1040 A.D. the Chinese develop gunpowder . . . technology? yes . . . technology necessary for warfare . . . protection . . .

in 1041 A.D. a Chinese inventor develops movable type . . . for printing . . . which is a forerunner for later printing presses . . . and can you imagine a world without newspapers . . . books? . . . those were a busy two years in China . . .

moving along . . . and don't imagine that nothing happened in the next 600 years . . . it's just impossible to mention everything . . . anyway in 1608 . . . the first telescope is developed in Holland . . . opening up new possibilities in the exploration of the universe . . .

OK . . . now that we're well into the Industrial Revolution . . . I have to be even more general because we see mechanical technology now proceeding at an incredible speed . . . machines for creating clothing . . . for mining . . . for farming . . . for communicating . . . so I'll just mention some of the ones that are especially relevant to your lives as students . . . we'll get into the industrial technology of the 19th and 20th century much later on in this class . . . so here are a few odds and ends . . .

in 1876 . . . Alexander Graham Bell invented the telephone . . . not much more than a century ago . . . and imagine life without a phone . . .

in 1879 . . . Edison discovered how to make a practical electric light . . .

in 1903 . . . the Wright brothers flew the first successful airplane . . .

in 1908 Henry Ford introduced the Model T . . . the first affordable automobile . . . think how that has changed our lives . . .

in 1926 . . . the television was invented . . . though it was many years before it was available in the average home . . .

in 1937 an American invented the first method of photocopying . . . something that you as students probably take advantage of regularly . . .

in 1963 audiocassettes are introduced . . .

in 1975 the first personal computer . . . PCs . . . were marketed . . . and these were marketed not as computers to take home and plug in . . . but in build-it-yourself kit formats . . .

how about one more? . . . let's see . . . in 1982 CDs . . . and compact disc players are introduced . . .

I could go on and on . . . as you see . . . I haven't even talked about rockets going into space . . . computers . . . robots . . . medical technology . . . it would all be impossible in a short lecture . . . each one of those has its own sequence of discovery . . . and I did try to cover more than a couple of million years . . . we've sure come a long way from stone tools, haven't we?

Using Your Notes Audioscript, page 40

For question 1, read or play each statement. Have students decide whether the statements are true or false based on their notes. For question 2, have students write eight statements—some true, some false—about the lecture based on their notes. Have students work in small groups or as a class; one student reads his/her statement; the other student(s) listen and decide if it is true or false based on their notes.

a. The first interior bathrooms were built in 20,000 B.C.
b. The first stone tools were invented more than 2 billion years ago.
c. The Egyptians started to mine copper in about 5000 B.C.
d. The first windmills were built in Iran in 600 B.C.
e. The Chinese developed gunpowder in 1014 A.D.
f. The first TV was made in the 19th century.
g. People started using glass before they started making paper.
h. A Japanese inventor developed moveable type for printing.

Answers:
1. a. F b. F c. T d. F e. F f. F g. T h. F

Defining Vocabulary Audioscript, page 41

1. <u>objective</u>: He isn't very clear about his career objectives. He really has no idea about what he wants from a job or career.
2. <u>implement</u>: A cook's implements must include a good set of carving knives.
3. <u>turning point</u>: The divorce was a turning point in her life. From that point on, she realized that she needed to take care of her family herself.
4. <u>to estimate</u>: No one is sure exactly how many blue whales exist nowadays, but scientists estimate their numbers at about 11,000.
5. <u>ancestor</u>: His ancestors came to the U.S. from Japan, but that was over a hundred years ago when his great-great grandparents emigrated.
6. <u>to weave</u>: Some American Indian groups are well known for weaving beautiful blankets and rugs.
7. <u>to mine</u>: When gold was discovered in California in the 19th century, many people rushed there to try and mine it.
8. <u>to rely on</u>: You can rely on her; she'll always be there when you need her and she always keeps her word.
9. <u>forerunner</u>: The Wright brothers flew the first successful airplane in 1903. That first airplane was a forerunner, helping to pave the way for later designs.

Answers:
1. goal   2. tool   3. a decisive moment   4. to approximate; to guess an inexact amount   5. a family member from a previous generation, usually earlier than grandparents   6. to make cloth by interlacing threads   7. to take minerals (or ores) from the earth   8. to depend on   9. a person or thing that comes before in time

Lecture 5: Immigration to the United States

Lecture Outline for Listen and Note, page 44
Use this outline if you'd like to deliver the lecture yourself.

INTRODUCTION: The U.S. is a land of immigrants. Only the American Indians—Native Americans—can be considered true Americans—although their ancestors can also be traced back to immigrants! At one time, the U.S. was called a "melting pot"—a place in which the "ingredients"—or cultural groups, in this case—mixed together so that one can't be separated from the other or identified separately from the other. Others called it a "stew"—meaning a place where there are many "ingredients" but where the ingredients or the cultural groups, retain their identity even while mixing with other groups. Whatever the case, immigrants continue to come to the U.S., some adjusting and blending in, others staying in separate communities.

The goal of this lecture is to give some statistics re immigration to this country throughout its history; in particular, to give statistics about immigration from 1820 to 1995 and then in 1995 alone.

I. Immigration by location of last residence
   A. From all countries
      1. From 1820 to 1995, the total number of immigrants was 60,602,091.
      2. In 1995 alone, the total was 720,461.

   B. By continent
      1. From Europe
         a. From 1820 to 1995, the number coming from Europe was 36,262,871 (59.8% of all immigrants during that period).
         b. In 1995 alone, the number was 128,185 (17.8% of immigrants in 1995).
      2. From Asia
         a. From 1820 to 1995, the number from Asia was 7,732,596 (12.7% of all immigrants during that period).
         b. In 1995 alone, the number was 267,931 (37.2% of all immigrants in 1995).
      3. From North, South, and Central America
         a. From 1820 to 1995, the number from North, South, and Central America was 15,604,541 (25.7% of all immigrants during that period).
         b. In 1995 alone, the number was 277,192 (38.4% of all immigrants in 1995).
      4. From Africa
         a. From 1820 to 1995, the number from Africa was 508,680 (0.8% of all immigrants during that period).
         b. In 1995 alone, the number was 42,456 (5.9% of all immigrants in 1995).
      5. From Oceania (Australia, New Zealand, and Pacific Islands)
         a. From 1820 to 1995, the number from Oceania was 221,154 (0.36% of all immigrants during that period).
         b. In 1995 alone, the number was 4,695 (0.7% of all immigrants in 1995).

   C. By individual countries in 1995
      1. Mexico—89,932 (12.5% of 1995 total)
      2. Philippines—50,095 (7.1% of 1995 total)
      3. Vietnam—41,752 (5.8% of 1995 total)
      4. Korea—16,047 (2.2% of 1995 total)
      5. Dominican Republic—38,512 (5.3% of 1995 total)
      6. Cuba—17,937 (2.5% of 1995 total)
      7. Ukraine—17,432 (2.4% of 1995 total)
      8. Canada—12,932 (1.8% of 1995 total)
      9. India—34,748 (4.8% of 1995 total)
      10. China, including Taiwan—35,463 (4.9% of 1995 total)

CONCLUSION: As you can see, immigration statistics reflect changes in the immigrating populations. As for the future, who knows?

Lecture Audioscript for Listen and Note, page 44
This audioscript shows one speaker's delivery of the lecture, as recorded in the audio program. Use it as a resource.

OK as you all know . . . the U.S. is a nation of immigrants . . . and the only people who can be considered true Americans are Native Americans or American Indians . . . even though the American Indians' ancestors were also immigrants . . . so it depends on how far you want to go back . . . at one time the U.S. was called a "melting pot" . . . a place where all cultures came together and mixed . . . intermarried . . . until eventually everyone became the same . . . American . . . however others call it a "stew" reflecting the idea that cultures come together and mix but that they never lose their true ethnic identity . . . whatever the case . . . immigrants continue to come to the U.S. . . . some adjusting and blending immediately . . . others staying in separate communities . . . what I'd like to do is just talk about in general some of the trends that have occurred in immigration over the last . . . 170 . . . 180 years . . . and then in particular focus on the year 1995 . . . as an example of the present times . . . OK first . . . what about from all countries? . . . from 1820 to 1995 the total number of immigrants to the U.S. . . . was 60,602,091 . . . that's 60,602,091 . . . in 1995 alone the total was 720,461 . . . 720,461 . . .

let me tell you about continents so you can get an idea about how this is broken down . . . from Europe . . . between 1820 and 1995 . . . the number coming from Europe was 36,262,871 . . . 36,262,871 . . . and that was 59.8% of all immigrants . . . so over those 175 years clearly the majority of immigrants were from Europe . . . and that is why even now a majority of Americans are of European descent . . . OK . . . in 1995 . . . from Europe . . . the number was 128,185 . . . 128,185 . . . and that was only 17.8% of all immigrants . . . in 1995 . . . so you can see . . . over . . . in the long run . . . Europeans were the majority of immigrants but now they're certainly not . . . they're nowhere near the majority . . .

What about Asia? . . . from 1820 to 1995 . . . the number of immigrants from Asia was 7,732,596 . . . 7,732,596 . . . and that was 12.7% of all immigrants . . . a very small percentage over 175 years . . . what about 1995 alone? . . . well in that year alone the number was 267,931 . . . 267,931 . . . and that was a quite substantial 37.2% of all immigrants . . . so more than one-third of the immigrants in 1995 were of Asian descent . . .

OK what about North, South, and Central America? . . . between 1820 and 1995 there were 15,604,541 North, South, and Central Americans immigrating . . . 15,604,541 . . . what percentage was this of all immigrants over those years? . . . they were 25.7% of all immigrants over that 175-year period . . . in 1995 alone there were 277,192 North, South, and Central American immigrants and that was 38.4% of all immigrants in 1995 . . . again more than one-third of the immigrants . . . this time coming from the Americas . . .

OK let's go to Africa . . . from 1820 to 1995 there were 508,680 immigrants from Africa . . . 508,680 . . . and that was 0.83% of all immigrants . . . a very small percentage . . . in 1995 alone there were 42,456 immigrants from Africa . . . 42,456 . . . and that was 5.9% of all 1995 immigrants . . .

OK Australia and New Zealand and the Pacific Islands . . . grouped as Oceania . . . from 1820 to 1995 . . . there were 221,154 immigrants from Oceania . . . 221,154 immigrants . . . and this was 0.36% of all immigrants . . . in 1995 . . . there were 4,695 immigrants from this region . . . and that made up 0.7% of all immigrants . . .

OK that's from major areas . . . continents . . . what about individual countries? . . . anyone want to guess which gave the most? yes, Mexico . . . the highest number came from Mexico . . . and that was with 89,932 people . . . in 1995 . . . from Mexico there were 89,932 people immigrating to the U.S. . . . and this was 12.5% of the total '95 immigration . . . OK and this probably doesn't count illegal immigration . . . just legal . . .

OK . . . the next one down . . . any guesses? . . . Philippines . . . there were 50,984 immigrants from the Philippines . . . 50,984 and this is 7.1% of the total . . . OK Vietnam was next with 41,752 immigrants . . . 41,752 immigrants . . . and this was 5.8% of the total . . . OK . . . now I'm not going to go in any particular descending order . . . Korea . . . from there, there were 16,047 immigrants in 1995 . . . 16,047 from Korea . . . 2.2% . . . of the 1995 total . . . from Cuba came 17,937 immigrants . . . and this was 2.5% of the total . . . again 17,937 immigrants . . . 2.5% of the total number of immigrants in 1995 . . . from the Dominican Republic came 38,512 immigrants . . . 38,512 immigrants . . . and this was 5.3% of the total . . . from the Ukraine . . . in the former U.S.S.R. . . . came 17,432 immigrants . . . 17,432 immigrants . . . and this was 2.4% of the total number of immigrants who arrived in 1995 . . . from Canada came 12,932 immigrants . . . 12,932 immigrants . . . and this was 1.8% of the total . . . from India came 34,748 immigrants . . . once again . . . 34,748 immigrants . . . and this was 4.8% of the total . . . last . . . China including Taiwan . . . from there came 35,463 immigrants . . . 35,463 immigrants . . . 4.9% of the 1995 total who immigrated that year . . .

OK as you can see . . . immigration trends change . . . depending on so many factors . . . and by looking at these statistics we can see how the United States' population is gradually changing . . . as for the future . . . who knows?

Using Your Notes Audioscript, page 45

For question 3, read or play each statement. Have students decide whether the statements are true or false based on their notes.

    a. The number of immigrants from Asia in 1995 was higher than the number of immigrants from North, South, and Central America during that same year.
    b. The total number of immigrants from Europe in 1995 was higher than the total number of immigrants coming from Asia in 1995.
    c. In 1995, approximately three-quarters of all immigrants came from Asia or the Americas.
    d. The majority of immigrants coming to the U.S. between 1820 and 1995 were from Asia.
    e. The number of immigrants coming to the U.S. in 1995 from Cuba and the Dominican Republic was approximately the same.
    f. In 1995, 15,095 immigrants came to the U.S. from the Philippines.
    g. In 1995, 402,456 immigrants came to the U.S. from Africa.
    h. In 1995, 1.8% of the immigrants came to the U.S. from Canada.
    i. In 1995, more people came from the Philippines than came from all of Africa.
    j. There were almost three-quarters of a million immigrants coming to the U.S. in 1995.
    k. Between 1820 and 1995, there were approximately 6 million immigrants coming to the U.S.

l. Immigrants from Asia made up more than one-third of the total immigrants to the U.S. in 1995.
m. Immigrants from North, South, and Central America made up more than one-third of the total immigrants to the U.S. in 1995.
n. In 1995, 7% of the immigrants were from Oceania.
o. In 1995, approximately the same number of immigrants came from Korea, Vietnam, and Canada.

Answers:
1. a 2.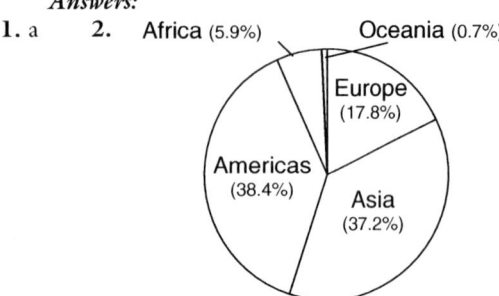

3. a. F b. F c. T d. F e. F f. F g. F h. T i. T j. T k. F l. T m. T n. F o. F

Using Vocabulary Audioscript, page 46

My grandparents and great-grandparents came from eastern Europe—primarily Poland and the former Soviet Union. They each came for different reasons. Some of them came to the U.S. because they desired opportunities and adventure. Others left their homeland because of persecution and discrimination. They chose New York City because it was a port and thus was a place where people from a great variety of racial and national groups lived. They hoped that this variety of people would allow them to mix in with the crowds without standing out too much. However, although New York City was supposedly a place where people from all cultures could "blend together" as Americans indistinguishable from one another, this was really not true. In reality, New York City was a place where many ethnic and national groups lived and interacted, never really losing their special ethnic identity. As for my grandparents and great-grandparents, I don't think they ever completely got used to their new life.

Answers:
1. ancestors 2. immigrated 3. emigrated 4. ethnic diversity 5. blend in 6. melting pot 7. retained their ethnic identity

UNIT 5 LISTENING FOR ORGANIZATION IN LECTURES

Unit Summary: Unit 5 provides information and exercises that increase students' awareness of lecture organization—introductions, conclusions, tangents, and nine specific organizational plans. Students become aware of cues that lecturers use to signal lecture organization. They also listen to authentic lecture excerpts to gain practice recognizing the relationship between lecture ideas and take notes on them.

The excerpts in Unit 5 come from authentic lectures primarily given to native-speaker audiences. Very occasionally, the originals were altered by adding paraphrase, simplifying vocabulary, or omitting certain comments. However, because of the value for students of hearing *real* lecture language, adaptations were kept to a minimum.

Because these lecture excerpts are authentic and come from lectures directed to native-speaker audiences, the vocabulary is occasionally difficult. Vocabulary that is essential to comprehending the lecture excerpt is glossed in the text. However, there may be other words that the students don't know. Rather than trying to teach students every word in every excerpt, it is more realistic to help students see that it is not necessary to understand all the words in order to take notes. Encourage students to guess and create meaning from what they do understand.

Additional recommendations follow.

- Avoid going straight through Unit 5. At the end of each organizational plan in Unit 5, recommended lectures in Unit 6 are listed for additional practice. Go back and forth between Units 5 and 6.

- Feel free to cover the organizational plans in any order.

- For each organizational plan, have students read the description of the plan, discuss how the sample notes visually represent that plan, read the cues and suggest contexts in which they have heard them, and take notes from the excerpt.

- It is often helpful for students to listen to the excerpt once, compare notes, and then listen to the excerpt a second time.

Exercise Audioscript, pages 50–51

Example
all over the world the question of women's role in society is becoming . . . or is an emotionally charged issue . . . women are questioning their previous roles and exploring new roles . . . everyone seems to have an opinion about it . . . one good thing that has come out of this is that women now feel that they have control or more

control over the direction of their lives . . . but this has caused some conflict . . . in fact . . . some people are saying that there is more strain on women than ever before . . . in any case . . . at least in the United States and many other countries . . . women must now decide a major question . . . whether to work outside of the home . . . pursue a career . . . or whether to stay at home and raise a family or whether to do both . . . I must add that this is the dilemma of a lucky few women . . . here in the U.S. nowadays the majority of working women must work outside of the home and it is no longer a luxury . . . but anyway what I would like to focus on in this lecture are some of the factors a woman might want to take into account when deciding whether to enter the job market or not . . . a major question would be which one is emotionally and physically more beneficial . . .

1. scientists are discovering things every day . . . things that are bad for you . . . twenty years ago it was smoking . . . fifteen years ago it was saccharine . . . a few years ago it was eggs . . . high cholesterol . . . caffeine . . . and we all get nervous when we hear these things but usually don't change our habits that much . . . a time though when people are concerned about what they eat and what they put in their body is usually when a woman is pregnant because not only at that time do the drugs or the food affect her but they also affect the fetus . . . what I'd like to tell you about is a recent study that was done concerning the effect of the mother's eating habits on the fetus . . . in particular the effect of alcohol on the fetus . . .

2. now I'd like to talk about ecosystem structure because ecosystems have a very consistent structure irrespective of which ecosystem you are dealing with . . . they all have the same basic structure . . . you have first of all . . .

3. I'm going to be talking about marriage and divorce trends ranging over a period of time . . . I know people . . . especially non-Americans . . . think that in the U.S. people get married easily and get divorced easily . . . people get married five times . . . divorced five times . . . but is this true? Has it always been the same? . . . what I'd like to do is show you a little about how the marriage trends have changed over the years and I'll give you some statistics dating back to 1900 and going all the way up to 1984 . . . OK . . .

4. OK . . . so what we want to start talking about and we want to finish talking about is . . . prenatal development . . . and then we're going to talk about physical growth and that'll be . . . from the time when the kid gets born all the way up to adolescence 'cause it's hard to talk about just isolated periods because . . . a lot of what's going on only makes sense when you contrast what goes on let's say when you're two years old to what goes on let's say when you're eleven or twelve . . . OK . . . so what we'll be talking about then is what goes on before you popped into the world and then what goes on as far as your bones and muscles and height and weight and all that stuff after you've popped into the world . . . so . . . that's that . . .

5. I want you to know that all around this state within Asian-American communities people are saying that this campus really welcomes Asian-American students and not only do you seem to welcome Asian-American students but you're doing a great deal to make people more aware of our backgrounds and our needs and I know this for a fact because I have been invited to several other things here . . . and I know many segments of this university are really sitting up and looking at this new population and trying to learn from what the students can bring us as well as trying to give them the best education possible . . . now the people who organized this conference asked me to address three questions and those are . . . give a broad history of immigration of Asians into this country and also to talk about the cultural and psychological characteristics of each of the groups and then assess the present status of each group . . . now I want you to know that that's the subject matter of three separate courses that I teach so I can't possibly pack all of that into half an hour or forty minutes but I'll do what I can . . .

6. what I'm going to talk about today is information . . . I'm not going to talk about a particular subject . . . a particular academic discipline . . . like I'm not going to give you a talk on foreign policy in Latin America . . . that is a distinct unique sort of clearly-defined subject . . . I'm going to talk about something much broader . . . information . . . OK? so not on a particular topic but what I'm going to be talking about is the seeking of information . . . looking for information . . . looking for information as a process . . . and what we call the process of looking for information is research . . . and I'm going to deal with a particular type of research . . . what we call in the jargon of my field which is information science . . . we call that library-based research . . . and all that means is looking for information . . . facts . . . data . . . ideas if you will . . . in a library . . . I have two major goals for this talk . . . the first is to offer a broad definition and in a way to make that definition of information distinct . . . unique . . . from the definition of knowledge because I see information and knowledge as two separate things . . . two entities so I want to start off by defining information and defining information sort of in relation to a definition of knowledge . . . and the second thing I'd like to do is provide some general outlines . . . this gets much more specific much more mechanical . . . to make your search for information in a library setting easier . . . OK?

7. now the basic purpose for this class is not just an introduction to ecology . . . it's an effort to relate to you . . . uh to give you . . . a reasoned approach to the relationship between the human species and its environment . . . and I use the term "reasoned approach" because all too often discussions of ecology or conservation of the environment tend to be overemotional . . . I'm a great believer in educational TV but some of the stuff they put out is so emotional . . . I will try to make this as factual as I can without making any demands on you in terms of scientific background . . . in other words, I will assume nothing.

Answers:
1. c   2. a   3. b   4. d   5. b, c, d   6. c, d   7. b

Exercise A Audioscript, page 54
Example
there are several essential abiotic . . . nonbiological . . . factors necessary to life in an ecosystem . . .

1. I see information and knowledge as two separate things . . . two entities . . .
2. an important part of the Indian household is called the chula or the hearth . . . the cooking center . . . small area in the courtyard . . .
3. there are organisms which are not capable of converting solar energy . . . and there are two sorts of these . . . and you need to be aware of these terms . . . the herbivores . . . the organisms which eat green plants directly . . . in other words . . . the plant-eaters . . .
4. you're figuring out what terminology . . . what vocabulary . . . to use a less polite word . . . what jargon . . . this topic is discussed in . . .

Possible Answers:
1. separate things   2. cooking center   3. plant-eaters   4. vocabulary

Exercise B Audioscript, page 54
Example
now the test was designed to study who was emotionally stronger . . . the women in the job market or the housewives . . . the researchers defined emotional strength as . . . the degree . . . of psychological distress . . . to which someone reacts . . . to a life crisis . . . let me repeat that . . . the degree . . . of psychological distress . . . to which someone . . . reacts . . . to a life crisis . . . in other words how much psychological distress did they show when there was a crisis in their lives? . . .

1. now exogamy is marriage outside of one's kin group . . . one's family group . . . it can also operate with respect to other social groups . . . the town . . . the race . . . and so on . . . marriage outside of some kind of group . . . and endogamy is marriage within a given group . . .
2. we need to know one important distinction here before you start work on your homework assignment and that is just a concept of "emic" and "etic" and again it's in your text but let's make sure we have it clear . . . emic means the point of view of a member of the culture or an insider's view of a culture . . . a subjective view from within a culture . . . whereas an etic analysis would be from the point of view of an outsider . . . a person outside the culture or subculture . . . supposedly an objective person perhaps a scientific observer . . .
3. metabolism is one way of distinguishing between the growth of a crystal and the growth of a living organism . . . by metabolism I mean the use of external energy and as you'll see before this course is over the ability to use energy is rather fundamental in the whole of the living system . . .
4. irritability [on board] . . . now that means more than just yelling OUCH when you sit on a pen . . . you react to stimuli of all sorts . . . you react to light . . . you react to heat . . . and living organisms have this capacity to react to features in the environment and obviously if you're going to look at the relationship between man, the human species, and its environment . . . then you've got to look at irritability . . .
5. what do we mean by life? . . . well the most obvious feature of life is reproduction . . . living organisms reproduce to repeat themselves . . . so that reproduction [on board] is obviously one criterion of life but reproduction itself is not enough . . . you can reproduce crystals in an appropriate solution . . . you can reproduce diamonds if you're so inclined . . . and living things don't behave quite like crystals or diamonds or anything else . . . living things have a capacity to metabolize . . . so metabolism [on board] is one way of distinguishing between the growth of a crystal and the growth of a living organism . . . by metabolism I mean the use of external energy and as you'll see before this course is over the ability to use energy is rather fundamental in the whole of the living system . . . and finally . . . irritability [on board] . . . now that means more than just yelling OUCH when you sit on a pen . . . you react to stimuli of all sorts . . . you react to light . . . you react to heat . . . and living organisms have this capacity to react to features in the environment and obviously if you're going to look at the relationship between man the human species and its environment then you've got to look at irritability so there you have three criteria . . . reproduction is not enough . . . metabolism and irritability distinguish the living from the nonliving.

Possible Answers:
1. a. marriage outside of group (family, town, etc.)   b. marriage inside of group (family, town, etc.)   2. a. insider's view of culture   b. outsider's view of culture   3. use of external energy   4. ability to react to environment   5. three criteria—reproduction, irritability, and metabolism

Exercise Audioscript, pages 56–57
Example
you might ask well how did the researchers judge psychological distress? . . . they used five measures . . . the first measure was anxiety . . . how much anxiety did the woman report in her life? . . . how often did she complain of anxiety? . . . the second one . . . irritability . . . how often did she complain of being irritated? . . . the third one . . . somatic complaints . . . somatic meaning bodily . . . complaints relating to the body . . . in other words . . . how often did the woman complain about having headaches or backaches? . . . the fourth one

. . . depression . . . how often did the woman complain about being depressed . . . feeling depressed? . . . the fifth one was problems in thinking and concentrating . . . how often did the woman complain about having this sort of problem? . . . added together these measures formed a way of judging how much psychological distress was in someone's life . . .

1. there are certain essential abiotic . . . nonbiological . . . factors necessary to life in an ecosystem . . . and the sorts of things with which we're concerned obviously are going to be . . . light . . . because there's the driving force for the whole of energy . . . you're going to need temperature . . . you're going to need nutrients . . . you're going to need moisture . . . and you can keep on going quite a way because those factors . . . those abiotic factors which I've just been talking about often interact with one another . . . you see the availability of nutrients for plants often depends upon the soil and the amount of moisture . . . so those are very simple categories with which to begin the discussion . . .
2. so roughly two things are happening as you survey your topic and clarify unfamiliar terms . . . one . . . you're getting a broad picture of the topic and testing out your interest in that topic . . . am I really interested in doing research on this topic? . . . and secondly . . . you're figuring out what terminology . . . what vocabulary . . . to use a less polite word . . . what jargon this topic is discussed in and you're allowing yourself then to go and define words that are not familiar to you . . . so when you start reading more in depth on a particular topic in more scholarly literature . . . you understand the language . . . you're comfortable with what you're doing . . .
3. and a lot of things have to be done to keep a baby born around the sixth or seventh month of pregnancy alive . . . one is constant monitoring of oxygen levels so that the oxygen levels are maintained at a high enough level so the kid gets enough oxygen in and out while breathing on its own and also that the oxygen levels don't get so high that it causes damage to the fetus . . . OK . . . one of the things that's very common among premature babies . . . quite common . . . has been blindness . . . which is caused by damage due to overoxygenation during the period that the kid is kept in the incubator . . . it's also very important to constantly maintain the kid's temperature at the appropriate level because the kid isn't capable at this point outside of the womb of maintaining body temperature . . . so you have to keep things warm and make sure that the kid is OK that way . . . hmmmm . . . variety of other stuff that I won't go into now . . .
4. OK . . . now during all of these stages lots and lots of growth is taking place and there's basically three kinds of things that are happening . . . the big thing is that cells are multiplying like crazy . . . and the rate at which they multiply changes over time . . . in the initial stages it's relatively slow . . . as you get . . . as you sit in that womb longer and longer . . . the growth becomes greater and greater and greater . . . and in fact it's in the last three months of the pregnancy that the kid exhibits the most growth . . . OK . . . we'll see that in a second . . . so the last half of the fetal period is when you really grow . . . um . . . so there is cell proliferation . . . cells are dividing . . . they're proliferating like mad . . . so the initial two cells end up to be millions and millions and billions of cells . . . OK . . . that's a lot of growth a lot of division . . .

OK . . . there's also things happening to those cells . . . as the . . . kid grows . . . they're differentiating . . . different cells . . . the two cells that started out initially united . . . divide . . . divide . . . divide . . . divide . . . and then they start to change their properties . . . different cells end up in different places in the embryo and the fetus and because they've ended up in that particular fate . . . place . . . they change . . . they change in certain ways . . . so some of those cells . . . which all came from the same two cells remember . . . are going to end up being cells which make up all those fancy organs which have all sorts of different cells in them . . . some are going to make up the skin . . . some are going to turn into bones . . . some are going to turn into blood . . . some are going to turn into brains and a variety of other stuff . . . so there's a lot of differentiation of the cells . . . OK . . . and by and large . . . what determines what a cell is going to look like when it starts to grow up in effect is where it ends up . . . where it is in the embryo or in the fetus . . .

OK . . . there's also some really bizarre things that go on that people hadn't noticed until about thirty or forty years ago . . . that is . . . not only are these cells proliferating like mad and changing themselves and differentiating but there's also movement of the cells . . . some of the cells sit around . . . differentiate . . . and then they creep around a little bit . . . it turns out they get not quite in the right place . . . so what happens they have to move to get into the appropriate place . . . OK . . . so they do that . . . and there are various mechanisms which particular kinds of cells have for recognizing their . . . their kin . . . in effect . . . so . . . you've got migration of cells . . . they kind of move around . . . suddenly they bump into a bunch of cells that are just like them and they say . . . ah . . . this is where I live and they stay there . . . so . . . that's the kind of stuff that's going on at the cellular level . . . OK . . . complicated stuff this . . .

Example Notes, pages 56–57
1. Essential abiotic factors for life in ecosystem
    1. light   3. nutrients
    2. temperature   4. moisture
2. While surveying topic and clarifying terms
    1. get broad picture of topic
       test interest in   ″
    2. find out vocab. of   ″

3. What needs to be done to keep a premature kid alive?
    1. monitor oxygen (too much → blindness)
    2. maintain body temperature
4. Three things that happen during prenatal period
    1. cells multiply faster
    2. cells differentiate—change properties
        —turn into brain cells, blood cells, etc.
    3. cells move

Exercise Audioscript, pages 59–60

Example

the seventh step is very similar to the second step . . . the second step broke the topic up into subtopics . . . in this next step you're looking at a topic and trying to see it in terms of its broadest possible . . . in the broadest possible way . . . and it asks you to think about all the academic subjects . . . the academic disciplines . . . that might have something to say . . . that might have something to contribute . . . to a discussion on your particular subject . . . and one of the reasons for doing this is different academic disciplines . . . different academic subjects . . . look at the same topic from very different vantage points . . . they have very different views of the same topic . . . and sometimes if you are deciding on an approach to a topic . . . how you want to discuss it in your particular paper you may decide to approach it from an economics viewpoint rather than a political science viewpoint . . . a religious viewpoint rather than a legal viewpoint . . . so think about academic disciplines academic subjects that might have something to say about your topic and think about the different ways that they might address the issues that are discussed in your particular subject . . .

1. OK . . . let's go to 1940 . . . and you know that 1940 was pretty much close to the beginning of World War II . . . it was prewar more or less . . . what do you think happens before a war? . . . any ideas? . . . people get married yes . . . I think that a lot of times people get married much more quickly than they would have in normal times because men are going off to war . . . they want to get married first . . . and then they go . . . well that's what happened . . . the marriages in 1940 . . . there were 1,595,879 marriages . . . and this occurred at a rate of 12.1 per 1,000 . . . so that you can see the great increase in the number of marriages . . .

2. so far we haven't seen any great increases in divorces . . . OK . . . but 1945 . . . what happened then? the men came home . . . the men who did come home . . . what do you think happened then? . . . well let's look at marriages first . . . the marriage rate stayed about the same . . . there were 12.2 per 1,000 and the number of marriages was 1,612,992 . . . that was about the same as in 1940 . . . the number of divorces was 485,000 and that occurred at a rate of 3.5 per 1,000 . . . so you can see that the divorce rate soared . . . and we can probably draw some conclusions about what separations do for marriages . . . some people think . . . what's the saying? . . . absence makes the heart grow fonder? other people think . . . out of sight out of mind . . . and I think the last one might hold better as seen in these statistics . . .

3. and the third wave of immigration started after 1965 when the U.S. changed its immigration laws . . . previously . . . the number of Asians had been kept very small because there was a quota . . . a limit . . . on people from certain parts of the world coming . . . and each Asian country . . . even after a restriction was lifted could send only about a hundred people into the country each year . . . but after the laws were changed each Asian country was allowed a quota of 20,000 immigrants under the quota and more . . . outside of the quota . . . people who were dependents . . . so the people started coming from many countries . . . a very rapid increase in Asian immigration . . .

4. OK as we know acid rain has increased with industrialization . . . we have not always had acid rain . . . when they look at glaciers from about 200 years ago they find that the water had a pH close to what we'd expect of theoretically pure water . . . so what can we do about this problem of acid rain then? . . . we do need to put some controls . . . or possibly put some controls on the production of acid rain . . . perhaps by shifting to alternative nonpolluting sources of energy . . . solar power . . . wind power . . . and so on . . . or . . . another way is to create technology to reduce the release of sulfur and nitrogen . . . the two chemicals which are primarily responsible for acid rain . . . technology to prevent these chemicals from being released into the atmosphere . . . the problem with both of these ideas is that they both cost money . . . so the costs and benefits need to be weighed . . .

Example Notes, pages 59–60

1. 1940—close to beg. of WWII (prewar)
    ↓
    people get married quicker
    ↑ in # of marriages
    Why? men go to war, want to marry first

2. 1945—men come home from war
    ↓
    divorce
    Why? "out of sight, out of mind"?

3. 1965—US changes immig. law
      ↓   (previously # of Asians small because quota ~100 people per country/yr.)
         raise quota to 20,000/country + dependents
         rapid ↑ in Asian immig.
   4. Acid rain ↑ w/ indust.
      Solutions? control production of a.r.
                 shift to nonpolluting energy?
                 create tech. to reduce sulfur & nitrogen?
      BUT both cost $!

Exercise Audioscript, pages 62–64
Example

now the levels of light which plants can tolerate varies enormously . . . there are shade plants which require very low light intensities . . . the sort of things that you grow in the hallway and in your office . . . and if you were to put them outside in the sun . . . they would die very quickly because the light intensity would be too high . . . and there are other plants which are perfectly happy sitting out in the sun all day . . . it's not just temperature . . . it's usually light intensity . . . so you've got to look at the light intensity . . .

1. with the cold-blooded plants and animals the chemical reactions depend upon the temperature of the environment . . . their body temperature depends on how cold or how warm the surroundings are . . . they don't have a stable temperature as humans do . . . now if you go in the desert at night you'll find that lizards are virtually asleep . . . it is so cold . . . they can't do anything . . . as the morning warms up . . . then the lizards and other things like that all begin to start moving . . . until you get into the heat of day and they then use up so much energy by any activity at that temperature that once again they are torpid . . . they're asleep . . . so the temperature requirements of a lot of animals in the desert have to be very carefully manipulated by their environmental habits . . . going into the shade during the day . . . going into a hole in the ground during the night . . .
2. we might note that cousin terms . . . terms for cousins . . . vary a great deal in languages and we'll be coming back to this . . . in English cousins of both sexes are referred to as a *cousin* . . . in Spanish you differentiate by sex . . . you say *primo* and *prima* . . . male cousin and female cousin . . . in Chinese it turns out that there are going to be eight terms for cousins . . .
3. the second step is to look at your topic and see if you can figure out what it's made up of . . . if you can break it up into simple subtopics . . . all topics are made up of really sort of connecting subtopics . . . for example let me think of a topic . . . uh take a topic like divorce . . . four students in my own class are writing their term papers on divorce . . . a very popular topic . . . if you break that broad topic . . . divorce is a very broad topic . . . you need to look at that broad topic and figure out what it's made up of . . . what are the subtopics that enter into a discussion of divorce . . . you can break it up in terms of thinking about who are the people affected . . . a husband a wife children . . . those are all subtopics or subideas . . . component parts of the broad topic of divorce . . . are you going to talk about divorce in terms of financial money issues? . . . that's another subtopic or component part . . . are you going to talk about it in terms of legal issues? . . . is it a religious problem or a religious issue? . . . break your topic up . . . sometimes you can break your topic . . . some topics you can break up very simply . . . breaking them up in terms of geography . . . what part of the world or parts of the world are affected by the particular topic? . . . breaking it up by chronology . . . periods of time . . . OK . . . so break your topic up see what it's made up of . . .
4. now endogamy is also sometimes built into marriage patterns . . . this is having to marry within the boundaries of some social category . . . within the family . . . within the village . . . within the religion . . . and so on . . . and I guess the most common example . . . the most well-known example of endogamy . . . is the caste system in India . . . where one has to marry within one's caste . . . there are also places where there is village endogamy . . . in southern Mexico for example there is pressure to marry within one's village that is the norm . . . that is what the society enforces . . . in the U.S. as well many people have analyzed southern race . . . racial cultures as endogamous groups . . . that blacks and whites in the American South at least in the past were endogamous . . . they married within their own social category or racial category . . . ethnic group endogamy is also a common thing especially among new immigrant populations . . . perhaps Korean immigrants to the U.S. are an endogamous group not marrying outside that category still . . .

Example Notes, pages 62–64
1. w/ cold-blooded animals, chemical reactions depend on temperature of the environment
      e.g., lizards—night/cold—can't move
                  day warms—↑ active
                  too hot—sleep
2. terms for "cousin"—vary in diff. lang.
      e.g., Eng.—both sex—same word
            Span.—diff. for ♀ ♂
            Chin.—8 terms

3. 2nd step—break topic into subtopics
         e.g., divorce
               who affected?
               financial issues?
               legal   " ? . . .
   4. Endogamy sometimes in marriage patterns
         marry w/i boundaries of soc. category
               e.g., caste sys. (India)
                     village endogamy (S. Mex.)
                     race   "   (S. U.S.—past?)
                     ethnic   "   (new immig.—Koreans?)

Exercise Audioscript, pages 65–67
   Example
      we are all cousins . . . if you trace our ancestry back far enough . . . you find . . . that all of us . . . ultimately come . . . from a small area . . . in East Africa . . . the species *Homo sapiens* began there . . . a few hundred thousand years ago . . . the human family began there . . . a few million years ago . . . initially we were . . . small . . . struggling . . . groups of family members . . . itinerant . . . wandering . . . following the game . . . our numbers were few . . . our powers were feeble . . . in the intervening years . . . we have expanded . . . to every continent on earth . . . some of us even reside at the ocean depths . . . and for brief periods . . . a few hundred miles overhead in space . . . we now number 5.6 billion of us . . . and our powers have reached formidable . . . if not awesome . . . proportions . . .

   1. OK . . . the embryonic period . . . during the first month . . . one of the critical things that happens is the life-support systems start to get formed . . . and in particular . . . the system of blood vessels . . . starts to form . . . so that all sorts of little tunnels start to form inside this developing thing which looks a whole lot like a tadpole or a fish at this point . . . um . . . and by the end of the month a heart has formed . . . primitive but recognizable as a heart . . . and the system of blood vessels connecting to it has also formed . . . OK . . . so we've got that happening . . . during the second month of this period . . . OK . . . the embryo gets a little bigger . . . gets to be about 2½ centimeters long . . . OK . . . an inch . . . it's still pretty tiny . . .
   2. there are three great pandemics of plague in history . . . or recorded history . . . the first occurs in the 600s . . . um . . . first noticed in the Middle East . . . first really big death toll comes in Egypt . . . which is the first densely populated place that the plague hit . . . coming from Arabia . . . and it's still raging a hundred years later in Ireland . . . the second is the one we're going to talk about today . . . the medieval outbreak . . . and the third . . . which we don't think about . . . is going on now . . . plague was cited in about . . . well in 1892 . . . in southwestern China . . . by 1896 it had reached India where it killed roughly 6 million people . . . and then something interesting happened . . . something that had never happened before . . . which is that since India at that point was a British colony . . . shortly after that it reached . . . England . . . but there it killed very few people . . . plenty of people *got* it . . . but in the 20th century . . . we have various medical treatments . . . and you *still* once in a while hear about plague . . . uh . . . it's also endemic to parts of New Mexico for instance . . . but . . . once you identify it today . . . you give people tetracycline . . . it clears up . . . its no longer deadly but it's still around . . .
   3. the fourth step asks you to estimate the quantity . . . the amount of information . . . that you're going to need to write a paper . . . the quantity of information is often based on the length of the paper . . . if you have to write a 10-page paper you'll need to do less research than if you're asked to write a 300-page paper . . . at least I think that's true . . . quantity also depends on what's available . . . sometimes because a lot of people choose to do their research on topics that are relatively new . . . they're in the news right now . . . they're just now happening . . . so there's not going to be 100 years' worth of scholarship or thought or writing on a particular topic . . . so quantity is sometimes determined by availability of information . . .
      often when you hear the word quantity people automatically think of its partner word which is *quality* . . . quality and quantity are often thought of in the same sentence . . . so after you've estimated the quantity of information or material that you need, you need to think about the quality of the information that you're going after . . . quality in terms of information which you find in a library can be judged in a couple of different ways . . . you can find out who wrote the book you're thinking about reading . . . is this person a scholar? is this person well-known or well thought of in her field? OK? so who wrote the book can say something about the quality of it . . . our library subscribes to 15,000 different periodicals . . . magazines . . . journals . . . newspapers . . . and they're of different quality . . . you get different types of articles in these different periodicals . . . so quality can sometimes be determined just by the magazine or the journal that you've read a particular article in . . . so you need to think about quantity in terms of amount of information and quality in terms of the value of that information . . .
      the next of these steps . . . the sixth step . . . is the one that I personally have the hardest time with and that's thinking about budgeting my time . . . think about all the things I have to do in terms of writing a research paper . . . in terms of doing research . . . processing the information . . . converting the information into useful usable knowledge . . . and then of course sitting down and writing the paper in absolutely flawless beautiful English . . . you have to budget your time because each of those aspects or elements takes a lot of

time . . . so the sixth step is to look at everything you have to do to get this paper written . . . and think about the amount of time it will take you to do each of these steps . . .

4. OK now so far I've mentioned norms about very basic things . . . I've mentioned some norms for things like talking . . . things like eating . . . and these are rather simple norms . . . there are of course more complex ones . . . which involve a series of actions . . . or a series of behaviors . . . and these norms are called rituals . . . all right rituals are a set or series of actions which . . . take place in a certain order . . . and they together form a certain kind of norm . . . one example of this is quoted by a British psychologist named Michael Argyle . . . Argyle had studied the rituals in various societies . . . including British society . . . and he has identified a number of steps . . . that take place in different rituals . . . one ritual that I'd like to mention is called . . . is what he calls the new-neighbor ritual . . . all right in the new-neighbor ritual . . . as he calls it . . . we have a typical set of . . . set of behaviors . . . when a new family moves into a neighborhood . . . shortly after that . . . the housewives in the immediate area will come over to the house . . . and through a series of actions . . . introduce themselves to the new housewife in the neighborhood . . . and according to Argyle these are the steps . . . OK? these are the steps in this particular ritual . . . first there is the invitation . . . an old neighbor invites the new neighbor to come over . . . OK that's the first step . . . the second step is that there is the greeting at the door . . . hello how are you please come in . . . the visitor is invited into the house . . . that's the third step . . . the fourth step the visitor has to admire the house . . . gee that's a lovely . . . lovely furniture you have here . . . next the hostess will serve tea and biscuits . . . then they will sit down . . . and will exchange information . . . essential in this exchange . . . they must exchange information about their husbands . . . what their husbands do . . . where their husbands work . . . what their husbands like to do in their free time . . . and finally . . . after a fixed period of time . . . maybe fifteen minutes is appropriate . . . the new neighbor must take the initiative . . . and say it's time to go . . . gets up . . . says farewell . . . we'll have to see each other again . . . OK now these steps together form what we call . . . a ritual . . . or a ritualized norm . . . OK not only . . . in a ritual not only must all the steps be there . . . but they must be there in a certain order . . . for example in the new-neighbor ritual . . . the hostess won't immediately serve tea and biscuits . . . without giving a tour of the house . . . nor will the person who comes to the house . . . immediately start talking about her husband . . . OK the point here is that in a ritual the steps must be there . . . and must be there in a certain order . . . Argyle the British psychologist and others . . . claim that it is a knowledge of rituals that make . . . us skillful . . . that make us socially skillful . . . that make us socially skillful in a given society . . . so learning the rituals is part of learning to be an acceptable member of our society . . .

Example Notes, pages 65–67

1. Embryonic period
    1st mo.: life-support system starts, esp. blood vessels
        looks like fish/tadpole
    by end of 1st mo.: heart formed (primitive) → blood vessels
    2nd mo.: bigger ~2.5 cm.

2. 3 great pandemics of plague in recorded history
    1st: 600s (Mideast) Egypt
            700s Ireland
    2nd: medieval outbreak
    3rd: now
            1892—SW China
            1896—India (6 million dead)
            ↓
            England—killed few people
                Why? medical treatment

3. 8 steps to writing research paper
    1. survey topic (look for broadest discussion) and clarify unfamiliar terms
    2. break topic into simple subtopics
    3. look for types of info. needed to research subject
    4. estimate quantity of info. needed
    5. estimate quality   "   "   "
    6. budget time

4. Rituals—set or series of actions take place in certain order—form norm
    e.g., from Argyle (British psychol.), identified steps in "new-neighbor ritual" (when new family moves into neighborhood)
        1. invitation (old neighbor invites new)
        2. greeting at door
        3. visitor invited in
        4. visitor admires house
        5. hostess serves tea & biscuits
        6. talk about husbands
        7. visitor (after ~15 min.) gets up to go
    Knowledge of rituals makes us skillful in given society

Exercise Audioscript, pages 69–70

Example

anyway the households and its constituents are a very good thing to look at cross-culturally . . . let me just review the types quickly that the book gives us . . . well first of all . . . patrilocal with the husband's father . . . where the newly married couple goes to live with the husband's father . . . this patrilocal extended family would be living together . . . "virilocal" . . . another term . . . V-I-R-I . . . local . . . this means going to live with the husband's family or any of his relatives . . . that is with his family not with his father . . . any of the husband's relatives . . . obviously a bigger range of possibilities than just going to live with the husband's father . . . similarly with the next two terms . . . "matrilocal" . . . going to live with the wife's mother . . . and "uxorilocal" . . . going to live with the wife's family or any relative . . . your book has a whole little chart of these . . . I'm just giving the main important types . . . another important type that we'll be talking a bit more about on Thursday . . . is "avunculocal" [on board] what does that mean? . . . uncle . . . OK . . . going to live with the man's mother's brother . . . so if this couple got married . . . they'd go to live with his mother's brother . . . the husband's uncle on his mother's side . . . I'll talk about this more on Thursday . . . this is what half of the world's matrilineal societies do . . . and this keeps the men of a matrilineage together . . . and finally "neolocal" . . . just the nuclear family going off and establishing a new household . . . independent household . . . not bothering with the parents on either side or with the mother's brother . . .

1. what people normally do is they divide up the period of development in the womb into three basic periods . . . the first one is what's called the germinal period . . . that's G-E-R-M-I-N-A-L, germinal . . . which basically encompasses the first two weeks . . . so it's a period which lasts from conception to about two weeks later . . . the second period is the embryonic period . . . that's E-M-B-R-Y-O-N-I-C . . . the embryonic period . . . which lasts longer . . . from about the second week on until the third month . . . and finally we've got what's called the fetal period which runs from the third month on to term . . . usually the ninth month . . .

2. the third step means . . . you need . . . asks you to look at types of information that you might need to successfully research this particular subject . . . and by types of information I mean something very specific here . . . two very specific types of information . . . one type that's known as primary information . . . and another type which is known as secondary information and in terms of a very simple and not exactly accurate definition, primary information or a primary source is an eye-witness account . . . somebody who was actually there at the time is reporting on an event as it happened . . . there are all kinds of primary sources . . . an interview with somebody is a primary source . . . somebody's diary or personal papers are a primary source . . . if you're a scientist and you keep a laboratory notebook that charts every step in an experiment . . . that's a primary source . . . secondary sources or secondary information is that which from a distance in time has looked at the primary source and has analyzed it, criticized it, worked it through some sort of critical process and written about it . . . most of what we read in journals, magazine articles, textbooks, encyclopedias are secondary source documents . . . so you have to think about your particular topic . . . whatever subject you're going to do research on . . . and think about the available primary and secondary sources of information . . .

3. there are two kinds of polygamy which is plural spouses . . . there is polygyny . . . P-O-L-Y-G-Y-N-Y . . . polygyny . . . where the plural spouses are women and polyandry, P-O-L-Y-A-N-D-R-Y . . . polyandry . . . where the plural spouses are men . . . now for polygyny again there are two kinds . . . there's general polygyny where the women are not specially related to each other in any way . . . they're co-wives but they may be from very different origins from very different places and there's the very special kind of polygyny which is sororal polygyny [on board] where the co-wives are sisters . . . and this is fairly common especially among Native Americans . . . now the general type of polygyny is more common in Africa and in Melanesia . . . and again there are two kinds of polyandry . . . and as you might guess with our example from polygyny the first kind . . . fraternal polyandry where the co-husbands are brothers . . . we already had some discussion of this in the last lecture in the Himalayan example of fraternal polyandry . . . the co-husbands are brothers . . . the other case being nonfraternal and this is very rare unlike the case with general polygyny which is quite common where the co-wives are not sisters . . .

4. OK if we move on to marriage payments . . . and here's an idea that emphasizes the family aspect of marriage arrangements . . . it's most common in arranged marriage systems . . . it's an alliance between families who are cooperating to arrange a marriage . . . and to . . . compensate each other for work and reproductive potential that's being exchanged here . . . when a man and woman are getting married . . . the first kind of marriage payment is a bride price . . . and this is most commonly required in marriage systems when women make important economic contributions . . . and their male kin control their marriages . . . so that when a daughter is lost her work is lost to her family of birth . . . her reproductive potential is lost to her family of birth and the man and his family who are taking her as a bride have to make payment . . . have to make compensation . . . another kind of marriage payment is the dowry . . . D-O-W-R-Y . . . dowry . . . and here . . . this is most common when women make unimportant or make less important contributions to the household's economic livelihood and their male kin also control their marriages . . . here money or goods has to be given along with the bride to her new family to help set up a new household or to help her move in to a joint household . . . often . . . she has to bring resources with her . . . OK a third kind of marriage payment . . . bride service . . . and here the husband and his family don't compensate by contributing cattle or money as a bride price but they go and give labor to compensate to make up for the loss of the woman's

labor in her family . . . so you might find a husband here going and working two years in the household of his prospective bride and then they can get married and live together . . . so bride service is another way that many societies work this bride . . . this marriage . . . payment . . .

Example Notes, pages 69–70
1. 3 periods of development in womb
   —germinal   —first 2 wks.
   —embryonic   —2nd wk.→ 3rd mo.
   —fetal   —3rd mo. → birth

2. 3rd step—look for types of info. needed to research subj.
   —primary info.—eye witness
       e.g., interview, diary
   —secondary info.—looks at prim. source, analyzes it
       e.g., journals, mag.

3.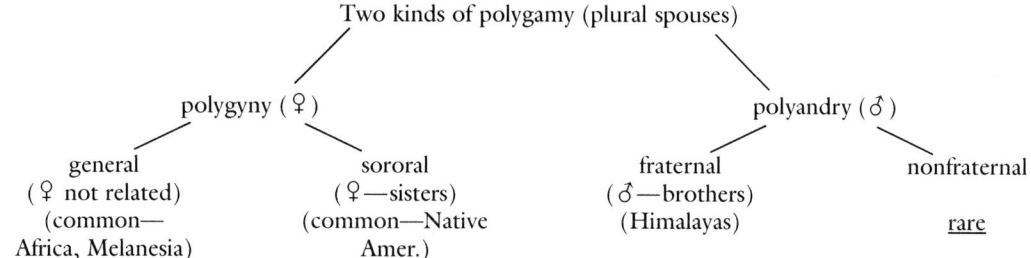

4. Marriage payment—most common in arranged marriages
   —alliance betw. families to compensate other for work & reproductive potential
   Types of payment:
   —bride price (where ♀ important economically & ♂ control marriage)
      ♂ pays ♀'s family
   —dowry (where ♀ unimport. econom. & ♂ control marr.)
      ♀ brings $/goods → ♂'s family
   —bride service (♂ & family work for bride's family to compensate for loss)

Exercise Audioscript, pages 72–73
Example

each house has two beds inside it . . . if we were to draw the inside of the house you'd see a man's bed and a woman's bed . . . the man's bed is not for the husband to sleep in . . . it's for male guests . . . it's for adult sons . . . these beds are built on platforms with cowhide on top . . . there's a little wood fire in the middle of the house . . . there aren't really windows in these houses . . . there are small airholes near the beds which are stuffed with rags if it's cold outside . . . so you have a lot of smoke . . . the wood fire is kept going constantly and it's very smoky inside . . . the dimensions here are about twenty-five feet long and about fifteen feet wide . . . fairly small houses . . . and usually goats and sheep . . . goats and sheep are penned up at one end of this house . . . so this is what the house looks like . . .

1. now in a typical deciduous woodland . . . you have got *large trees* . . . you've got *small shrubs* . . . and you have got *vegetation* at ground level . . . it's obvious that the light intensity . . . the amount of energy which is available . . . varies enormously . . . because there's going to be a lot of screening . . . so you've got tall trees which absorb direct sunlight up here and plants which occur down here at the ground which are essentially shade plants . . . they barely get any sun . . . so here you are in a complex woodlands such as this . . .

2. during the second month . . . OK . . . the embryo gets a little bigger . . . gets to be about 2½ centimeters long OK . . . an inch . . . it's still pretty tiny . . . OK . . . and things have been differentiating and things have been forming and folding in on themselves and so on and so forth . . . to the point where the embryo starts to have recognizable features . . . it's got a recognizable head . . . it's got recognizable limbs . . . it's got recognizable buds on the ends of its hands and feet that are eventually going to turn into hands and toes . . . and so on . . . OK . . . so . . . so . . . we get that . . . it starts to be recognizable of something other than just a blob . . .

3. OK . . . during the fourth and the fifth month . . . now we've got stuff that's spread out over a number of months . . . we start to see completion of the basic body structures . . . so that is basically one of the reasons that it's starting to look more and more like a little baby . . . OK . . . the face is basically complete at this point . . . so nose, lips, eyes, mouth, all that stuff, OK . . . um . . . the bones . . . bone structures are starting to form . . . they're at least getting outlined at this point . . . but they're soft and rubbery . . . real soft and real rubbery in fact . . . OK . . . but they're there . . . you can see them . . . OK if you x-ray the fetus or use various other kinds of imaging techniques . . . OK you're starting to get blood forming . . . which can race around inside the blood vessels . . . and the head now gets the ability to move independently

from the trunk . . . so we've had the kid capable of sort of waving the arms and legs around independently . . . now the kid can nod . . . OK and wiggle its head . . .

Example Notes, pages 72–73
1. Typical deciduous woodland
    —tall trees
    —small shrubs
    —vegetation on ground
    —light varies from top to ground
2. 2nd month of embryo development
    —gets bigger—2½ cm. (1")
    —starts have recognizable features
        —head
        —limbs
3. 4th–5th month of fetal development
    —looks more like baby
    —face complete
    —bones start form (soft)
    —blood   "   "
    —head moves independently (nod)

Exercise Audioscript, pages 75–77
Example

and we move now . . . I should say about . . . 12 to 14 million years later . . . we have fossils of another kind of being . . . it's called *Australopithecus* and . . . this fossil was or is representative of men and women . . . it's very clear huh? . . . it walked upright um . . . every indication it . . . every indication shows that they looked essentially like us . . . there were some differences . . . *Australopithecus* did not have this great uh uh bulbous development up here . . . this cranium development . . . *Australopithecus* was very flat here . . . when you go home today grab . . . grab a hold of the first alley cat you see and take a look at it . . . their nose is here and right from the nose the head line goes back . . . it's very flat from the nose . . . the nose is there . . . and there's no . . . there's no cranium . . . no bulbous cranium . . . *Australopithecus* was like that . . . also . . . *Australopithecus* did not have a chin . . . *however Australopithecus* walked upright just like we do and not like this ape . . .

1. now in a typical deciduous woodland . . . you have got *large trees* . . . you've got *small shrubs* . . . and you've got *vegetation* at *ground level* . . . it's obvious that the light intensity . . . the amount of energy which is available *varies* enormously . . . because there's going to be a lot of screening . . . so you've got tall trees which absorb direct sunlight up here and plants which occur down here at the ground which are essentially shade plants . . . so in this sort of deciduous woodland you have a complex series of plant species . . . a very complex ecosystem . . .
    . . . and if you go into coniferous woodland . . . the situation is slightly different . . . it's much more open . . . there is not the heavy shade . . . the trees are more widely spaced . . . light reaches the ground level more easily . . . you still have got vegetation on the ground but this has a very different look to it . . . very different from the deciduous woodland . . .
2. psychologists sort of fall into various camps that sort of line up pretty much according to particular philosophical lines . . . but the big thing is the debate between [on board] the empiricists . . . empiricism . . . and the nativists . . . these are extreme positions . . . basically the empiricist position says everything is learned . . . everything is the result of experience . . . the nativist says no . . . it's all wired in . . . we're born with certain predispositions . . . um so for the empiricist if there's any regularity in development . . . in behavior . . . in thought patterns . . . or whatever . . . it's because the world out there is regular . . . and those regularities have been detected in some way . . . have been impressed upon the individual and that's why the individual's behavior is regular . . . the nativist says no . . . no . . . the reason why behavior is regular is because people are regular guys . . . they've got these innate predispositions to organize experience in a particular way . . . and it's because of what's inside not outside that people organize experience and organize the world in that particular way . . .
3. the critical difference between digging stick, hoe agriculture, which is called horticulture . . . and plow agriculture are these characteristics . . . it tends to be true that with digging stick agriculture . . . with horticulture . . . people move to fresh land . . . every three or four years . . . they don't keep using the land . . . they use the land for three or four years . . . and then move on . . . cut down trees on some new land that's kind of fresh and productive and move on to that . . . leaving the old one to grow over again and kind of refresh itself . . . um . . . this means that you need more land per person than you would under a system where you're intensively using the same land . . . um . . . and so this technology tends to limit the group size . . . not as much as hunting-and-gathering technology but quite a bit . . . so again group size is 500 to 5,000 . . . the next transition, the big one, is the plow . . . and that has a lot of implications which I'll go into detail later . . . so that anthropologists . . . usually distinguish between plow agriculture and horticul-

ture . . . and the plow agriculture tends to be associated with societies that have urban centers . . . they're more settled . . . they tend to be very large societies . . .

Example Notes, pages 75–77

1. typical deciduous woodland — large trees
   small shrubs
   vegetation—ground, shade plants
   tall trees absorb light

   typ. coniferous woodland — more open
   no heavy shade
   ground veg. diff.

Example Rewritten Notes

	Deciduous	Coniferous
Vegetation	tall trees short shrubs ground—shade plants	trees—widely spaced
Light	absorbed by trees	reaches ground

2. Empiricist view　　　　　　　　　　　　Nativist view
   　—everything learned from experience　　—knowledge built in
   　—world regular ∴ people similar　　　　—people similar because innate tendencies

3. Diff. betw. horticulture (digging stick/hoe agriculture) & plow agricult.
   　　　　　　　／　　　　　　　　　　　　＼
   —move every 3–4 years　　　　　　　　　—settled
   —need more land per person ∴ limits size (500–5,000)　—urban center
   　　　　　　　　　　　　　　　　　　　　—large society

Example Rewritten Notes

	Horticulture	Plow Agriculture
Use of land	move every 3–4 yrs.	reuse land; settle
Size of society	500–5,000; ltd. because need land	larger urban society because reuse land

Exercise Audioscript, pages 80–81

Example

a major question would be which one is emotionally and physically more beneficial . . . let me first look at the physical side of the question . . . previously we knew that men had a higher heart attack rate than women did and that most people blamed that on the fact that they worked outside of the home and women didn't . . . work in the job market being more stressful than staying at home . . . however . . . now with more than 50% of women in the job market and still there is an uneven heart attack rate . . . this theory has lost credibility . . . in fact research has shown that women who work outside the home appear to be at no greater risk than women who stay at home . . . for heart disease at least . . . so . . . it seems that physically there is no benefit in working outside the home or not . . . they seem to be about equal . . .

1. the first question is . . . do drugs improve memory in any way and let me answer with a decided yes because there is extensive evidence and I will show you that in a couple of minutes that drugs can influence learning and memory in laboratory animals . . . there's no doubt about that . . . that's been amply demonstrated . . . as a matter of fact that's been known for almost seventy years . . . the first study on this topic was published by Carl Ashley . . . many of you know who he is . . . he's an important contributor to psychobiology . . . he founded a journal by that name . . . this article . . . I've always liked especially that it was the first article to show that drugs can improve memory . . . now what did he show? . . . what he showed is important because it sets the problems that we have to face in this field . . . he did several experiments in which he injected rats with a drug . . . strychnine sulfate [on board] . . . each day a few minutes before they were trained in a relatively simple alley maze . . . that is a maze with a bunch of alleys . . . each day they got a few training trials in that maze and they were put back in the cages . . . and the next day they were injected with the drug . . . and given some more training and so on . . . and he measured the number of errors that they made over the course of each day's training and what he found was that the animals who were injected with strychnine made fewer errors than the animals that were injected with the saline control solution . . . now . . . that's a very interesting finding and it raises dozens of questions because the conclusion that we can draw from that is that the performance of the animals in the maze is improved by the injection of the drug and the problem faced in science then is to figure out why that happened . . .

2. now . . . there are cases . . . I don't know exactly how many . . . where a bilingual . . . you know . . . someone who speaks two languages fluently . . . where bilinguals have suffered brain damage . . . and they've lost their first language completely . . . but they can still speak their second language . . . and this seems to mean that the two languages are stored in different parts of the brain . . . but at the moment we're not sure about that . . .

3. OK . . . um the first point that I'd like to make is that when you're talking about Asian-Americans or Asian-Pacific-Americans you're really talking about a very heterogeneous population . . . um . . . in the 19th century people from five different Asian countries came to the U.S. . . . and those were China . . . Japan . . . Korea . . . the Philippines . . . and India . . . now the descendants of those five groups are . . . the ones who make up the second, third, fourth, and fifth generation of Asian-Americans and they're really quite a distinct group from the more recent immigrants . . . in the 19th century, people did not come from all over China or all over Japan or all over Korea . . . they came from very small limited areas . . . specific localities . . . and I don't have time to go into the reasons there . . . but people from those particular areas in the country had a lot in common and they spoke in particular kinds of dialects . . . which are different from the dialects and languages that are being spoken by many of the more recent immigrants . . .

Example Notes, pages 80–81

1. Drugs improve memory
   —1st study—70 yrs. ago
      —inject rats w/ strych. sulf. before go in maze and trained
      —repeat
      —rats w/ chem.—fewer errors than control
   Problem—why?

2. case of bilingual —brain damage
      —lose 1st lang. but keep 2nd lang.!
   ∴ 2 langs. stored diff. parts of brain???

3. Asian-Americans—heterogeneous group
      19th c.—immigrated fr. China, Japan, Korea, Phil., India
               fr. specific areas, not whole country
   recent imm.— " fr. diff. parts of these countries; diff. dialects

Exercise Audioscript, page 82

1. this theory agrees with the idea that man in fact did come from some kind of chimpanzee . . . some kind of a monkey . . . but that there was a long . . . something like 12 million years of aquatic evolution . . . the idea that men and women were in the water . . . and the suggestion of this theory is not that he was a deep-sea creature not like a . . . shark or a deep-sea fish . . . but rather a seashore creature . . . a creature of the seashore that lived on the beach and found his food in the water diving for his food and living a great deal of time in the water along the shore . . . so . . . if you go down to the beach on any Sunday and take a look at that crowded beach with people all around the beach and then some of them playing and swimming in the water, you'll have a very accurate scene of . . . what perhaps this theory suggested millions and millions of years ago . . . the only thing wrong would be the bikini bathing suit which I don't think existed then . . .

2. now why should water have such a moderating effect on climate? . . . the answer is because of its physical properties and there are two particularly that you need to know about . . . the specific heat [on board] is the amount of heat it takes to raise the temperature of one gram of water by one degree Celsius . . . this is the calorie . . . now don't confuse this with the calorie of the calorie counter . . . the calorie of the calorie counter is a bigger unit . . . and just as the meter and the kilometer are related in this way . . . the kilometer is 1,000 meters . . . the calorie of the calorie counter is in fact a thousand of the little calories I've just been talking about . . . and I know you'd never be able to sell a can of diet soda if you advertised it as containing 1,000 calories . . . which in fact is scientifically correct . . . the food calories should be spelled with a capital C or kilocalories should be used in its place . . . the other two heat factors that need to be considered are the two latent [on board] heats . . . these are the amount of heat energy needed to convert solid water . . . that's ice . . . to liquid . . . on the one hand . . . and to convert the liquid water to steam on the other . . . without raising temperature . . . just simply convert it from solid to liquid to gas . . . and all of those three . . . the specific heat and the two latent heats . . . for water . . . are higher than for any other fluid . . .

3. well we know what killed people in the 14th century was bubonic plague . . . 'cause it has very distinctive symptoms . . . particularly large black blobs that appear on you . . . which are called "bubos" . . . thus the term "bubonic plague" . . . and the agent that causes it . . . it's a bacillus . . . whose normal host is either the blood stream of an animal or the stomach of a flea . . . and actually in general the plague prefers rodents . . . it usually stays with them . . . especially rats . . . and the outbreak of the great pandemics . . . always seems to be linked to the migration of rats out of their normal areas . . . we don't really understand why this happens but it does . . . in the Middle Ages . . . the chief of these emigres was one of these guys . . . the black rat . . . *Ratus ratus* . . . um . . . there he is . . . in case you were wondering this belongs to a colleague of mine who was *given* this by his mother-in-law . . . after he started talking about the plague at her house one day . . . so this is a lesson for you . . . if you go home at Thanksgiving . . . and talk about

what you are learning in History 21A . . . *watch* under the tree at Christmas . . . and you never know . . . but anyway . . . the . . . the black rat by nature is nomadic . . . and its original home . . . seems to be in Central Asia . . but it's in Europe by 1100 at least . . . uh . . . introduced again . . . largely by increased trade contacts . . . so there are rats . . . but you have to get the bacillus out of the rat population and into the humans . . . and the agent that does that is a special flea . . . the Latin name of which I cannot pronounce so I won't try . . . which lives on household rats . . . and can also live on humans . . .

4. there are three types of marriage payments . . . the first kind of marriage payment is a bride price . . . and this is most commonly required in marriage systems when women make important economic contributions . . . and their male kin control their marriages . . . so that when a daughter is lost her work is lost to her family of birth . . . her reproductive potential is lost to her family of birth and the man and his family who are taking her as a bride have to make payment . . . have to make compensation . . . another kind of marriage payment is the dowry and here . . . this is most common when women make unimportant or less important contributions to the household's economic livelihood and their male kin also control their marriages . . . here money or goods has to be given along with the bride to her new family to help set up a new household or to help her move in to a joint household . . . often . . . she has to bring resources with her . . . actually the U.S. was a bridal . . . was a dowry system and we have vestiges of that . . . you get hope chests . . . some people still keep hope chests building up household goods to take with them into their marriage . . . wedding gifts are a vestige of this . . . usually at weddings it's the bride's family in this country that pays for the wedding . . . you get more relatives from the bride's side . . . more gifts from the bride's side . . . I think if you went out and did analyses of weddings going on last week, next week, you would find that this is generally true . . . it still represents a greater investment, a greater contribution, on the part of the bride's family reflecting the past when a dowry was part of the American marriage system . . . I should say that we had arranged marriages too in the 19th century and one of the ways that you can tell the change . . . in arranged marriage systems the girls all marry in birth order eldest daughter first . . . second daughter next . . . third daughter next . . . because the parents are arranging them very nicely and in birth order . . . when you begin to get your second daughter marrying before your first one or the fourth before the second then you know that that system is breaking down and you're moving from an arranged marriage system to some kind of a choice or love marriage system . . . I'm sure that we would find that the dowry system was changing at the same time . . . OK . . . a third kind of marriage payment . . . bride service . . . and here the husband and his family don't compensate by contributing cattle or money as a bride price but they go and give labor to compensate to make up for the loss of the woman's labor in her family . . . so you might find a husband here going and working two years in the household of his prospective bride and then they can get married and live together . . . so bride service is another way that many societies work out this bride . . . this marriage payment . . .

Answers, page 82:
1. info. about the bikinis on the beach **2.** info. about calories of diet soda **3.** info. about mother-in-law's gift of rat **4.** info. about arranged marriages in the U.S.

UNIT 6 LECTURE COMPREHENSION AND NOTE-TAKING PRACTICE

Unit Summary: Unit 6 enables students to practice listening and note-taking skills such as listening for the larger picture, recognizing organizational plans and taking notes accordingly, and using notes to answer test-type questions. They also learn and use both discipline-specific and general vocabulary in reading/writing and speaking/listening activities. Lectures in this unit are from five to twenty minutes in length.

Lecture 6: How To Deal with Stress

Pre-Lecture Reading and Discussion, pages 83–85

Answers:
1. Answers will vary. **2.** No. There are a number of items (e.g., vacation, Christmas, marriage) that most would consider positive. **3.** Answers may vary. Some may point out the preponderance of items relating to adult life events and issues; a scale for teens would probably put more emphasis on dating, friendship, relations with siblings and parents, and school. Some may point out that there is a cultural bias in the scale as shown, for example, by the inclusion of Christmas and the concept of mortgages. **4.** This research alone would not be sufficient to prove a cause-and-effect relationship. Answers may vary regarding the reason. Some possibilities: It is only one study and would need more research; one might question how the study was conducted and whether the procedures were sound; additional research would need to be done to show that stress, in fact, was the key and causal factor in the development of the major illness rather than anger or another factor. **5.** Answers may vary. Students might suggest specific dietary changes (e.g., drinking herbal tea), lifestyle changes (e.g., waking up early to meditate), attitude changes (e.g., giving people the benefit of the doubt more frequently).

Lecture Outline for Listening for the Larger Picture, page 85
Use this outline if you'd like to deliver the lecture yourself.

INTRODUCTION: It's easy to relax when there's nothing causing tension—no problems, no school, no job. But life without stressors (things that cause stress) is virtually impossible. No one is immune to stress. So if we have to live with stress, we may as well find out more about it—what it is, how it can be dealt with.

I. What is stress?

    A. The term was originally used in physics to describe the force exerted between two touching bodies.

    B. In the thirties, Dr. Hans Selye of Montreal first adapted this term to describe the body's nonspecific response to any demand placed on it, pleasant or not.
        1. This response includes accelerated breathing and heart rate, increased blood pressure, and muscle tension.

    C. Stress may be both negative and positive.
        1. Positive stress (*eustress*) occurs in a life situation toward which one feels positively.
            a. e.g., Pressure in a job may give some people added incentive and excitement.
            b. e.g., Notice on the "stress test" that you did that items such as "vacation," "Christmas," "marriage," and "outstanding personal achievement" all have stress values. Even though these events are considered good or happy events, they still cause stress.
        2. Negative stress occurs in a life situation toward which one feels negatively.
            a. e.g., test-taking, a close friend's death

    D. Stress, in itself, is not hazardous; rather, the danger is in the individual's reaction to the stress.

II. By developing appropriate ways to cope with stressful situations, individuals can reduce the physiological harm caused by stress.

    A. Find ways to deal with stress appropriately.
        1. Learn to recognize stress signals.
            a. Individuals should monitor themselves for stress signals so that attention can be focused on minimizing or acknowledging stress before it becomes out of control.
            b. Common early signals include irritability, insomnia, rapid weight loss or gain, increased smoking or drinking, increases in small or "dumb" errors, physical tension, nervous tics, and tightness of breath.
            c. Individuals can consider ways to protect themselves when confronted with early signs of stress. This might involve withdrawing from the stressful situation or rewarding themselves with equal amounts of low-stress activity time.
        2. Pay attention to demands of the body.
            a. Exercise and good nutrition can decrease the effect of stress on both the body and mind.
            b. Exercise often provides a stress-free environment away from the usual stressors.
        3. Make plans and act when appropriate.
            a. Rather than wasting energy on worrying, an individual can direct his/her energy to plan steps and act.
            b. Not only does the process of planning and acting decrease stress, but the results of one's plans and actions may actually serve to remove or weaken the source of one's stress; that is, the worrisome job might get done!
        4. Hand in hand with acting when appropriate, learn to accept situations that are out of one's control and cannot be acted on.
            a. Individuals need to distinguish between those situations that are worth the energy invested in changing them and those situations that are unchangeable regardless of the energy invested in them.
                (1) e.g., Lateness caused by traffic is out of the hands of an individual.
                (2) It only increases stress to waste energy trying to resist what is inevitable.
        5. Pace activities.
            a. Break a task into manageable parts and start fresh each day.
            b. Recognize that there are twenty-four hours in a day and set reasonable daily goals for yourself.

    B. Remember that the problem is not in stressful experiences themselves; the problem is in one's reactions to these experiences.

CONCLUSION: Each individual has his/her own limits for stress, his/her own ways of coping with stress, and his/her own ways of balancing the costs and benefits of stress. Perhaps your strategies were mentioned in this lecture; perhaps you have your own ways that you would like to share with the class.

Lecture Audioscript for Listening for the Larger Picture, page 85
This audioscript shows one speaker's delivery of the lecture, as recorded in the audio program. Use it as a resource.

OK . . . as you all know it's easy to relax when there's nothing causing tension . . . when you have no . . . uh . . . problems . . . no school . . . but that's pretty unrealistic . . . life always has stressors . . . uh things which are causing us stress . . . and living without stress is virtually impossible . . . and no one is immune to stress . . . *so* . . . if we have to live with stress we may as well find out more about what it . . . what it is . . . how we can deal with it and so on . . . OK . . . um what *is* stress? . . . the term was originally used in physics . . . to describe . . . the force . . . exerted . . . between two touching bodies . . . uh it was strictly a term describing a physical reaction . . . in the 1930s um . . . a doctor named Hans Selye . . . S-E-L-Y-E . . . of Montreal . . . first used this term to describe a human's reaction to a demand placed on it . . . the human body's reaction . . . its *non*specific response . . . to any demand placed on it . . . pleasant or not . . . let me repeat that . . . the body's *non*specific response . . . to any demand placed on it . . . pleasant or not . . . so uh he really didn't put any value judgment on that . . . and he included in this response things like um accelerated breathing . . . accelerated heart rate . . . uh increased blood pressure . . . muscle tension . . . and so on . . . a . . . and notice that I said that stress can be pleasant or not . . . this response can be pleasant or not . . . and stress can be both negative and positive . . . and positive stress . . . he named "eustress" [on board] . . . and eustress occurs in a life situation towards which one feels positively . . . and as you saw in the exercise at the beginning . . . uh you saw on the stress scale things like Christmas . . . um getting married . . . usually positive events . . . but still stressful nonetheless . . . um another example is that pressure in a job can give some people incentive to work and excitement but it still is stress . . . or as I said before Christmas . . . marriage . . . achievement . . . are all positive things but they certainly add stress to your life . . . *negative* stress is what most of us think of when we think of stress and negative stress occurs . . . logically enough . . . in situations toward which one feels negatively . . . and those examples could be uh . . . test-taking . . . uh a friend's death . . . and um so on . . . but a thing to remember is that stress in itself is not hazardous . . . rather the danger is in the individual's reaction to the stress . . . so stress is not a negative or a positive word . . . it's not dangerous in itself . . . the danger is in the individual's response to the stress . . . and psychologists have found that if we develop appropriate ways to cope with stressful situations . . . individuals can reduce the physiological harm which is caused by stress or which *can* be caused by stress . . . and that's what I want to talk a bit about . . . what are these appropriate ways to deal with stress . . . to minimize any negative reactions? . . .

the first thing that most psychologists suggest is to learn . . . to recognize . . . your own stress signals . . . OK and we all have different types of stress signals but individuals should monitor themselves for stress signals . . . so that they can focus on minimizing or acknowledging the stress before it gets out of control . . . and common early signs for many people include irritability . . . uh insomnia . . . weight loss . . . weight gain . . . smoking . . . drinking . . . increases in small or "dumb" errors . . . uh tension . . . tics . . . tightness of breath . . . all kinds of things . . . that people get which could be an early signal of stress . . . and if you're aware of *your* early signs of stress . . . and as I said people might have *different* early signs of stress . . . you can consider ways to protect yourself when you start seeing these signs coming on . . . so you might decide to withdraw from a stressful situation . . . or uh reward yourself with equal amounts of low-stress activity time . . . but once you recognize the stress signals you can do something . . . to prevent them . . . from getting out of hand . . . so that's really the first . . . important way to deal with stress appropriately . . .

a *second* very important way to deal with stress is to pay attention to your body's demands . . . most psychologists are finding that a good exercise program . . . good nutrition . . . decreases the amount of stress . . . or the effect of stress . . . on the body . . . in the mind . . . *and* this seems quite apparent because exercise can provide a stress-free environment away from your usual stressors and it keeps your body busy and preoccupied with non-stressful things . . .

OK . . . uh . . . the *third* thing psychologists suggest should be done to reduce stress . . . is to make plans and act . . . when appropriate . . . and I'll get back to that "when appropriate" comment, OK? . . . but what they suggest is rather than wasting energy on worrying . . . an individual can direct his or her energy to plan the steps and act . . . and often just the planning of the action helps to reduce the stress because it reduces the worrying . . . and also the *results* of the plans or actions may serve to remove or weaken the original cause of the stress . . .

OK but notice that I said *when appropriate* . . . and this next suggestion has to do with that idea "when appropriate" . . . the third suggestion was to make plans and act when appropriate rather than just sit around and worry . . . but the fourth plan . . . or fourth idea says to learn to accept situations which are out of your control . . . which you can*not* act on . . . OK . . . these two then go hand in hand . . . they're very important . . . you can make plans and act when it's *appropriate* . . . *but* . . . when it's *not* appropriate . . . or when it's impossible . . . the only way . . . the thing to do is to learn to accept that some things are unchangeable and out of your hands . . . OK? . . . so for example if you're in traffic . . . lateness caused by traffic is out of your hands . . . there's no sense in getting really all crazy about that . . . *other* things are . . . well . . . just in general it only increases your stress to waste energy trying to resist what's inevitable . . . what can't be avoided . . .

the *last* item that psychologists suggest is to pace your activities . . . and by pace I mean . . . give yourself some manageable task to do at a regular . . . uh a reasonable speed . . . don't try to jump into something all at a whirlwind speed . . . then get exhausted and burnt out . . . but go at a speed that you can handle . . . break your task into manageable parts rather than try to deal with the whole task all at once . . . so as an example in your lives as students . . . a whole term paper might feel overwhelming . . . but if you say to yourself "today I'm going to go to the library and gather resources" . . . "tomorrow I'm going to read three articles" . . . and so on . . . you'll have broken this one large task . . . writing a term paper . . . down into many smaller and more manageable tasks . . . reducing your stress . . . and the important thing to do is recognize that there are only twenty-four hours in a day . . . you can't possibly do more than is feasible in twenty-four hours a day . . . so plan a manageable amount of items to do in a period of time . . . and start fresh each day . . . OK . . . so remember . . . the problem is not in the stressful experiences themselves . . . we all experience stress and stressful events . . . the problem is in one's reaction to these experiences . . . and each of us has our own limits for stress . . . our own ways of coping with stress . . . our own way of balancing the costs and benefits of stress . . . stress can be positive for some . . . more positive for others . . . negative for some . . . etc. . . . perhaps your strategies for dealing with stress were mentioned in this lecture . . . and perhaps some of you have your own ways that you'd like to share with the class . . . so uh why don't we open the floor to comments . . . suggestions . . . questions from you before we go on.

Answer, page 85: c

Defining Vocabulary Audioscript, pages 86–87

1. <u>virtually</u>: Life without stress is virtually impossible.
2. <u>immune</u>: He thought that he would never get sick if he took vitamins every day and exercised. However, when everyone in the office got the flu, he got it, too. That taught him that no one is immune to disease!
3. <u>to adapt</u>: She bought a computer that was on sale, but she needed to adapt it because it really didn't fit her needs in her office. She added additional power and a larger monitor.
4. <u>incentive</u>: The boss promised him a thousand-dollar raise if he sold two cars in one day. That gave him an incentive to work harder.
5. <u>hazardous</u>: Smoking is hazardous to your health.
6. <u>to monitor</u>: The doctor was worried about the development of the baby. Therefore, she asked the parents to bring him into her office each week so that she could monitor his development.
7. <u>regardless of</u>: Regardless of the amount of work I do, I can never satisfy my boss. I think it's impossible.
8. <u>out of one's hands</u>: I know you really want that job, but now that the interview is over, you should just relax because the decision is out of your hands.
9. <u>inevitable</u>: Everyone experiences the loss of a loved one sometime. Death is inevitable.
10. <u>to pace</u>: Long-distance runners know not to run at the maximum speed at the beginning of a race. They need to pace themselves so that they have energy left if they have to speed up toward the end of the race.

Answers:
1. b   2. a   3. c   4. b   5. c   6. b   7. a   8. c   9. c   10. a

Note-Taking Practice, page 87
See page 204 of Appendix C in the textbook for example notes.

Using Your Notes, page 88
Answers:
1. c   2. physics   3. stress caused by events about which one feels positively   4. learn to recognize stress signals; pay attention to demands of body; make plans and act when appropriate; learn to accept situations which are out of your control; pace activities   5. False

Using Vocabulary Audioscript, page 89
Group A
1. He had virtually no sleep last night.
2. Because of his insomnia, he is very irritable today.
3. There is a lot of noise outside of the window. However, his wife seems to be immune to it.
4. Traffic speeds by outside regardless of the hour of night.
5. The husband is now in the process of monitoring the noise levels so that he can support his case when he complains to the city council.

Group B
1. "Burnout" is a term used to describe physical and emotional exhaustion as a result of long-term stress. It's a feeling of not wanting to or not being able to cope with all or part of one's life.
2. Psychologists warn that burnout may be inevitable if people do not know how to pace themselves.

Answers:
Group A: **1.** a **2.** a **3.** b **4.** c **5.** b   Group B: **1.** b **2.** a

 Lecture 7: Acid Rain

Pre-Lecture Reading and Discussion, page 91
Answers:
1. LaBastille mentions the following effects around her home: her lake has grown increasingly clear with a strange layer of algae spreading across the bottom; certain fish, frogs, and birds are now rare; a large number of the spruce trees have died; the lake is measuring a more acidic pH; copper and lead plumbing has corroded. She mentions the following effects worldwide: Certain fish and trees/forests are threatened; buildings are being damaged; certain animal organs are unfit to eat.   **2.** Answers will vary.

Lecture Outline for Listening for the Larger Picture, page 92
Use this outline if you'd like to deliver the lecture yourself.

INTRODUCTION: As you read in the introductory reading in this section, acid rain has caused direct damage to architectural structures, corroding such famous monuments as the Acropolis in Greece, the Taj Mahal in India, and the Lincoln Memorial in the United States.

And as you also read, acid rain is not just a problem for man-made objects. We see the damage to materials, forests, agriculture, and aquatic ecosystems as well.

What is this substance that is causing so much damage? What is acid rain? That is what I would like to talk about today.

I. Acid rain is any form of precipitation—rain, snow, sleet, fog—that contains high levels of acid, particularly sulfuric acid and nitric acid.

   A. The scale for measuring acidity is the pH scale—with a pH of 7 being considered neutral.

   B. Theoretically pure rain water has a pH of 5.6.

   C. Near L.A., scientists have found water with a pH of 2.8—almost 1,000 times more acid than usual—dripping from pine needles.

   D. The most acidic rainfall in the United States to date is pH 1.4 in West Virginia—this is not much above battery acid, which has a pH of 1.

   E. Monitoring has shown that broad areas of North America as well as most of Europe and other industrialized regions of the world are regularly experiencing precipitation that is between 10 and 1,000 times more acidic than usual.

II. What causes acid rain?

   A. When nitrogen and sulfur are released into the atmosphere, they combine with oxygen and hydrogen in the atmosphere to form nitric acid and sulfuric acid.
      1. The chemical symbols are HNO_3 and H_2SO_4, respectively.

   B. The nitrogen and sulfur necessary for this chemical reaction come from a few different sources.
      1. Nitrogen sources are as follows—and these are statistics from the United States.
         a. 44.5% of nitrogen emissions come from transportation—cars, trucks, buses, etc.
         b. 50% of nitrogen emissions come from electric utilities, that is, from the fuels burned to produce electric power.
         c. 5.5% of nitrogen emissions come from other sources.
      2. Sulfur sources are as follows—again, statistics from the United States.
         a. 88% of sulfur emissions come from electric utilities—mostly coal-burning power plants.
         b. 8.7% of sulfur emissions come from other industrial sources.
         c. 3.3% of sulfur emissions come from transportation.
      3. On the whole, air pollution from the burning of fossil fuels—gas, coal, oil—is the major cause of acid rain. Power plants burn coal and oil to produce electricity. We burn oil and gas to heat our homes. Cars, trucks, and planes use gasoline, another fossil fuel.

III. The effects of acid rain are numerous.

    A. Fish populations decrease or disappear in certain areas. As water in aquatic ecosystems—such as lakes, ponds, and streams—becomes acidified, there is a rapid dying of many organisms, either because the acidified water kills them or because it keeps them from reproducing.

        1. In Norway and Sweden, fish have died in at least 6,500 lakes.

        2. In Ontario, Canada, approximately 1,200 lakes now harbor no life.

        3. The physical appearance of such lakes is deceiving. From the surface, they are clear and blue—the outward signs of a healthy condition. However, under the surface, there is not a sign of life.

    B. Forests become damaged.

        1. Certain trees die in great numbers (spruce, pine, aspen, birch) because the acidity strips them of their protective waxy surface, leaving the trees vulnerable to water loss and disease.

        2. In the 1970s and 1980s, this was a major issue. However, there is evidence that the damage to forests due to acid precipitation has leveled off—primarily because sulfur emissions have been declining due to greater pollution controls.

    C. Architectural structures are damaged.

        1. Monuments and buildings that have stood for hundreds or even thousands of years with little change are now dissolving and crumbling.

        2. This costs billions of dollars a year for replacement in the United States.

    D. No adverse health effects are directly attributed to acid waters, but there is concern that highly acidic levels of water can lead to illness because the acidity can leach toxic metals (such as lead) from pipes.

CONCLUSION

    A. Acid rain has increased with industrialization.

        1. Water (preserved in glaciers) from 200 years ago (prior to the Industrial Revolution) has a pH of approximately 5—close to the pH of theoretically pure rainwater.

    B. In order to put some controls on the production of acid rain, we need to consider shifting to alternative, nonpolluting energy sources and/or creating technology to reduce the release of sulfur and nitrogen.

        1. This is happening worldwide, though the problem is still a serious one.

            a. Laws and policies have been created with specific goals and plans for the reduction of pollutants in the atmosphere.

            b. There have been agreements between countries to reduce emissions that cross national boundaries.

            c. Improved pollution-control devices are being placed on cars. (However, the effects are not as dramatic as they could be because, at the same time, the number of cars is increasing greatly.)

    C. Remember: Because acid rain is airborne, it is a problem that has no national boundaries. All need to be concerned.

Lecture Audioscript for Listening for the Larger Picture, page 92
This audioscript shows one speaker's delivery of the lecture, as recorded in the audio program. Use it as a resource.

    acid rain . . . that's what I'm going to talk about today . . . and as you've read, this thing called acid rain has caused direct damage to architectural structures by corroding very famous monuments . . . such as the Acropolis in Greece . . . the Taj Mahal in India . . . the Lincoln Memorial in the United States . . . and . . . as you also read . . . architectural damage is not all that it does . . . it has also damaged forests . . . agriculture . . . aquatic ecosystems . . . health and water systems . . . OK? . . . so what I'd like to do is talk about this substance that is causing so much damage . . .

    first . . . what is it? . . . acid rain is any form of precipitation . . . that is rain . . . snow . . . sleet . . . fog . . . any form of precipitation . . . that contains high levels of acid . . . particularly sulfuric acid and nitric acid . . . now the scale for measuring acidity is called the pH scale . . . and on this scale a pH of 7 is considered neutral . . . rainwater . . . theoretically pure rainwater has a pH of about 5.6 . . . now just so you can get an idea of how bad the problem of acid precipitation has gotten . . . imagine that the most acidic rainfall in the United States to date had a pH of 1.4 . . . that was in West Virginia . . . to get an idea of how acidic that is . . . consider that battery acid has a pH of 1! . . . another example was near Los Angeles where scientists have found water with a pH of 2.8 dripping from pine trees . . . this is almost 1,000 times more acid than usual . . . and this is not only a problem affecting the United States . . . monitoring has shown that broad areas of North America . . . as well as most of Europe . . . and . . . other industrialized regions throughout the world . . . are *regularly* experiencing precipitation that is between *10* and *1,000* times more acid than usual . . . OK . . . so there's a big . . . this is something that we're talking about that really is affecting many of us . . .

where does this come from? . . . acid rain comes from nitrogen and sulfur that is released into the atmosphere . . . what happens when this occurs? . . . when nitrogen gets released into the atmosphere it combines with oxygen and hydrogen to form . . . what? . . . nitric acid . . . the chemical symbol for that is H . . . N . . . O . . . 3 [on board] . . . H . . . N . . . O . . . 3 . . . when sulfur gets released into the atmosphere it also combines with oxygen and hydrogen to form an acid . . . sulfuric acid . . . and the chemical symbol for that is H . . . 2 . . . S . . . O . . . 4 [on board] . . . sulfuric acid . . . H . . . 2 . . . S . . . O . . . 4 . . . so where does all this nitrogen and sulfur come from in the first place? . . . it comes from a few different sources but as you'll see in a minute, there are a couple of sources that dominate . . .

first of all . . . the nitrogen . . . 44.5% of all nitrogen sources in the United States come from transportation . . . cars . . . trucks . . . buses . . . and so on . . . our convenience comes at a price . . . 50% of nitrogen emissions come from electric utilities . . . that is . . . from the fuels burned to produce electric power . . . when coal and other fuels are burned to generate power, nitrogen is released into the atmosphere . . . eventually forming nitric acid . . . finally . . . 5.5% of nitrogen emissions come from a miscellaneous category . . . other sources . . .

as for sulfur . . . 88% of sulfur emissions in the United States come from electric utilities . . . mostly coal-burning power plants . . . so just as nitrogen is released into the atmosphere as a result of fuel combustion . . . so is sulfur . . . you can see that the predominant source of sulfur emissions . . . at least in the U.S. is the burning of fuel to generate power . . . the remainder of sulfur comes from . . . well 8.7% comes from other industrial sources . . . and 3.3% comes from transportation . . . transportation-related sources . . .

so in general we can say that the major cause of acid rain is air pollution caused by the burning of fossil fuels . . . coal . . . oil . . . gas . . . this is the general cause . . . what happens is that power plants burn coal and oil to produce electricity . . . the electricity that we use daily . . . and the electricity that industry uses daily . . . day in . . . day out . . . we also contribute when we burn oil and gas to heat our homes, businesses, and factories . . . cars, trucks, and airplanes use gasoline . . . another fossil fuel . . . so what it all comes down to is that acid rain is caused by the burning of fossil fuels . . . by the pollution created by this burning . . . and we all contribute to it . . .

OK . . . as I said . . . the effects have been pretty numerous . . . it's caused architectural damage . . . ecological damage . . . and for example . . . it has caused fish populations to decrease or disappear in certain areas . . . what happens is . . . as water in aquatic ecosystems . . . such as lakes . . . ponds . . . streams . . . becomes acidified . . . what happens is that there is a rapid dying of organisms . . . either because the acidified water kills them or because it keeps them from reproducing normally . . . as an example . . . in Norway and Sweden . . . fish have died in at least 6,500 lakes . . . in Ontario, Canada, approximately 1,200 lakes now harbor no life . . . and the physical appearance of these lakes can be deceiving . . . you look at them and they appear clear and blue . . . beautiful . . . outwardly they seem healthy . . . but under the surface . . . there's no life . . . no life . . .

other ecological results are that forests and trees . . . certain trees . . . are damaged . . . certain trees have died in great numbers . . . particularly some types of spruce, pine, aspen, and birch . . . what happens is that these trees are sensitive to the acidity and it destroys their protective waxy surface . . . their protection . . . and this leaves the trees vulnerable to water loss and disease that kills the trees . . . in the 1970s and '80s this was a major issue . . . however . . . now . . . there appears to be evidence that the damage to forests due to acid precipitation has leveled off . . . primarily we think because sulfur emissions have been declining due to greater pollution controls . . .

what else? architectural damage . . . I mentioned before . . . monuments and buildings that have stood for hundreds or even thousands of years with little change are now dissolving and crumbling . . . there's a picture of that in your book . . . and repairs and replacements are expensive . . . the United States alone . . . billions are spent each year to replace and repair damage to structures caused by acid rain . . .

as for your question as to whether there are any health risks . . . so far scientists haven't found any adverse health effects . . . *directly* attributed to acid rain . . . notice I said *directly* attributed to acid rain . . . there *is* concern that there could be an indirect influence . . . so for example . . . the acid rain could leach . . . or remove some kind of toxic metal from pipes . . . such as lead . . . and then this toxic metal can contaminate our drinking water . . . so it's not a direct result but it could be an indirect result . . .

OK . . . as we know . . . acid rain has increased with industrialization . . . we have not always had acid rain . . . OK? . . . when they look at glaciers from about 200 years ago . . . they find that the water had about a pH of about 5 . . . that was close to theoretically pure rainwater . . . so 200 years ago rainwater wasn't yet acidified . . .

OK . . . what can we do . . . we do need to put some controls . . . or possibly put some controls on the production of acid rain . . . perhaps by shifting to alternative nonpolluting energy sources . . . harness the energy of the sun or the wind, for example . . . or we need to create technology to reduce the release of sulfur and nitrogen into the atmosphere . . .

this *is* happening worldwide . . . though the problem is still a serious one . . . nations are passing laws and creating goals for reducing pollution emitted by industry and by cars and other vehicles . . . there have been agreements between countries to reduce emissions that cross national boundaries . . . much has been successful

. . . but with the world's continuing and increasing demand for power and transportation . . . we still have work to do in this area . . .

the important thing to remember is that this is not a problem that just concerns one area . . . OK? . . . acid rain is not a problem that has boundaries . . . everyone really needs to be concerned.

Answers, page 92: acid rain; b, c, d, e

Defining Vocabulary Audioscript, pages 92–93

1. <u>corrosion</u>: When engineers plan to build a metal structure that will stand unprotected outdoors, they must consider the possibility of corrosion caused by rain.
2. <u>ecosystem</u>: An ecosystem is a delicate balance. For example, in a low desert ecosystem, if there is an extremely cold winter, one species of plant may suffer. The loss of that one species can cause the loss of food for one small animal. If this animal dies in great numbers, this can affect a higher order species and so on. In an ecosystem, all parts are interrelated and interdependent.
3. <u>precipitation</u>: Last year was a record year for precipitation in the desert. More than six inches of rain fell.
4. <u>source</u>: If he loses his job, he will have no money. His job is his only source of income.
5. <u>emission</u>: Some people are urging the government to put more controls on automobile emissions. They warn that if this is not done, air pollution will only get worse.
6. <u>vulnerable</u>: Nations are especially vulnerable to an attack when they are unprepared or preoccupied with internal difficulties.
7. <u>to level off:</u> The cost of new homes has leveled off. For a while, it seemed that prices would never stop rising, but now they have stayed at the same price for a few months.
8. <u>adverse</u>: Smoke not only has adverse effects on smokers but also harms people around smokers.
9. <u>to attribute</u>: People attributed his death to the fact that he smoked four packs of cigarettes a day.
10. <u>toxic:</u> All toxic material should be kept on high shelves so that small children do not drink or eat dangerous substances.
11. <u>glacier</u>: Visitors to Alaska often take boat trips to view the many glaciers that exist there. If you're on a boat that pulls close to a glacier, you may feel surrounded by blue walls of ice, pieces of which occasionally break off and splash into the water.
12. <u>alternative energy</u>: Many believe that alternative energy, such as energy from the sun, wind, tides, heat of the earth, is too expensive to use on a large scale.
13. <u>airborne</u>: I was nervous before we got on the plane, but once we were airborne I seemed to relax.

Answers:
1. b   2. b   3. a   4. a   5. a   6. a   7. c   8. a   9. c   10. c   11. b   12. a   13. a

Note-Taking Practice, pages 93–95
See pages 205–206 of Appendix C in the textbook for example notes.

Using Your Notes, pages 95–96
Answers:
1. HNO_3 2. 44.5% from transportation, 50% from electric utilities, 5.5% from other sources   3. 88% from electric utilities, 8.7% from other industrial sources, 3.3% from transportation   4. a. F   b. F   c. F   d. F   e. F   f. F   g. F

Using Vocabulary, page 96
Use this outline if you'd like to deliver the mini-lecture yourself.

I. The effects of acid rain in southern Norway

    A. Acid rain has had a negative effect on the fish population over a 33,000-square-kilometer area.

        1. Within this 33,000-square-kilometer area, there are 13,000 square kilometers where all the fish have died.

    B. Acid rain plays an indirect and a direct role in this damage to the fish population.

        1. Directly, the acid rain enters the lake and thus raises the acid level of the water.

        2. Indirectly, the acid in the acid rain causes aluminum in the soil to leak into the lake, which then raises the acid level of the water.

    C. There are far-reaching effects of this damage.

        1. Because of the loss of the fish, higher-level animals are losing a major source of food and the ecosystem is being disrupted.

Answers:
1. vulnerable   2. adverse effects   3. attribute   4. toxic   5. ecosystem   6. source

Lecture 8: Archaeological Dating Methods

Pre-Lecture Reading and Discussion, pages 98–99
Students' answers will vary; allow them to conjecture and consider the different possible sources of information. For example, for number 2, perhaps the researchers found bright beaded necklaces at the site, and perhaps they found females buried with these necklaces.

Lecture Outline for Listening for the Larger Picture, page 100
Use this outline if you'd like to deliver the lecture yourself.

INTRODUCTION: In the previous activity, you read a composite sketch created to demonstrate the wealth of information that archaeologists are able to discern from remains. Clearly, in a short lecture, I cannot go into all the methods that they use in order to get this information, so what I would like to do is just focus on some of the major methods used to date material.

I. Tree-ring dating—"dendrochronology"—one of oldest dating techniques

    A. A cross section of each tree shows a series of concentric rings consisting of alternating pale and dark rings.
        1. The pale rings indicate spring.
        2. The darker rings indicate winter.
        3. The light/dark pattern is repeated for each year of the tree's life.

    B. Each year, trees grow a new layer that varies in size with climatic changes.
        1. Thin rings mean a drought or cold spell that stunted growth.
        2. Thick rings mean abundant water and sunlight.

    C. Scientists don't need to count all the rings to date an object; rather, they start at outer layers, where the rings can be matched with recorded climatic events and work back from that point.

    D. Using dendrochronological methods, archaeologists have been able to date objects thousands of years old.

II. Carbon-14 dating method

    A. This method is based on the concept that all living things contain radioactive C-14 isotopes, which are unstable and disintegrate.
        1. NOTE: An isotope is an element with the same number of protons but a different number of neutrons. (e.g., Chlorine-35 has seventeen protons and eighteen neutrons, while chlorine-37 has seventeen protons and twenty neutrons.)

    B. Beginning at death, an organism's C-14 level diminishes at a fixed rate (one-half of the total every 5,730 years).
        1. The point at which one-half of the C-14 diminishes is called the "half-life."

    C. Using a Geiger counter, a scientist can tally the C-14 electric signals emitted by an ancient specimen and compare this with the signals emitted by a living sample.
        1. e.g., If the live sample emits 75 disintegrations per minute and the ancient sample emits 37.5, the scientist knows the find is 5,730 years old.
        2. The problem with this method is that it requires a relatively large sample, which is destroyed in the process of dating—up to ten ounces of some materials—and some objects are too important to be destroyed.

    D. Recent advances have focused on measuring the C-14 atoms themselves rather than the electric signals emitted by C-14 deterioration.
        1. This uses a method called accelerator mass spectrometry (AMS).
        2. The advantage of this latter method is that it requires much smaller samples—1,000 times smaller (just one to two milligrams) than systems that measure the electric signals.

    E. Carbon-14 dating is limited to about 60,000 years.
        1. This is because past that date, there is an extremely small amount of C-14 present in the sample (since ten half-lives have passed).

    F. Items older than 60,000 years must be dated by other techniques.

Lecture Comprehension and Note-Taking Practice

CONCLUSION

    A. There are other methods; this list is not conclusive.

    B. For most accuracy, methods are cross-checked.

        1. e.g., An estimate based on C-14 dating would be cross-checked with a dendrochronological estimate of the age of other materials found at the site.

Lecture Audioscript for Listening for the Larger Picture, page 100
This audioscript shows one speaker's delivery of the lecture, as recorded in the audio program. Use it as a resource.

OK . . . what you just did is you looked at a composite sketch which as I said is really not a real sketch . . . most of the time in one site they're not going to get all of this information . . . this was taken from pieces of information from many different sites . . . but they're all pieces of information that the sites were able to give at some point . . . in this short lecture that I'm going to give and I can't go into all the methods that archaeologists use . . . but I'm going to focus on some of the major methods used to date materials . . .

OK . . . the first method I'd like to look at is a method called dendrochronology and that's D-E-N-D-R-O-C-H-R-O-N-O-L-O-G-Y . . . and someone might remember what exactly that was . . . and it was the study of . . . tree rings . . . the concentric circles in tree rings . . . and using them . . . these concentric circles . . . to draw conclusions about the age of objects . . . and that is the oldest method of dating . . . materials . . . or dating remnants . . . OK? . . . and part of this method is the assumption that every year that a tree grows . . . it grows a new ring . . . and this ring varies in size depending on changes in climate . . . OK and so if you look at a cross section . . . of a tree . . . you would see variations in the tree rings . . . it would vary from pale to dark . . . thick to thin . . . and these variations mean something . . . OK so in the spring the tree rings would be pale . . . in the winter they would be darker . . . OK . . . and, and it's repeated every year for the tree's life . . . and thin rings then would mean a drought . . . or a cold spell . . . that stunted the growth . . . and thick rings would mean abundant rain . . . that could increase the growth . . . OK? . . . and you might think . . . oh come on . . . are scientists going to count all of these rings? . . . no they don't need to do all that . . . what scientists do is they look for what they're sure of . . . so if they're sure of a certain climatic change . . . say in . . . the year 1000 A.D. . . . that means they can just look for . . . let's say a thick pale ring at this time and then date back from there . . . so they don't always have to recount . . . they can tell . . . they can match trees and say "AHA!" . . . that year we know there was a drought . . . so we can find that particular ring and date back . . . OK this method is the oldest but it's certainly not the most efficient because . . . archaeologists can only work back a few thousand years with it . . . OK . . . but a few thousand years really doesn't get us that far with archaeology . . .

now the second method that I want to talk about is something called the C-14 [on board] or carbon-14 dating method . . . now this is more modern technology for dating material . . . some of you might know that all living things contain an isotope called C-14 . . . carbon-14 . . . which is radioactive . . . all right . . . and this radioactive isotope then is unstable and it disintegrates . . . and beginning at death then . . . the organism's level of C-14 decreases . . . or diminishes . . . at a fixed rate . . . and this rate is . . . half of the total of the C-14 decreases every 5,730 years . . . every 5,730 years the organism loses half its total C-14 . . . the term for this is "half-life" . . . the time it takes for one-half of a specific isotope to undergo radioactive decay . . . so the half-life for C-14 is 5,730 years . . . anyway using a machine similar to a Geiger counter . . . an archaeologist can tally the carbon-14 electrical emissions that come out of a specimen and compare this with what would normally come out of a living specimen . . . and . . . let me give an example . . . if the live specimen emitted 75 disintegrations per minute . . . and the ancient sample emitted 37.5 . . . how old would this be? . . . any idea? . . . if the live sample emitted 75 . . . and the ancient sample emitted 37.5 . . . and then one-half of the total disintegrates every 5,730 years . . . how old would the item be? . . . it would be 5,730 years old . . . does that make sense? . . . because the specimen had half the number of carbon-14 emissions . . . so that's equal to one half-life . . . 5,730 years . . .

now there are drawbacks to this method . . . one of the drawbacks is that it requires a large sample . . . or a relatively large sample . . . which is destroyed in the process . . . and you can imagine that if the archaeologists find something that is very important . . . the last thing they would want to do is destroy it by dating it . . . OK and you can imagine for example . . . there's a shroud in Italy . . . that people claim is the shroud of Jesus . . . that's the garment worn when one dies . . . no one is going to want to try to date it to prove its authenticity by this method . . . because in the process they would destroy it . . . all right . . . so that's a drawback to this method . . .

now there have been some improvements in this dating technique . . . and what they do is rather than measuring the *emissions* . . . it measures the *atoms* of C-14 themselves . . . they use a smaller sample . . . a much smaller sample . . . about 1,000 times smaller . . . usually one or two milligrams is sufficient . . . the term for this new measuring technique is accelerator mass spectrometry [on board] . . . AMS for short . . .

now the carbon-14 dating methods . . . whether using techniques which measure the electrical signals or using techniques which measure the C-14 atoms themselves are limited to dating back only to about 60,000 years . . .

this is because past that date, there is an extremely small amount of C-14 present in the sample . . . if one half-life equals 5,730 years . . . then we're talking about more than ten half-lives . . . and by that time there's just not that much C-14 left in the sample . . . so items older than 60,000 years must be dated by other techniques . . .

OK there certainly are other methods . . . this just gives you an idea of some of the methods used . . . and for most accuracy . . . most methods are cross-checked . . . so if they're going to do a dendrochronological analysis for example . . . archaeologists would usually check it with another kind of analysis to make sure they're accurate.

Answers, page 100:
1. dendrochronology; C-14 dating; improvements   2. See outline section I for information about dendrochronology. Because students are listening for the larger picture in this exercise, they don't need to get all the details. The important information is that it is a method of dating objects through the examination of the color and size of tree rings.   3. See outline section II for information about C-14 dating. Because students are listening for the larger picture in this exercise, they don't need to get all the details. The most important information is that it is a method of dating objects through the measurement of C-14, which decreases at a fixed rate beginning at death.

Defining Vocabulary Audioscript, pages 100–101

1. climatic: Some scientists fear that a nuclear war would cause climatic changes over much of the earth. In particular, they say that the earth's temperature would generally get colder.
2. cross section: The cross section taken from the tree clearly showed signs of disease that had not been apparent when looking at the outside of the tree, the bark.
3. drought: The recent drought in Africa forced many people to leave their land in search of food and water.
4. cold spell: We thought that spring had arrived. Then suddenly, there was a cold spell that lasted for two weeks when the temperature dropped below the freezing point.
5. abundant: That location is very desirable for farming. It's close to a freshwater pond and always has an abundant supply of water.
6. unstable: Don't sit on that chair. It's unstable and you might fall.
7. to disintegrate: The letter was so old that when I finally found it, it disintegrated in my hands. It fell apart and all I was left with was some dust in my hands.
8. to diminish: The sound of the train diminished as it got farther away.
9. to tally: The workers tallied the votes and declared her the winner.
10. to emit: The sun emits heat.
11. drawback: Nothing is perfect. Everything has some drawbacks.
12. to cross-check: If you want to be more certain of the results of your experiment, I would recommend cross-checking your results. You can compare them with other people's results, use a different type of test to see if the results are the same, and so on.

Answers:
1. relating to climate or weather   2. a surface made by cutting across something, especially at right angles to its length   3. a long period of dry weather when there is insufficient water   4. a long period of cold weather   5. in large quantities   6. easily moved, upset, or changed; not firm   7. to break into very small pieces   8. to get smaller   9. to count   10. to release; to send out   11. a limitation; a disadvantage or difficulty   12. to find out the correctness of something by using a different method, standard, or information from other places

Note-Taking Practice, pages 101–102
See page 207 of Appendix C in the textbook for example notes.

Using Your Notes, pages 104–105
Answers:
1. a. F   b. T   c. F   d. T   e. F   f. F   g. T   h. F   i. T   2. b   3. e   4. 5,730 years   5. The new method requires much smaller samples.   6. They match rings to known climatic events; then, they count from that ring. (They don't count all the rings.)

Using Vocabulary Audioscript, page 105

1. According to stories that have been passed down from generation to generation, a race of supermen lived at this particular spot. Archaeologists have dug up the area in order to find remnants and, thus, to find out the truth.
2. An analysis of a cross section of the tree indicates that there was a long period of time without water during the year 2000 B.C., which caused the food supply to get smaller and smaller.
3. The primary disadvantage of the older C-14 dating method is that it requires a fairly large sample.
4. In 1450, there was a great deal of rainfall, and this caused the people who lived in the area to move to higher ground.

Answers:
1. legends; site; excavated   2. drought; diminished   3. drawback   4. abundant; inhabitants

Lecture Comprehension and Note-Taking Practice   45

Lecture 9: Amnesty International

Lecture Outline for Listening for the Larger Picture, page 108
Use this outline if you'd like to deliver the lecture yourself.

INTRODUCTION: Amnesty International (AI)

    A. Founded in 1961

    B. One of the largest and most active human rights organizations

    C. In 1998, had 1,100,000 members with supporters in 160 countries

    D. In 1977, received the Nobel Peace Prize

    E. In 1978, was given an award by the United Nations for outstanding achievement in the field of human rights

    F. Concerned strictly with prisoners
        1. Seeks release of prisoners of conscience (any persons detained for nonviolent expression of political or religious beliefs, or because of color, ethnic origin, race, or sex)
        2. Works for fair trials within reasonable time periods for *all* political prisoners
        3. Acts for protection of all persons against torture
        4. Works for abolition of death penalty

    G. Has been successful and has earned high international respect
        1. The reasons for AI's success lie in certain principles that underlie its activities.

I. The eight principles underlying AI's activities

    A. A limited mandate (command, field of authority)
        1. AI does not act in respect to violations of all rights set out in the Universal Declaration of Human Rights.
        2. AI concentrates only on political imprisonment, torture, and execution.
        3. This does not mean that AI believes those rights are more important than others.
            a. There has been pressure to expand work to other civil and political liberties (voting, censorship) and social rights (poverty, hunger, etc.).
        4. AI says, "If someone takes away your bread, he suppresses your freedom at the same time. But if someone seizes your freedom, rest assured, your bread is threatened, because it no longer depends on you, but on the pleasure of your master."

    B. Focus on the individual prisoner
        1. According to AI, general information about political imprisonment and related human rights violations is not enough.
        2. AI is after the names of individual prisoners and specific details of each case.
        3. This principle is exemplified in AI adoption groups—the basic unit of AI.
            a. These adoption groups are local groups of individuals who get together to take action on behalf of specific prisoners.
            b. These adoption groups focus their efforts on this one prisoner, trying to find out details of his/her situation, corresponding with the prisoner and his/her family, making contact with people who might be influential in securing a fair trial for the prisoner, and so on.

    C. Action grounded in fact
        1. AI recognizes the necessity of initiating action only when it has reliable information.
        2. At the heart of AI's activities is research.
        3. AI is aware that its credibility rests on the reliability of its information.

    D. Based on member participation
        1. AI believes that without the concerted effort of individual men and women, little would be accomplished in human rights.
        2. AI believes that human rights will not be protected if left solely to governments.

3. AI believes that the individual can make a difference.
4. The structure of AI is built on the effort of individuals.

E. Moral persuasion with governments
1. AI does not seek conflict with any government. It seeks dialogue wherever possible.
   a. Its goal is to point to a better way.
2. AI does not urge the isolation of governments or military or economic sanctions against governments.
3. AI wants feedback and comments from governments on its reports.

F. Strict impartiality in all work
1. AI believes that whenever men and women are deprived of their freedom of expression, their right not to be tortured, their right to life, AI will do what it can.
2. AI believes that no external considerations, whether political, religious, or ideological will be allowed to influence or to inhibit AI in the pursuit of this task.
3. AI refuses to compare or rank countries.
   a. It believes that there is no point in trying to judge which human rights violations are "better" or "worse."

G. Full independence in policy and finances
1. AI is independent, without links to state, political body, or ideological or religious group.
2. Its sole authority is worldwide membership.
3. AI has adopted rules to protect this independence.
   a. No AI member who occupies a high post with any government can at the same time hold a leading position in AI.
   b. No member of the executive committee of AI can take part in decisions affecting his/her country.
   c. No AI section or group is allowed to work for prisoners or to issue public statements about human rights violations in its own country.
4. All finances come from subscriptions or contributions of members.
   a. No gift is accepted which has "strings attached" that are inconsistent with AI goals.
   b. No grants are taken from governments except for relief funds.

H. Commitment to the international responsibility of human rights
1. AI does not recognize geographical or political frontiers where human rights violations are concerned.
2. AI does not accept the argument that questions of human rights are entirely the affair of the nation or state concerned.
3. AI believes that human rights are the birthright of every individual.
4. AI believes that it is the duty of every person to seek the defense of human rights wherever and whenever they are violated.
5. According to AI, noninterference in the internal affairs of a state has no place in questions of human rights.

CONCLUSION: Working with these eight principles, AI has survived since the early 1960s and has been successful, gaining high international respect.

Lecture Audioscript for Listening for the Larger Picture, page 108
This audioscript shows one speaker's delivery of the lecture, as recorded in the audio program. Use it as a resource.

what I'm going to be talking about in this lecture is an organization . . . Amnesty International [on board] . . . and I know that some of you have heard of this organization and others of you haven't . . . some of you have heard about it from me . . . others of you haven't . . . well let me start with some details about the organization . . . it was founded in 1961 . . . and what it is . . . it's one of the largest and most active human rights organizations . . . in 1998 it had 1,100,000 members . . . and these members were spread out among about 160 countries . . . so it's very international . . . in 1977 it was given the Nobel Peace Prize . . . and in 1978 it was given an award by the United Nations . . . for outstanding achievement in the field of human rights . . . so it's very very well-known . . . very widespread . . . and quite recognized . . . it's concerned strictly with prisoners . . . and I'll tell you a little more about that . . . it seeks the release of what they call "prisoners of conscience" [on board] . . . they seek the release of these prisoners of conscience . . . and the way they define the term . . . is they say it's any person . . . who is detained . . . for the *nonviolent* expression . . . of political . . . or religious beliefs . . . *or* . . . because of color . . . ethnic origin . . . race . . . or sex . . . and I'll repeat that definition for you because I'd like you to get that . . . they seek the release of all prisoners of conscience . . . and the way they define prisoners of conscience is any person . . . who is detained . . . for the nonviolent expression . . . of political or religious beliefs . . . *or* . . . because of color . . . ethnic origin . . . race . . . or sex . . . they also do a couple of other things on behalf of prisoners . . . they work for fair trials within reasonable time periods for *all* political prisoners . . . they also work to protect all people from torture . . . because they believe that no one has the right or *no one* should be tortured . . . and finally . . . they work for the abolition of the death penalty . . . that is . . . they're against the death penalty . . . OK . . . as I said before . . . this organization has been very very successful and has earned high international respect . . . among a wide range of countries . . . not just West . . . not just East . . . but worldwide . . . OK . . . what I'm specifically going to focus on in this lecture . . . now that I've told you a little bit about the organization . . . are some of the specific principles that underlie some of Amnesty International's activities . . . and probably contribute to its success . . . OK? . . . and there are eight principles in particular that I'm going to talk about . . .

[end of introduction]

OK . . . the *first* principle is that it has a limited mandate . . . and that is . . . it has a limited field of authority . . . it doesn't try to do too much . . . it limits its field . . . of work . . . so as you might have noticed . . . it doesn't act in respect of *all* violations of *all* rights . . . but it specifically works for particular kinds of rights . . . specifically focuses on political prisoners . . . torture . . . execution . . . OK . . . and they don't believe that other rights are *less* important . . . but they just believe that in order to do good work they need to limit their focus to those particular areas . . . and in the past there has been some pressure on them to expand their work to include other civil and political rights such as voting . . . censorship . . . poverty . . . hunger . . . so far they've resisted . . . and basically . . . their belief is . . . and this is a quote . . . quote . . . "if someone takes away your bread . . . he suppresses your freedom . . . but if someone takes your freedom . . . rest assured . . . your bread is threatened . . . because it no longer depends on you . . . but on the pleasure of your master" . . . end quote . . . OK . . . so that's how they justify their work specifically in terms of political freedom . . .

now the *second* basic principle is that they focus on the *individual* prisoner . . . according to Amnesty International . . . it's not enough just to get general information . . . just to find out about general human rights violations . . . OK? . . . they're particularly concerned about the names of individual people . . . individual prisoners . . . and specific details about each case . . . and this principle is exemplified in the basic structure of Amnesty International which is the "adoption group" [on board] . . . and these adoption groups are made up of members of Amnesty International in a specific locale . . . for example there might be an adoption group made up of Amnesty International members from one city . . . or state . . . or country . . . or even neighborhood . . . and these adoption groups take on specific prisoners' cases . . . so it's a very personal operation . . . rather than an abstract operation . . . so these particular adoption groups will have the name of the prisoner . . . information about his or her case . . . information about his or her condition . . . his or her family and so on . . . and the adoption group writes letters . . . raises money . . . and does whatever it feels it can do to help this one prisoner . . .

OK the *third* principle of Amnesty International is that all action is grounded in fact . . . and part of the reason for this is that they recognize that in order to take action it is necessary to have reliable information . . . in order to be respected you need to have reliable information . . . so at the heart of their activities is good research . . . they conduct fact-finding missions to countries to find out the truth of what's going on . . . and most countries *do* let them in . . . because they know that this is a fairly nonpartial organization that is respected worldwide . . . and so it would look very bad in terms of worldwide opinion to *not* let them do research in a country . . . OK . . . and Amnesty International is aware that *its* credibility rests on the reliability of its information . . .

OK the *fourth* principle . . . Amnesty International is based on *member* participation . . . if you remember the second principle I said that they are concerned with individual prisoners . . . now this fourth principle is concerned with their membership . . . OK? . . . it says that it's the members . . . the individual members . . . that are very important . . . and I'm sure you've heard of "top-heavy" organizations in which all of the power really rests on the top level . . . well Amnesty International you might call a "bottom-heavy" organization because really . . . the *key* work is done by the members themselves . . . OK . . . and as far as Amnesty International is concerned . . . the individual makes a difference . . . and so it's the effort of individuals that make up the organization . . . and they feel that without the efforts of these individuals . . . of these individual men and women . . . little would be accomplished . . . it's these people who take the actions . . . according to Amnesty International . . . if it were left solely to governments . . . human rights would not be protected . . . OK . . .

OK . . . the *fifth* principle is moral suasion . . . or persuasion . . . with governments . . . Amnesty International is not a conflict-seeking organization . . . rather what they like to do is initiate dialogue . . . with the governments . . . with the people involved . . . they'd rather point to a better way . . . rather than punish the government . . . OK? . . . so therefore they don't urge the isolation of a government . . . or they don't urge economic sanctions . . . or any kind of punishment against a country . . . rather what they want is they want dialogue . . . they want feedback . . . and they want some action . . .

OK? . . . the *sixth* point . . . and the sixth one I think is very very important for an international organization . . . and that is that it's strictly *impartial* in all of its work . . . as far as Amnesty International is concerned . . . *wherever* men and women are deprived of their freedom . . . or their right to not be tortured or their right to life . . . that's where they will go . . . it doesn't matter if the country is capitalist . . . communist . . . religious . . . nonreligious . . . it doesn't matter . . . so as far as they're concerned . . . there is no other consideration to be taken into account when these rights are being violated . . . OK? and that helps because that way if you're a communist country you don't need to feel that this is a capitalist organization . . . a capitalist country doesn't feel that it's a communist organization . . . very impartial . . . and in order to *keep* this impartiality . . . Amnesty International refuses to compare or rank countries . . . so they don't compare countries . . . they don't rank countries . . . and they feel that there's no use in saying X is better than Y when they're talking about human rights . . .

OK . . . *another* important consideration . . . another important *principle* is that Amnesty International is fully independent in policy and finances . . . this is the seventh principle . . . it has no links . . . state . . . political bodies . . . religious bodies . . . it has no links to anyone except its membership . . . and there are certain rules that Amnesty International has adopted to protect its independence . . . for example . . . if an Amnesty International member occupies a high post in a government . . . he or she cannot occupy a high post in Amnesty International . . . because that would . . . or could . . . be a conflict of interest . . . as another example of laws Amnesty International has taken to protect its independence is the fact that no Amnesty International group can work for prisoners in its own country . . . for example . . . if I'm in an adoption group in the United States . . . I can't work on behalf of American prisoners . . . I might work on behalf of prisoners in other countries . . . who would work for prisoners in the United States? . . . Amnesty International members from other countries . . . remember there are members in over 160 countries . . . in this way again there are no conflicts of interest . . . OK . . . finally . . . all finances . . . I'm sorry . . . this is still part of the seventh principle . . . all . . . finances come from subscriptions or contributions of members . . . Amnesty International doesn't take any grants from any governments . . . and they don't take any gifts that have any kind of strings attached . . . any conditions . . . that are inconsistent with the organization's goals . . .

OK . . . and finally . . . the last one . . . is that a basic belief of Amnesty International is that all people have a responsibility in . . . terms of human rights . . . what does this mean? . . . it means that according to Amnesty International . . . geography . . . political frontiers . . . have nothing to do with human rights violations . . . so we can't just say "oh . . . that's going on in another country . . . it's none of my business" . . . we have to realize that what is going on in other countries . . . if it's a human rights violation . . . *is* our business . . . they believe that human rights are the birthright of every individual and that it's the duty of every person then to seek the defense of those rights whenever they're violated . . . OK? . . . and they believe that noninterference is just as bad as acceptance . . .

OK . . . so you can see that these eight principles have helped Amnesty International to survive since the early 1960s . . . to grow to a membership of over 1 million . . . and to gain very very high international respect . . . quite an achievement.

Answers, pages 108–109:
1. a limited mandate   2. focus on the individual prisoner   3. action grounded in fact   4. based on member participation   5. moral suasion with governments   6. strict impartiality in all work   7. full independence in policy and finances   8. commitment to the international responsibility of human rights

Defining Vocabulary Audioscript, page 109

1. abolition: In the 19th century, many young children worked long hours in factories. People demanded the abolition of this type of child slavery, and eventually laws were passed to limit child work hours.
2. death penalty: People question the ethics of the death penalty. They ask, "Should we murder someone because he murdered someone else?"
3. mandate: The union members voted to give their representatives a limited mandate. The representatives could negotiate salary but not working conditions. This mandate definitely restricted their power.
4. on behalf (of someone): The woman was in prison, so she couldn't go to a meeting. The prisoner's husband, therefore, went on behalf of his wife.
5. appeal: The mother of the guilty murderer made an appeal to the judge for mercy. She begged the judge not to sentence him to death.
6. grounded in fact: The police department does not take action unless that action is grounded in fact. That is, the department makes sure that its information is accurate and complete before doing anything.
7. credibility: That newspaper has lost credibility ever since it was found guilty of making up two newspaper articles.
8. concerted effort: They made a concerted effort to get the job done. It was not always easy working together, but they did it.
9. economic sanctions: Sometimes when one country has violated international law, other countries will place economic sanctions on that country. They may place a heavy tax on all imports from that country, or refuse to import or export to that country.
10. persuasion: Some people believe that the best way to teach children how to behave is to punish them when they behave poorly. I, however, think that persuasion works better than punishment. I'd rather convince my child of my way of thinking.
11. impartiality: It's not easy to be a good parent. One important quality is impartiality when it comes to your children. All children in the family should feel equally loved and not feel that there is a preference for any one child.
12. to pursue: He pursued his goal to be president without rest. He would not stop for anything or anyone in pursuit of that goal.
13. ideology: A major ideological split among the countries of the world is along the lines of capitalist ideology versus Marxist ideology.
14. sole: His sole relative is his mother now, because the rest of his family was killed in an earthquake.
15. with no strings attached: I said I would only take the gift if there were no strings attached, because I didn't want to feel that I owed anybody anything.

16. <u>relief funds:</u> World health organizations usually provide relief funds for the victims of natural disasters to be used for food, shelter, and medical care.
17. <u>frontier:</u> Geographical frontiers are the physical borders between countries. Political frontiers are more psychological and involve the borders that divide people because of political differences.
18. <u>birthright:</u> Every citizen of the United States has, as his or her birthright, freedoms that are stated in the Bill of Rights. Each person has rights simply because he or she was born in this country.

Possible Answers:
1. bringing a law or condition to an end   2. execution as a result of conviction of a crime   3. the right and power given to a group of people/organization to act according to the members' wishes   4. in the interests (of someone); for (someone)   5. very strong request (for help, assistance)   6. based on actual information   7. the quality of being trustworthy   8. an attempt made with others (rather than individually)   9. economic actions taken against a country that has broken a law or rule   10. the ability to influence others; the ability to cause others to do something by reasoning, convincing, begging, etc.   11. the state of not being biased, not taking sides   12. to continue steadily with   13. a set of ideas, typical of a social or political group   14. only   15. with no limiting conditions (on something agreed upon or received)   16. money designated to assist people in need (of money, shelter, food, etc.)   17. border; limit (especially where the land of two countries meets)   18. a privilege granted a person, simply for having been born

Note-Taking Practice, pages 110–111
See pages 208–209 of Appendix C in the textbook for example notes.

Using Your Notes, page 112
Answers:
1. a. F   b. F   c. F   d. F   2. a, b, f, g, h, i   3. local group working on particular prisoner's case   4. See outline G3 and G4.

Using Vocabulary Audioscript, page 113

1. He was detained by the police and no one took any action on his behalf.
2. When they voted on the new law, Mary's vote was the only dissenting one.
3. People in many parts of the world are working to abolish the death penalty.
4. The judge lost credibility when people discovered that she was not as impartial as she was supposed to be.
5. The police held him in custody for having allowed human rights violations to occur.
6. They appealed to the governor to prevent the execution of the criminal.
7. The funds were given to the organization with no strings attached.
8. Her father persuaded her to pursue her goals.

Answers:
1. b   2. a   3. c   4. a   5. b   6. b   7. a   8. c

Lecture 10: Pheromones

Lecture Outline for Listening for the Larger Picture, page 117
Use this outline if you'd like to deliver the lecture yourself.

INTRODUCTION: Animals obviously communicate with each other, yet they do not communicate with words as humans do. One way they communicate is by emitting a chemical substance that sends signals to other members of the species. This substance is called a pheromone.

I. Definition of *pheromone:* Chemical substance released by an organism into the environment to evoke a response from the other members of the same species [repeat once]

   A. These chemicals may be detected by either the sense of smell or taste.

   B. These pheromones are widely used within the animal kingdom in a variety of species ranging from one-celled animals to higher primates (a group including monkeys, apes, and humans).

   C. Special characteristics of pheromones
      1. Pheromones are highly sensitive—an animal can release one microgram of a pheromone and get a response.
      2. Pheromones are highly specific—each species is responsive to only its own species' pheromones and those pheromones have no effect on members of other species.

II. Two types of pheromones

    A. Primer pheromones: cause physiological changes in the organism and affect its development and later behavior

        1. e.g., The queen bee gives off a primer pheromone that prevents the reproductive development of female worker bees.

    B. Releaser pheromones: produce rapid and reversible responses and immediate changes

        1. There are four types of releaser pheromones divided along functional lines that are *not* mutually exclusive.

            a. Alarm pheromones: used to warn others of danger; released in response to a threatening situation such as an attack by any enemy

                (1) Response to an alarm pheromone may be dispersal to an area of safety or gathering followed by aggressive behavior.

                (2) e.g., A mouse releases an alarm pheromone and this odor causes other mice to flee.

            b. Aggregation pheromones: used to call members to one locale

                (1) This pheromone may be for the purpose of food, shelter, or mating, among other things.

                (2) e.g., Honeybees recognize the entrance to their specific colony by an odor (which is distinct from one colony to another). This odor not only enables identification of the correct home colony, but it also acts as a stimulant causing the returning insects to enter the nest.

            c. Sex pheromones: used to sexually arouse and attract members of the species

                (1) e.g., Mature female snails emit a sex pheromone to attract immature sexually undifferentiated (neither male nor female) snails to them. Once the immature snail attaches itself to the female snail, the female releases a primer pheromone, which causes the immature snail to develop into a male so that they can mate.

            d. Terrestrial trail pheromones: used as a navigational guide for others to follow

                (1) This pheromone is "terrestrial" because it is deposited on a solid base and "trail" because species maintain contact with the pheromone while they move along a trail.

                (2) e.g., An ant moving from a food source toward its nest deposits a secretion on the ground as it moves along. Ants follow this trail to reach the food source. When they return from this food source, they deposit additional terrestrial trail pheromones as long as there is still food remaining at the source. Once the food source is exhausted, the returning ants no longer deposit terrestrial trail pheromones and the pheromone dries up.

CONCLUSION

    A. The study of pheromones is very important to agriculture because pheromones can be used to control animal behavior for protecting crops.

        1. Pheromones can lead insects to traps where they can be killed or away from crop locations.

        2. Traditional insecticides contain poisons (which can harm helpful animals and can harm people who eat food sprayed with the insecticide), but pheromones cannot harm other species.

    B. Pheromone communication clearly is not comparable to human language, but each system does have its own complexity and usefulness.

Lecture Audioscript for Listening for the Larger Picture, page 117
This audioscript shows one speaker's delivery of the lecture, as recorded in the audio program. Use it as a resource.

OK as we discussed earlier when we were looking at the studies of ants . . . bees . . . etc. . . . animals obviously communicate with each other . . . and yet we know that they don't communicate with words as humans do . . . and one way they communicate is by emitting a chemical substance . . . which sends signals to other members of the species . . . and this substance is called a pheromone [on board] . . . OK . . . what *is* a pheromone? . . . and I'm going to give you a regular scientific definition of that . . . a pheromone is . . . a chemical substance . . . released by an organism . . . into the environment . . . to evoke a response . . . from the members of the same species . . . let me repeat that . . . it's a chemical substance . . . released by an organism . . . into the environment . . . to evoke a response from the other members of the same species . . . and these chemicals may be detected by either the sense of smell or taste . . . and as I'll talk about later on . . . you'll see that these pheromones are widely used within the animal kingdom . . . in a *variety* of species ranging from one-celled animals all the way to higher primates . . . a group which includes monkeys, apes, and man . . . and the *special* characteristics of pheromones . . . and that I'll talk about again later . . . are that *one* . . . they're highly sensitive . . . an animal can release one microgram of a pheromone and get a response and one microgram as you probably know if you've done scientific experiments is extremely extremely small . . . and the other special characteristic is that it's highly specific . . . each species responds *only* to its own species' pheromones . . . and these pheromones have no effect on members of other species . . . so if a pheromone is released by a bee . . . it will have an effect on other bees and not on other species . . .

OK I'm going to divide this talk up according to the different classifications that scientists have given pheromones . . . and primarily they divided pheromones into two types . . . primer pheromones . . . P-R-I-M-

E-R . . . and releaser pheromones . . . now the primer pheromones cause physiological changes in the organism . . . and affect its development and later behavior . . . now as an example of that and we talked about it . . . the queen bee . . . gives off a primer pheromone and this primer pheromone prevents the reproductive development of female worker bees . . . so it allows the queen bee to be the *sole* reproducer in the hive . . . OK so . . . her primer pheromone changes . . . causes physiological changes . . . in the other females . . . OK now the releaser pheromones on the other hand produce rapid and *reversible* responses . . . and immediate changes . . . so whereas the primer pheromones are long-range . . . not reversible . . . the releaser pheromones are rapid . . . immediate . . . and reversible . . . and there are four types of releaser pheromones that scientists have come up with and primarily they're divided along functional lines . . . and they're not mutually exclusive . . . so different pheromones or different activities can belong to a number of the different categories . . .

OK . . . the first type of releaser pheromone that the scientists have come up with is called an *alarm* pheromone . . . and as you can guess from the name . . . it's used to warn others of danger . . . and it's released in response to a threatening situation . . . such as an attack by an enemy . . . and usually the response to an alarm pheromone may be dispersal to an area of safety . . . or gathering followed by aggressive behavior . . . so for example . . . a mouse would release an alarm pheromone which would cause other mice to flee . . . another type of animal might release an alarm pheromone which would cause other animals to gather . . . and attack . . .

OK the second type of releaser pheromone is called an *aggregation* pheromone . . . let me write that [on board] . . . and again as you might guess by its name it's used to call members to one location . . . or one locale . . . and this could be for the purpose of food . . . shelter . . . mating . . . among other things . . . and primarily it's used to call members to one location . . . an example of this would be *honeybees* . . . who recognize the entrance to their specific colony by an odor . . . which is separate and distinct from one colony to another . . . so the honeybees know which colony is theirs by the odor which is present at the entrance of the colony . . . and this odor not only enables them to identify their home colony but it also acts as a stimulant to get them to return to their home colony . . . I'll bet some of your parents wish they had such a technique! . . .

OK . . . the third kind of releaser pheromone is the sex pheromone . . . and as you can see the names adequately describe each of these pheromones . . . the sex pheromone is used to sexually arouse and attract members of the species . . . and one of the most interesting examples I know of is the example of the snail . . . when a female snail is mature . . . a mature female snail . . . she emits a sex pheromone to attract immature . . . sexually undifferentiated . . . snails to her . . . so what she does . . . she's mature . . . she's female . . . she *attracts* immature snails to her . . . and immature snails are neither male nor female . . . they're sexually *un*differentiated . . . so she *attracts* these undifferentiated snails to her . . . and once she attracts this immature snail to her . . . she releases a primer pheromone . . . which causes the immature snail to develop into a male . . . so they can mate . . . OK so here's an example where pheromones work in two different ways . . . the sex pheromone attracts the immature snail to the female . . . and the primer pheromone changes the immature snail to a male . . . so that they can mate . . .

OK . . . finally . . . the last type of releaser pheromone is called a terrestrial trail pheromone . . . and terrestrial of course means having to do with the land . . . and this type of pheromone is used as a navigational guide for others to follow . . . and as I said . . . the pheromone is "terrestrial" because it's deposited on a solid base . . . on land . . . and "trail" . . . because the species maintain contact with the pheromone while they move along the trail . . . and you can probably guess the example I'm going to give you . . . *ants* . . . ants moving from a food source towards their nest deposit a trail pheromone on the ground as they move along . . . and this tells other ants to follow the trail to reach a food source . . . when they *return* from the food source they deposit additional trail pheromone as long as there's still food remaining at the source . . . and the interesting thing is that once the food source is exhausted . . . the returning ants no longer deposit the pheromone . . . and the pheromone dries up . . . and ants no longer follow it . . . so that explains how ants can follow this long path continuously . . . not getting lost . . . until the food dries up . . .

OK . . . you might wonder why the study of pheromones is so important . . . well it's very important to agriculture . . . among other things . . . of course it's very important to our knowledge about how species communicate . . . but in terms of a practical use it's very important to agriculture . . . and that's because pheromones can be used to control animal behavior to protect crops . . . so for example . . . they can lead harmful insects to traps where they can be killed . . . or they can lead helpful insects *to* a particular location . . . and they're much better than traditional insecticides which contain poisons . . . obviously these poisons in the traditional insecticides not only harm the insects which could hurt the plants but also could harm people who eat the plants or worked with the plants . . . but remember pheromones are highly specific . . . they have no effect on members of other species . . . so pheromones are much safer . . .

so pheromone communication clearly is not comparable to human language but each system does have its own complexity and usefulness . . . are there any questions?

Answers, page 117:
1. a, c, d   **2.** a, c, f, g   **3.** Primer pheromones cause physiological changes and affect the organism's development and later behavior; releaser pheromones produce rapid and reversible responses.   **4.** four

Defining Vocabulary Audioscript, pages 117–118

1. to emit: The skunk emitted a smell that was so powerful that everyone had to leave.
2. to evoke a response: Her screams evoked an immediate response from her neighbors; they were at her door in seconds.

3. <u>physiological</u>: That drug causes physiological changes such as an increased heart rate and a tightening of the muscles.
4. <u>mutually exclusive</u>: The two types of pheromones—primer and releaser pheromones—have opposing characteristics. One is reversible and immediate; the other affects later behavior and development. Because of these opposing characteristics, pheromones can never be both at the same time. They are mutually exclusive categories.
5. <u>to disperse</u>: At the scene of the crime, people gathered to watch. The police told the crowd to disperse because they were afraid that someone would get hurt if so many people stayed around.
6. <u>to flee</u>: The house went up in flames and the residents had to flee with only the clothes they were wearing. There wasn't a moment to waste.
7. <u>stimulant</u>: Caffeine in coffee is a stimulant. I wouldn't advise drinking coffee close to bedtime. You'll have a hard time falling asleep.
8. <u>to arouse</u>: Snails emit a pheromone which sexually arouses immature snails. This pheromone ensures mating and thus the continuation of the species.
9. <u>terrestrial</u>: Humans are basically terrestrial creatures, while fish are aquatic.
10. <u>navigational guide</u>: Sailors often use the stars as navigational guides while they are sailing the oceans at night. The position of the stars gives them directional information.
11. <u>to exhaust</u>: Some geologists believe that if we continue with our present use of oil and gas, we may eventually exhaust our supply.
12. <u>insecticide</u>: Insecticides must be powerful enough to kill specific insects. This may be a problem, however, because they may be poisonous to other useful species of insects as well.

Answers:
1. b   2. b   3. a   4. b   5. a   6. c   7. b   8. b   9. a   10. c   11. b   12. b

Note-Taking Practice, page 119
See pages 210–211 of Appendix C in the textbook for example notes.

Post-Lecture Reading and Discussion, page 120
Answers:
1. Answers will vary.   **2. a.** Three. Monti-Bloch and Berliner found pheromones that elicit an electrical response in humans. McClintock found that women who lived together tended to synchronize menstrual cycles. Researchers at the University of Bern found that women tend to choose T-shirts worn by men whose immune systems were most different from their own.   **b.** Because his research has not been replicated and because he seems to have rushed to make a profit.   **c.** No. It says that "supporting evidence is slowly accumulating" showing the existence of pheromonal responses.   **d.** The article seems to indicate that these claims are premature. ("Don't spend any money on a pheromonal spritz.") However, the article also seems to support the idea that pheromones do still exist in humans.

Using Your Notes, page 121
Answers:
1. chemical substances released by an organism into the environment to evoke a response from the other members of the same species   **2. a.** T   **b.** F   **c.** T   **d.** F   **e.** F   **f.** T   **g.** F   **h.** F   **3.** "Highly sensitive" means that only a tiny amount of the pheromone is required to evoke a reaction. "Highly specific" means that each species is responsive only to its own species' pheromones.   **4.** A primer pheromone causes physiological changes in the organism and affects its development and later behavior. A releaser pheromone produces rapid and reversible responses and immediate changes. The former is permanent and long-lasting; the latter is temporary and immediate.
5. An alarm pheromone warns others of danger (e.g., mouse pheromone warns other mice to flee danger); an aggregate pheromone calls members together (e.g., honeybee pheromone helps bees recognize their colony and causes them to return to it); a sex pheromone arouses and attracts members (e.g., snails attract immature undifferentiated snails for mating purposes); a terrestrial trail pheromone acts as a navigational guide (e.g., ants notify others of the existence and location of food through these pheromones).

Using Vocabulary Audioscript, page 122

1. Workers in a chemical company complained of stomach pains. When scientists examined the chemicals they were using, they found that these chemicals acted to speed up bodily processes.
2. The refugees were forced to run from their homeland but rather than leave together, they split up and went separate ways. This made them less noticeable as a group and thus was less dangerous. Of course, they hoped to be reunited in a new country. When people throughout the world heard of the situation of these refugees, they felt sorry for them and offered help.
3. The hikers were lost in the mountains and worried because their flashlight batteries were weak and thus were only giving off a faint light, and they were almost out of food. They tried to use a compass to lead them in the right direction and luckily, it did. They made it to the road. People were extremely curious and interested in their story, and many news articles were written about them.
4. The chemical used for killing insects worked well on land-based insects but did not work as well on water-based insects.

Answers:
1. stimulants; physiological changes   **2.** flee; disperse; evoked a response   **3.** emitting; exhausted; navigational guide; aroused   **4.** insecticides; terrestrial

Lecture 11: The Near Side of the Moon

Lecture Outline for Listening for the Larger Picture, page 125
Use this outline if you'd like to deliver the lecture yourself.

INTRODUCTION: It is hard to believe that the same moon that we see in the night sky is the moon that Apollo astronauts have walked on. Through these "moon walks," we have received firsthand information about what the moon's surface looks like and feels like. Though few of us will ever get the opportunity ourselves to see and touch this surface (though, who knows?), this talk is meant to familiarize you in some detail with the features of the surface of the near side of the moon (the side that is perpetually turned toward the earth) and to let you get an idea about what you would see and feel if you were on the surface of the near side of the moon.

I. Distinctive surface features of the near side of the moon

   A. The most obvious distinction that can be made in the surface features of this side of the moon is between the flat *lowlands* called *maria*/ma' riy uh/ (singular = *mare*/ma' ray/) and the *highlands* (mountain ranges).

   1. The lowlands—the dark areas of the picture
      a. The lowlands are called *maria*—which means "seas." But don't imagine "seas" as oceans and huge bodies of liquid water as we see on the earth—that doesn't exist on the moon.
      b. The lowlands are fairly smooth and represent valleys and basins that were filled in by molten lava at some stage in the moon's evolution.
         (1) Basalt (an igneous rock similar to lava on earth) is common in these maria.
      c. Certain of these maria are areas of high concentration of mass called *mascons* (the darkest of the dark areas of the picture).
         (1) Spacecraft flying over these mascons have experienced increased gravitational attraction.
      d. Circular maria (associated with mascons) may range in diameter up to 702 miles, with irregular maria being significantly larger.
   2. The highlands
      a. The highlands appear lighter in color and brighter than the maria.
      b. The highlands are dominated by *craters* (surface depressions).
         (1) These craters generally don't occur in maria.
         (2) These craters range in size up to 150 miles.
      c. The highlands extend for hundreds of miles and reach heights of over 3½ miles above the level of the maria.

II. The issue of water on the moon

   A. Up until recently, the scientific community was unanimous in its opinion that there was no water on the moon.
   1. It was believed that since the moon lacked an atmosphere, it could not maintain *liquid* water on the surface.
   2. It is because of the earth's atmospheric pressure that we have *liquid* water on our surface.

   B. However, the issue of water on the moon is much more in question now, with unmanned lunar probes in 1998 suggesting the possibility of frozen crystals of water in the soil.
   1. The probe sent back data indicating the possibility of ice crystals sprinkled sparsely and embedded in soil in the craters of the lunar poles—places where the temperature allows the ice crystals to remain permanently frozen.
   2. If this turns out to be true, the existence of ice crystals on the moon creates great possibilities for space exploration, because the ice could provide the basic components of rocket fuel on the moon's surface—a lunar refueling station.
   3. Scientists believe these data require more examination and stress that the technological know-how to mine and use these ice crystals is not available.
   4. In any case, the strong possibility of ice crystals on the moon's poles raises exciting questions and offers great potential.

III. Temperature of the near side of the moon

   A. There are drastic temperature changes on the moon.
   1. Temperatures on the moon range from 215 degrees F (102 degrees C) when it is directly under the sun to –285 degrees F (–176 degrees C) when it is at its coldest point.

    B. This wide variation of temperature can only occur on a body devoid of atmosphere.

        1. The earth's atmosphere provides a moderating blanket that limits the difference between daytime and nighttime temperatures.

IV. Light and darkness on the near side of the moon

    A. There is no such thing as twilight and dawn on the near side of the moon.

    B. When the sun rises or goes down, darkness or light is immediate except for a small number of reflections from nearby peaks above the observer's head.

    C. Again, this can be attributed to the moon's lack of atmosphere, which does not reflect light.

CONCLUSION: The moon is 238,600 miles away. Chances are slim that we ourselves will visit, but through the research of astronomers, we are able to "visit," at least in our minds.

Lecture Audioscript for Listening for the Larger Picture, page 125
This audioscript shows one speaker's delivery of the lecture, as recorded in the audio program. Use it as a resource.

OK . . . the picture that you have in your hand is as we said . . . is the moon . . . it's hard to believe that this moon is the same moon we see at night *and* the same moon that astronauts have walked on . . . but through these moon walks . . . we've gotten firsthand information about what the moon's surface looks like . . . and though few of us will get the opportunity ourselves to see this . . . in person . . . although who knows? . . . what this talk will do . . . or I'd like to do . . . is familiarize you in some detail with the features . . . the surface features of . . . the surface of the *near* side of the moon . . . the side closest to us . . . and to give you an idea of what you would see and feel if you were *on* that surface of the moon . . . and the near side is that side which is *perpetually* turned towards the earth . . . OK . . . so there are different features for each side but I'm going to talk about the near side of the moon . . . and I'm going to use a bit of subject-specific vocabulary that you really won't hear about unless you're talking about the features of the moon . . . 'cause they're specific for that . . . so I'd like you to listen for that and make sure you get those . . .

OK . . . if you were on the moon . . . the most *distinctive* things that you would see . . . and the most *apparent* things that you would see . . . would be the differences between the highlands and the lowlands . . . OK? . . . and these flat lowlands . . . and I'll I'll talk about each one separately . . . but the flat lowlands . . . are called mare [on board] . . . M-A-R-E . . . mare . . . and that's the singular form . . . the plural form is maria [on board] . . . spelled like the name . . . but pronounced differently . . . M-A-R-I-A . . . maria . . . and these are the flat lowlands . . . the highlands would be what we call here mountain ranges . . .

OK . . . these lowlands or maria are called "seas" . . . *maria* means "sea" in Latin . . . uh but don't imagine any oceans or great bodies of water on the moon . . . they're not there . . . so remember they mean "sea" but we're not talking about oceans or rivers or lakes . . . or even puddles . . . and I'm going to come back to this issue of water on the moon later because . . . well . . . recent moon explorations have raised questions and possibilities in this area . . . anyway I'll talk about that in a minute . . .

first . . . what do the lowlands look like? . . . well they're very smooth or fairly smooth . . . and they include valleys and basins that were filled in with molten lava at some stage in the moon's evolution . . . and most of the rock in these maria is basalt [on board] . . . B-A-S-A-L-T . . . basalt . . . and basalt rock . . . if you don't know . . . is . . . uh a rock that's found on the earth as well . . . and it's a rock that is . . . an igneous rock . . . a rock that is made of molten lava . . . molten lava is melted rock from volcanic activity . . . OK so these maria are associated with this kind of molten lava . . . this rock . . .

now there are specific types of maria called "mascons" [on board] . . . M-A-S-C-O-N-S . . . mascons . . . these are a certain type of maria . . . and what happened is when the spacecrafts flew over these mascons . . . they found that the gravitational pull was much stronger than usual . . . and these mascons are extremely *dense* portions of the maria . . . OK? . . . there's a high concentration of mass in these mascons . . . and if you look at the picture in fact I think you can see some differences . . . where's my picture here . . . here it is . . . so if you look at the dark areas these are the maria . . . and the darkest dark in the dark areas . . . are the mascons . . . OK you can't see the mascons very clearly in this picture but you can see some shadows . . . OK? . . . the darkest parts are the mascons . . . the dark parts are the maria . . . and all these areas that are lighter are the highlands . . .

OK . . . how big are the maria? . . . the circular maria . . . which are mostly associated with mascons . . . can range in diameter up to 702 miles . . . and irregular maria are even larger . . .

what about the highlands? as you can see from the picture there's definitely a difference . . . the highlands appear lighter in color and brighter than the maria and if you were on or in . . . the highlands . . . you would see that they are dominated by craters . . . and a crater . . . if you've ever seen a volcano . . . is the part of the volcano . . . the hole from which the lava had erupted? . . . OK . . . so the highlands are dominated by these craters . . . and these craters range in size up to 150 miles across . . . the highlands may extend for hundreds of miles and they reach heights of over 3½ miles . . . heights similar to some of our tallest mountains here on earth . . . 3½ miles above the level of the maria . . .

OK . . . now just a minute ago . . . I said I'd talk about the issue of water on the moon . . . very interesting . . . until recently . . . the past few years . . . scientists were generally unanimous in their belief that the moon was devoid of water . . . and this stems from the belief that since the moon lacks an atmosphere . . . it could not possibly maintain water . . . *liquid* water . . . on its surface . . . because it is *because* of the *earth's* atmosphere . . . the *pressure* created by the earth's atmosphere . . . that we . . . here on earth . . . can have liquid water on our surface . . . but the moon has no atmosphere . . . so therefore no surface water . . . but in 1998 an unmanned lunar probe sent data to the earth indicating the possibility of ice crystals . . . *frozen* water . . . permanently frozen water . . . not liquid . . . embedded deep in craters on the moon at the lunar poles . . . and sprinkled sparsely just at the north and south poles of the moon . . . so we're not talking about glaciers or ice sheets . . . we're talking about sprinklings of ice crystals . . . mixed in the rocky soil of the moon . . . in very low concentrations . . . still . . . this discovery has people excited because it provides the basic components of rocket fuel on the moon's surface . . . a lunar refueling station . . . though for the most part scientists believe this data requires much more examination . . . and even if it turns out to be true that there are water crystals on the moon . . . the ability to mine and use that water is still . . . um shall we say . . . light years away . . . anyway . . . a very exciting possibility . . . with enormous potential . . .

so what would you see if you were on the surface of the moon? . . . what would you feel? . . . well there are drastic temperature changes on the moon . . . OK 'cause *again* the moon has no atmosphere so there's no blanket . . . to keep heat in . . . or . . . to protect the surface from these extremes in heat when the sun goes down . . . heat and cold . . . so there are drastic temperature changes . . . temperatures on the moon range from 215 degrees Fahrenheit when it's directly under the sun . . . 215 degrees Fahrenheit . . . what's that in Centigrade? . . . um . . . about 102 degrees . . . and I'd hate to live under that . . . and it ranges to *minus* 285 degrees Fahrenheit when it's at its coldest point . . . minus 285 degrees . . . that's equal to minus 176 degrees Centigrade . . . OK . . . and this could all be in the passage of one day . . . these extremes in temperature . . . and as I said these wide variations in temperature could only occur on a body that is *devoid* of atmosphere and our earth's atmosphere provides a moderating blanket for us . . .

OK . . . another very interesting thing that you'd probably notice if you were on the surface of the moon is that there's no twilight and dawn . . . we think of twilight . . . we think of dawn . . . as these periods when we can watch the transition between day and night . . . OK? . . . but on the moon there's no atmosphere to reflect light . . . and so the time . . . there is very little . . . switching time OK? . . . you might see a little bit of reflection but on the whole . . . when the sun rises or goes down . . . darkness and light would be immediate except for a very very small number of reflections from some nearby peaks over the observer's head OK? . . . but you wouldn't have that feeling of twilight and dawn which is a lengthy period of time on earth because of the reflection of light on the earth's surface . . .

OK . . . in this short lecture I tried to give you a little bit of a feeling of what it would be like to either be on the moon's surface . . . or . . . be an observer . . . the moon is 238,600 miles away . . . and chances are slim that we ourselves will . . . visit but through the research of astronomers and some of the work of astronauts . . . we're able to at least visit in our minds.

Answers, page 125:
1. describe the features of the near side of the moon   2. **a.** maria (lowlands)   **b.** highlands; a, b, a, a, b
3. **a.** temperature   **b.** lightness/darkness

Defining Vocabulary Audioscript, pages 126–127

1. <u>firsthand knowledge:</u> It's usually not enough for a child to be told that fire is hot. The child often needs to learn this firsthand—by going near the flame and feeling heat. This firsthand knowledge stays with the child for a long time because it was experienced directly.
2. <u>perpetually:</u> Certain parts of the world are perpetually frozen. Because the ground water never melts, the area cannot support trees.
3. <u>molten lava:</u> Pictures of a volcanic eruption often show red, yellow, and orange lines coming from the crater. These are actually streams of molten lava, melted rock which is so hot that it burns in theses colors.
4. <u>to dominate:</u> Skyscrapers dominate the New York City skyline. A two-story building is very hard to find there.
5. <u>unanimous:</u> The new law passed without a single vote in opposition. The decision was unanimous.
6. <u>to be devoid (of something):</u> Areas in which the ground is perpetually frozen are devoid of trees. Imagine what it's like to look at a landscape without trees.
7. <u>to moderate:</u> The atmosphere moderates the sun's influence on the earth's temperature. Without the atmosphere, there would be great temperature extremes depending on whether the sun was up or down. With the atmosphere, heat can be retained by the earth and thus warm the air even when the sun is down.
8. <u>twilight:</u> The best colors of the sunset are during twilight, the time when the sun is no longer on the horizon but the sky is still lit.
9. <u>dawn:</u> We got up at the crack of dawn. Although we couldn't see the sun yet, the sky was lit up.
10. <u>to attribute:</u> The well-known doctor attributed her success to her family's support for her work and education.
11. <u>slim chance:</u> She thought her chances were good to win that scholarship when she applied. However, she found out that there were 10,000 applicants and only two scholarships. Now, she realizes what a slim chance she has!

Answers:
1. a   2. a   3. c   4. a   5. a   6. c   7. a   8. c   9. b   10. a   11. b

Note-Taking Practice, pages 127–128
See pages 212–213 of Appendix C in the textbook for example notes.

Post-Lecture Reading and Discussion, pages 128–129
Answers:
1. a. He is a hotelier.   **b.** He imagines "moonbound tourists traveling by space ferry to a Lunar Hilton with 100 guest rooms and a dining room serving everything from reconstituted martinis to freeze-dried steaks."   **c.** They have hired an architect to design a lunar hotel and have spent about $300,000 to explore building a glass-domed inn with thousands of pressurized guest rooms, galactic viewing platforms, and a medical center.   **d.** Skeptics are pointing out the huge costs, complex engineering challenges, and potential safety risk. Others consider the project feasible.   **2.** Answers will vary.

Using Your Notes, page 129
Answers:
1. a. lowlands of moon (pl.)   **b.** lowlands of moon (sing.)   **c.** maria with particularly high concentrations of mass   **2. a.** lowlands—smooth, basalt is common, valleys and basins, darker in pictures   **b.** highlands—appear lighter in pictures, dominated by craters   **3. a.** no liquid water because there is no atmospheric pressure   **b.** great temperature extremes because no atmosphere to retain heat after sun goes down   **c.** no twilight or dawn because no atmosphere to reflect light after sun goes down   **4.** c   **5.** ranging from 215 degrees F (102 degrees C) to –285 degrees F (–176 degrees C)

Using Vocabulary Audioscript, page 130

1. In January 1977, Voyager 2 was launched.
2. In 1986, it passed Uranus and its moons and took photographs. These photographs showed that Ariel, one of Uranus's moons, is dominated by broad, curving valleys and huge canyons.
3. Presently, a visitor to Uranus's south pole would experience something that would feel like perpetual sunlight, although it will only last about forty or so more years.
4. Scientists attribute this phenomenon to the fact that Uranus lies on its side with respect to the sun and the south pole is now facing the sun.
5. Uranus's atmosphere is probably devoid of oxygen. It consists primarily of hydrogen, helium, and methane.

Answers:
1. a   2. b   3. a   4. a   5. b

Lecture 12: Drink Your Green Tea!

Lecture Outline for Listening for the Larger Picture, page 133
Use this outline if you'd like to deliver the lecture yourself.

INTRODUCTION: If you go to Italy, you're likely to drink a lot of coffee. If you go to England, you're likely to be invited to have tea—afternoon tea, high tea, morning tea—and it's usually a black tea, often served with cream and sugar. In India, the English tradition has been continued—however, the Indian version is much sweeter than the average English tea. If you go to a Japanese restaurant or spend time in Japan, you're likely to be offered green tea.

In fact, in many Asian countries, including China, Japan, and India, green tea is held in high esteem. It is a brew thought to purify the body, delight the senses, and lift the spirits.

What I'd like to do in this lecture is talk specifically about green tea and its effects on our health. However, before I do that, I'd like to give a brief overview about teas, in general—where they are grown, the different types of tea, what makes them different—and then I'll talk in some detail about the specific health properties of green tea.

   I. How does green tea differ from other teas?

   A. All tea comes from *Camellia sinensis,* an evergreen with white blossoms that thrives in tropical and semitropical climates.

   B. There are three ways to process tea leaves, resulting in three kinds of teas: green, oolong, and black tea.

   1. Green tea is the virgin of tea manufacturing, the least processed, the youngest, the freshest.

>   **a.** To make it, the tea leaves are (1) immediately steamed and heated to soften them (and stop a process called oxidation—interaction with oxygen), then (2) rolled out under pressure (to remove most of the moisture) and (3) spread out and dried for a short period of time to dry a bit more.
>   **b.** The whole process—from steaming to drying—takes about three hours.
>   **2.** In contrast, black tea requires more elaborate processing.
>   **a.** Black tea requires a chemical process called fermentation, which means that the tea is allowed to interact with oxygen. This changes the chemical structure of the tea leaf.
>   **b.** Therefore, instead of steaming the tea leaves to soften them and prevent oxidation (fermentation), when manufacturers want to make black tea, they spread the leaves out in a cool, humid place to allow the leaves to interact with the oxygen and thus ferment. The leaves wither and change color as they oxidize.
>   **c.** Oxidation continues for a few hours.
>   **d.** Then the leaves are exposed to hot, dry air for fifteen to twenty-five minutes to stop oxidation.
>   **3.** To make oolong tea, the leaves are only semifermented, resulting in a green-brown leaf.
> **C.** In world tea production, only about 4% is oolong. Green tea represents about 20%, and the rest—about 75%—is black tea.

II. Green tea is good for you!

> **A.** Studies in China found that green tea could reduce the incidence of cancer of the esophagus (the long muscular tube that leads into the stomach).
>   **1.** The Chinese studies showed that the risk for esophageal cancer was reduced by 57% for men and by 60% for women by drinking green tea.
>   **2.** A tea drinker was defined as someone who drank at least one cup of tea per week for six months or longer.
>
> **B.** Studies in Japan have shown lowered rates of lung cancer, stomach cancer, and skin tumors, and lowered blood cholesterol among people who drink green tea every day.
>   **1.** Some researchers are suggesting that green tea may help explain why smokers in Japan have a lower rate of lung cancer than smokers in other parts of the world.
>
> **C.** Green tea also contains vitamin C; the amount varies depending on the type of leaf, but the average in two small cups of brewed tea is nearly equal to that in a cup of orange juice.
>
> **D.** A U.S. research team at the University of California, Berkeley, found a substance in green tea that may help protect against dental cavities.

III. Continuing research on green tea

> **A.** Green tea is on the list of foods being studied in the Designer Food Program of the National Institute of Health.
>   **1.** The forty foods on the list are thought to have unusually powerful disease-fighting abilities.
>   **a.** Other foods being studied include garlic, licorice, soy, cranberry juice, and carrots.
>   **2.** Scientists believe that if the disease-fighting elements in these foods were isolated and synthesized, they could be designed for use as preventative medication.
>   **3.** The problem is finding what element in any one food is the preventative agent.
>   **a.** The research is focusing on polyphenol, a main component of green tea.
>   **b.** Polyphenols are a class of compounds that seem to inhibit cancer cell growth.

CONCLUSION

> **A.** According to some researchers, green tea has no known toxicity; it's not going to hurt you, and it may very well help you.
>
> **B.** So next time you reach for a cup of coffee or a cup of black tea, consider green tea!
>   **1.** Green tea is a mild stimulant, but it contains less caffeine than black tea and half the caffeine of coffee.

Lecture Audioscript for Listening for the Larger Picture, page 133
This audioscript shows one speaker's delivery of the lecture, as recorded in the audio program. Use it as a resource.

if you go to Italy . . . you can't go anywhere without finding a cafe on the corner . . . you'll get a coffee there . . . a cappuccino . . . if you go to England . . . you'll find coffee . . . but what England is usually known for is the tea . . . tea is a tradition . . . you have afternoon tea . . . high tea . . . usually it's black tea and it's served with milk and sugar . . . if you go to India . . . the English tea tradition has been continued there except the tea that is served is much stronger and much sweeter with cream . . . if you go to a Japanese restaurant or spend time in Japan . . . you're likely to be offered green tea . . . in fact in many Asian countries . . . including China, Japan, and India . . . green tea is held in very very high esteem . . . it's a brew that's thought to purify the body . . . delight the senses . . . um lift the spirits . . . OK so . . . what do I want to do in this talk? . . . what I want to do is talk specifically about *green* tea . . . not about coffee . . . not about cappuccino . . . not about black tea . . . but green tea . . . and its effects on health . . . because there has been some surprising research that has been showing some positive connections between green tea and health . . .

um . . . before I do that . . . uh what I'm going to do first is I'm, I'm going to give a brief overview about tea in general . . . uh where it's grown . . . different types of tea . . . what makes them different . . . and then I'm going to talk in detail about the specific health properties of green . . . tea . . .

so . . . let's start . . . how does green tea differ from other teas? . . . well um all teas are the same in that they all come from the same plant . . . they all come from a plant called *Camellia sinensis* . . . [on board] . . . they all come from this same plant . . . it's a . . . it's an evergreen with white blossoms that thrive in tropical and semitropical climates . . . so all teas come from this particular genus . . . and as I said . . . it's an evergreen with white blossoms that thrives in tropical and semitropical climates . . .

how do you get your different teas? . . . well there are three ways to process tea leaves . . . and that results in three different *kinds* of teas . . . the three types are green tea . . . black tea . . . those are the ones that everyone knows . . . and one more type called . . . oolong . . . OK . . . and these are the three different types of tea and they simply result from the three different processes . . . applied to this *Camellia sinensis* plant . . .

uh . . . so let me talk first about green tea . . . green tea is the . . . virgin . . . of tea manufacturing . . . what do I mean by the virgin of tea manufacturing? . . . it's the least processed . . . it's the youngest . . . it's the freshest . . . of all of those teas . . . how is it made? . . . simply the tea leaves are gathered . . . and then they're immediately steamed and heated to soften them . . . and this not only softens them but it also stops a process called oxidation [on board] . . . oxidation means interaction with oxygen . . . and I'll talk a bit more later about what happens to tea when it oxidizes . . . but anyway . . . this heating and steaming prevents oxidation . . . and then the tea is rolled . . . it's rolled under pressure to remove most of the moisture . . . and finally it's spread out and dried for a short period of time to remove more of the moisture . . . that's all . . . so they gather the leaves . . . they heat and steam them . . . they roll them . . . and they dry them . . . that's the simplest process . . . OK . . . so it's gathered . . . it's steam heated . . . it's rolled up . . . and then it's dried . . . and this whole process . . . from steaming to drying . . . takes . . . about . . . three hours . . .

OK . . . black tea . . . is the one that takes the most processing and it requires the most elaborate processing . . . it requires a chemical process called fermentation [on board] . . . and fermentation means that the tea is allowed to interact with oxygen in a way that changes the chemical structure of the tea leaf . . . so . . . instead of steaming the tea leaves to soften them and prevent oxidation . . . which is what they do with green tea . . . instead of doing this . . . when manufacturers want to make black tea . . . they . . . spread the leaves out in a cool . . . humid . . . place just so that they can allow the leaves to interact with the oxygen and ferment . . . and what happens is that the leaves wither . . . and they change color as they oxidize . . . and they allow this oxidation or fermentation process to continue for several hours . . . OK so . . . so there's a process here . . . it's, it's much . . . there's a more complicated process . . . but what's important is that there's oxidation . . . there's a process of oxygen interacting with the enzymes in the leaves . . . so this interaction begins the process called oxidation . . . fermentation . . . and that continues until the leaves are heated to stop it . . . the leaves are exposed to hot dry air for about um fifteen to twenty-five minutes . . . and this stops the oxidation . . . so you can see that there's this process in there . . . which encourages um this process called fermentation . . . and what happens . . . as the leaves oxidize . . . they turn black . . . OK so all the leaves are the same to begin with . . . they're all green . . . but in the case of black tea . . . as the leaves are exposed to oxygen for a long period of time . . . as they ferment . . . they turn black . . .

all right um what about oolong tea? . . . it's just right in the middle . . . OK in this case the leaves are only *semi*fermented . . . so they're *partially* exposed to oxygen . . . they're partially fermented . . . and this results in a leaf that's greenish-brown . . . it's kind of in the middle of the other types . . . greenish-brown . . . OK so we have green tea . . . we have black tea . . . and then oolong is a green-brown tea . . .

all right then . . . in world tea production . . . only about 4% of tea is oolong tea . . . so only 4% of world production of tea is actually oolong tea . . . green tea makes up 20% of world production . . . and black tea . . . 75% . . . so that you can see that most of the world drinks black tea . . . 75% of the world's production is black tea . . .

but let's get to the important part of the lecture . . . because uh what I want to talk about is the idea that green tea is actually good for you . . . and that's what science and research are showing . . . OK . . . I . . . I want to tell you about some studies that were done . . . to show . . . that green tea . . . is good for you . . . uh the *first* ones . . . were done in China . . . and what they found is that green tea seems to reduce the incidence of cancer of the esophagus . . . so it's a specific type of cancer . . . uh but in these studies from China . . . they were able to see . . . there seems to be a relationship between drinking green tea . . . and a reduction . . . in the incidence of cancer of the esophagus . . . everyone knows what the esophagus is? . . . it's a um long muscular tube that leads into the stomach . . . these Chinese studies found that the risk of esophageal cancer in men was reduced by 57% and for women . . . by 60% . . . when they drank green tea regularly . . . and they defined a tea drinker as someone who drank at least one cup of tea per week for six months or longer . . . so *not* a great great amount . . . anyway that's one example of a study that seems to indicate that there is a relationship between drinking green tea and improved health . . .

OK . . . um there has *also* been research in Japan . . . where a lot of green tea is actually consumed . . . and studies in Japan have shown . . . among people who drink green tea . . . lower rates of lung cancer . . . lower rates of stomach cancer . . . lower rates of skin tumors . . . and lowered blood cholesterol . . . some researchers are even suggesting that green tea may help to explain why smokers in Japan have a lower rate of lung cancer than say . . . smokers in the United States . . . or in other parts of the world . . . so again . . . they're finding all of these factors among people who drink green tea every day . . . lower rates of lung cancer . . . lower rates of stomach cancer . . . lower rates of skin tumors . . . and lowered blood cholesterol . . . so a lot of benefits . . . this is a . . . a pretty good argument . . . it looks like for drinking green tea . . .

another thing you might want to know about green tea is that they found that green tea contains vitamin C . . . this is another bit of research that they've done . . . uh green tea contains vitamin C . . . and most people don't think of tea containing vitamin C . . . we think of . . . what contains vitamin C? . . . uh orange juice . . . citrus fruits . . . but they found that on average . . . two small cups of green tea . . . were nearly equal to a cup of orange juice . . . in vitamin C . . . two small cups of green tea were nearly equal to the vitamin C in a cup of orange juice . . .

and lastly . . . um a U.S. research team . . . at the University of California at Berkeley . . . found a substance in green tea . . . which they say . . . may help protect against dental cavities . . . wouldn't that be great . . . anyway . . . uh another area to research further . . . green tea's properties in protecting against dental cavities . . . uh we'll probably see green tea toothpaste soon . . .

OK . . . um where are they going with this research on green tea? . . . what's the future of the research? . . . right now . . . the National Institute of Health has a program called their Designer Food Program . . . and what they're doing is they're looking at forty different foods . . . that are shown to have powerful disease-fighting properties . . . they have a list of forty different foods that this particular program . . . the Designer Food Program of the National Institute of Health is looking at . . . um these forty foods that they think have disease-fighting properties . . . and some of the other foods they're looking at are . . . uh . . . garlic . . . licorice . . . um soy . . . carrots . . . cranberry juice . . . and green tea is one of those . . . and what the scientists want to do . . . is they want to see if they can . . . isolate . . . and then re-create . . . synthesize . . . the disease . . . fighting . . . content . . . or element . . . in these foods . . . OK so they're uh . . . what they're trying to do is to find out what is it in green tea . . . or what is it in carrots for example . . . that can fight disease . . . and what they'd like to do is isolate it . . . and synthesize it . . . or re-create it . . . why? . . . so they could use it in medicine . . . the problem seems to be that it's hard to find that one element . . . they know that the food itself seems to work . . . but they're not sure exactly what element in the food is the preventative agent . . . what is it exactly that is causing the disease-fighting characteristics? . . . the research is pointing to a class of compounds called polyphenols . . . [on board] . . . poly, P-O-L-Y, phenols, P-H-E-N-O-L-S . . . polyphenols . . . this class of compounds which seem to inhibit cancer cell growth . . .

OK . . . so . . . green tea . . . has no known toxicity . . . there's nothing that can hurt you with green tea . . . and . . . according to some researchers . . . it may very well help you . . . so the next time you reach for a cup of coffee . . . a cup of black tea . . . consider green tea . . . like the others, green tea is a mild stimulant . . . so it will wake you up a bit . . . but it contains less caffeine than black tea . . . and half the caffeine of coffee . . . so if you need a little pick-me-up . . . maybe green tea is a healthier answer.

Answers, page 133: a, c, e

Defining Vocabulary Audioscript, pages 133–134

1. <u>to hold in high esteem</u>: Everyone holds that artist's work in very high esteem. The art critics are praising her new show and people are willing to pay quite a bit for her paintings.
2. <u>steam</u>: After my eight-hour plane ride, everything in my suitcases was wrinkled. I didn't have an iron, so I turned on the hot water in the shower and closed the bathroom door. I hung all my clothes in the bathroom. In about five minutes, the steam had removed all the wrinkles.
3. <u>to roll</u>: In order to make a good pie crust, take flour, water, and butter and make a dough. Then, use a rolling pin to roll the dough into a thin and even crust.
4. <u>humid</u>: In deserts, the climate is often hot and dry. However, in tropical areas, the climate is often hot and humid.
5. <u>to wither</u>: The roses were beautiful on the first day. However, by the third day, the leaves and some of the petals had withered and fallen off.
6. <u>incidence</u>: The incidence of serious car accidents has increased because of the greater number of cars on the road.
7. <u>to isolate</u>: One of the horses on the ranch seemed very sick, so the rancher isolated it until it got better. He kept it in a separate stable because he didn't want the other animals to get sick.
8. <u>to inhibit</u>: I don't like wearing high heels because they inhibit my ability to move about freely and easily.
9. <u>toxicity</u>: Those chemicals have a high level of toxicity. You should wear a mask when you use them so you don't breathe in poisonous fumes.
10. <u>stimulant</u>: Don't drink coffee before you go to bed. It's a stimulant and will keep you awake.

Answers:
1. b   2. c   3. c   4. c   5. a   6. c   7. a   8. a   9. c   10. b

Note-Taking Practice, pages 134–135
See pages 214–215 of Appendix C in the textbook for example notes.

Post-Lecture Reading and Discussion, pages 136–137
Answers:
1. There have been no human studies to date in which people have been given green tea and then observed to see if they develop cancers at a lower rate. Rather, the evidence has been epidemiologic, that is, starting with people who have cancer and asking them to reflect on their consumption of tea (and then comparing the consumption rates of this group to the rates of a group without cancer). There are problems with this method of study: (1) people may not remember their tea consumption patterns accurately, and (2) there is no clear proof that it is the tea, and not something else in their lifestyle, that affected their cancer risk. Finally, another concern about the studies is that the results have been mixed. **2.** More and better controlled investigations in humans need to be done.
3. This is open for discussion. The article's tone and content seem to encourage readers to be cautious about accepting the findings 100% at this time, but they also seem to encourage optimism about the possibility that tea will be found to provide health benefits. The article also seems to encourage a balanced perspective, concluding that tea, even if found to be healthy, will not be a "miracle cure" and will never replace the importance of a healthy, balanced diet and a lifestyle including exercise. (The first two paragraphs clearly explain why readers should be skeptical. The third paragraph counters one of the concerns. The fourth paragraph is very optimistic, quoting a doctor who says "the evidence from studies thus far is encouraging enough to provide incentive for additional research in the area." The last paragraph reminds readers that exercise and a healthy diet are ultimately more important than tea consumption, regardless of the findings.)

Using Your Notes, pages 137–138
Answers:
1. a. T **b.** F **c.** F **d.** T **e.** F **f.** F **g.** T **h.** F **2.** b, d, e, g **3.** First, steam and heat the leaves to soften them and stop oxidation. Then, roll them under pressure to remove most of the moisture. Then, spread the leaves out and dry them for a short additional period. **4.** First, spread the leaves out in a cool, humid place to allow the leaves to ferment for a few hours. Then, expose the leaves to hot, dry air for fifteen to twenty-five minutes to stop fermentation. **5.** They hope to isolate the disease-fighting elements in these foods and then synthesize or re-create those elements for use in medicines.

Using Vocabulary Audioscript, page 138

1. The life expectancy in many countries is increasing because of improved diets.
2. The doctor is held in very high esteem.
3. Generally, vitamins are beneficial; however, consuming too much of certain vitamins can be toxic.
4. The factory regularly releases steam into the environment, which is reported to contain carcinogenic substances.
5. In one isolated island in the Pacific, there is a high incidence of birth defects.

Answers:
1. b **2.** c **3.** b **4.** b **5.** b

Lecture 13: Voter Turnout in the United States

Pre-Lecture Discussion, pages 140–141
Answers:
1. Answers may vary. However, students should notice that more people register than vote and that fewer and fewer people are voting (though the 1992 election showed a rise before a steep fall in 1996). The 1996 election had the lowest percentage of reported voters of all the years listed. **2.** Answers may vary. However, students should notice that females tend to register and vote more than men, whites more than blacks and those of Spanish origin, those with more education more than those with less education, and older people more than younger people.

Lecture Outline for Listening for the Larger Picture, page 142
Use this outline if you'd like to deliver the lecture yourself.

INTRODUCTION: Originally the right to vote in the United States was in the hands of a small group of property-owning white males.

The first step in the expansion of the right to vote went to white men without property. Then black men gained the right to vote. Finally in 1920, black and white women gained the right to vote.

No step in the battle for voting rights was easy. Often even after winning the right to vote, the actual voting was easier said than done.

With such a long history of struggle for voting rights, one might expect a high rate of voter turnout in the United States. In fact, voter turnout is remarkably low. To offer some examples from presidential election years, the actual voter turnout in 1960 was 64%; in 1988, it was 50%; in 1992, it was 55%; in 1996, it was 49%.

Why is this so?

I. Causes of low voter turnout

    A. People assume that the reason people don't vote is apathy, but this is basically not true.

    B. There are two main reasons for nonvoting: *institutional* reasons and *political* reasons.
        1. The institutional barriers are problems with the mechanism of voting, particularly problems with registration and absentee ballot requirements.
            a. e.g., People forget to register in time.
            b. e.g., People may have moved too recently to register.
            c. e.g., People may think registration is time-consuming.
        2. Far more important than the institutional obstacles and far more difficult to change are the political obstacles to voting.
            a. Millions of Americans fail to show up at the polls because they feel that it is not worth the trouble.
                (1) They feel that their real interest is not reflected in the "system."
                (2) They feel that there is no real choice between candidates or parties.
                (3) They mistrust politicians and believe they make promises that they fail to carry out.
            b. These people are not apathetic about politics; rather, they believe that politics is apathetic about them.

    C. A poll asking why people didn't vote was taken.
        1. 38% of respondents said they didn't vote because they didn't register. It is difficult to tell from this statistic whether the reasons for not registering were apathy, institutional reasons, or political reasons.
        2. 14% of respondents gave explicitly political reasons—e.g., they did not like the candidates.
        3. 18% of respondents gave explicitly institutional reasons—e.g., they were sick or disabled, new residents in an area, away from home, unable to leave their jobs, or unable to get to the polls.
        4. 10% of respondents stated that they were not interested in politics.
        5. 10% of respondents said they had no particular reason for not voting.
        6. The remaining 10% of respondents either were not U.S. citizens or gave other reasons.

II. Voter/nonvoter characteristics

    A. Generally, as education goes up, the likelihood of voting goes up regardless of race or ethnicity.
        1. Those who finish grammar school are more likely to vote than those who don't.
        2. High school grads tend to turn out more than grammar school grads.
        3. College grads turn out more than high school grads.

    B. Generally, those with higher incomes and with higher-status careers are more likely to vote than those with lower-status jobs.

    C. Generally, the older (until about age seventy-eight) you are, the more likely you are to vote.
        1. Persons eighteen to twenty-four and persons over seventy-eight have a very poor voting record.

    D. Generally, whites go to the polls more frequently than blacks, who go more frequently than Hispanics.

    E. Women are slightly more likely to vote than men.

    F. The general trend that emerges is that the poor, the uneducated, and members of racial minorities are seriously underrepresented in the voting booth.
        1. According to Burns, Peltason, and Cronin in their textbook *Government by the People,* their nonvoting is not accidental but is part of a larger political and psychological environment that discourages political activity by minority groups.

CONCLUSION

    A. Perhaps the picture is not as bleak as described above.

1. It should be noted that Americans conduct far more elections and types of elections than many other countries.
2. It also should be noted that Americans, in addition to having the right to vote, have the right not to vote. No one is forced to vote or threatened if they don't vote, as they may be in other countries.

B. Perhaps with the increased incidence of women and minorities running for higher office, some disillusionment with the system will decrease.

Lecture Audioscript for Listening for the Larger Picture, page 142
This audioscript shows one speaker's delivery of the lecture, as recorded in the audio program. Use it as a resource.

now you all know that yesterday was an election day . . . and it was the time of the primaries . . . but what they found was that the turnout was not . . . uh they knew the turnout was going to be very low . . . OK? . . . they expected about 47% . . . and I think actually the turnout was even much lower . . . like 30% . . . and you realize . . . uh you wonder why 60 or 50% of eligible voters don't vote . . .

so what I'm going to do is talk a little bit about voter turnout in the United States . . . OK? . . . originally . . . as you might know . . . that the right to vote in the United States was in the hands of a small group of property-owning white men . . . so it wasn't even *all* white men . . . and the first step in the expansion of the right to vote went to white men without property . . . now it's been a long struggle for voting rights . . . it hasn't been . . . giving the rights to everyone . . . it's been step by step . . . after that . . . black men gained the right to vote . . . finally in 1920 . . . black and white women . . . gained the right to vote . . . so you can see . . . it took hundreds . . . it took 200 years before everyone really had the right to vote in this country . . . and no step in the battle for voting rights has been easy . . . because even after winning the *right* to vote . . . often actually *voting* was difficult because people were prevented from voting . . . or prevented from registering . . . often by intimidation . . . so you would think that with such a long history of struggle to get voting rights . . . that we'd expect a high rate of voter turnout on election days . . . but the fact is that voter turnout is remarkably low . . . just to give you some examples . . . in presidential election years . . . let's see . . . the, the actual voter turnout in 1960 was 64% . . . in 1988 it was 50% . . . in 1992 it was 55% . . . in 1996 . . . it was 49% . . . I think this is pretty shocking because it indicates that close to *half* of the eligible voters in this country just don't vote . . . what I'm especially going to talk about is *why* this is so . . . and that's the main reason for this talk . . .

so . . . what are the causes of this low voter turnout? . . . OK? . . . most people assume that the reason people don't vote is apathy but this basically is not true . . . the main reasons not to vote are . . . well there . . . there are two particular reasons . . . one are institutional reasons . . . and the one are . . . um and the other . . . are political reasons . . . and we'll go into each one in particular . . . the institutional reasons have to do with the mechanism of voting . . . the procedures required to vote . . . for example people forget to register in time . . . people might have moved and they didn't register again . . . or they may think that registration is too time-consuming . . . or they don't know how to get an absentee ballot and they can't get to the polls . . . so institutional reasons then are the reasons . . . the reasons which are based on the mechanics of voting . . . the procedure required to vote . . . and the institutional reasons for not voting are the procedural problems that make it difficult to vote . . . OK . . . so it's not easy enough to vote . . . things like inconvenient hours for registration . . . early deadlines for registration . . . are primary reasons for lowering voter turnout . . . but in truth . . . these institutional reasons are not the main reasons . . . and far more important than the institutional blocks are political blocks to voting . . . for example . . . millions of Americans don't turn up at the polls because they feel that it's really not worth the trouble . . . for example . . . they feel that their real interest is not reflected in the system . . . they feel that the candidates don't reflect their interests . . . they feel that the candidates are the same . . . they don't believe that any candidate is honest . . . they mistrust politicians . . . you can see the difference between *this* . . . and apathy . . . these people are not apathetic about politics . . . but rather they believe that politics is apathetic about them . . . that politics does not really meet their needs . . . OK? . . . it's not that they don't care . . . but they don't feel that politics is meeting their needs . . . so these were the two *major* blocks that prevent people from voting . . . the institutional . . . and the political . . .

now let me tell you about a poll that was taken asking people why they didn't vote . . . listen to this . . . in this poll . . . 38% of the respondents said they didn't vote because they didn't register . . . now this could be an institutional reason . . . but it's really hard to tell from the statistic what the reason actually was . . . it could be apathy . . . it could be an institutional reason . . . it could be a political reason . . . we really can't tell . . . now . . . 14% of the respondents gave explicitly political reasons . . . that is they didn't like the candidates . . . they didn't think they were represented . . . they said they all seemed alike . . . OK? . . . 18% of the respondents gave explicitly institutional reasons . . . such as they were sick or disabled . . . they were new residents in the area . . . they were away from home . . . they couldn't leave their job . . . they had no way to get to the polls . . . etc. . . . OK . . . 10% of the respondents said that they were not interested in politics . . . so this is your apathetic group . . . they're simply not interested . . . another 10% said they had no particular reason for not voting . . . they just didn't vote . . . so we might say that they're apathetic too in a different way . . . OK? . . . and the remaining 10% of the respondents in the sample either were not U.S. citizens or gave some other reason . . . so it's not a great poll . . . it doesn't give you a lot of information but it does give you some idea of the different reasons that cause people not to vote . . .

well what are some characteristics of the voter versus the nonvoter? . . . generally we find that as education goes up . . . the likelihood to vote also goes up . . . and that's regardless of race or ethnicity . . . and you can see that at all levels . . . people who've finished grammar school are more likely to vote than those who don't

. . . high school graduates are more likely to vote than high school dropouts . . . college graduates go out more than high school graduates . . . they also find that those with higher income and higher-status careers are more likely to vote than those with lower-status jobs and lower income . . . OK . . . another factor they found is generally the older you get . . . and that goes until about the age of seventy-eight . . . so the older you get . . . the more likely you are to vote . . . and exceptions to this are people over seventy-eight . . . who have a very poor voting record . . . OK . . . so now they found that in terms of age . . . the range is from twenty-four to seventy-eight . . . is the best voting record . . . people below the age of twenty-four or above the age of seventy-eight . . . have pretty poor records . . . now . . . what about race? . . . generally whites go to the polls more frequently than blacks . . . who go more frequently than Hispanics . . . and I really don't have any statistics about Asians right now . . . I think that uh probably as the number of Asians in this country increases . . . the more frequently Asians become citizens . . . it might change . . . I don't know . . . OK . . . what about sex? . . . women are more likely to vote than men . . . OK . . . what kinds of trends can we see? . . . most times what most analysts see is that the general trend is that the poor . . . the uneducated . . . members of racial minorities . . . are *seriously under*represented in the voting booth . . . now . . . is this an accident? . . . again most analysts *don't* think that this is accidental . . . but they believe . . . or at least the author of your text believes that this is part of the larger political and psychological environment that discourages political activity by certain groups . . . so groups that do not have power in this country are not encouraged to vote . . . they're not encouraged to be represented . . . and this goes back to some of the political reasons for not voting that we talked about in the beginning . . .

so the picture does look a little bleak . . . but it's really not as bad as it sounds . . . there are two things we might want to note about American electoral policy . . . the first one is that Americans conduct far more elections and far more types of elections than many other countries . . . so we're looking at this as a really bad situation but when we realize that Americans vote one or two times *a year* . . . then maybe it's not that bad . . . so Americans vote far more . . . or they have far more *elections* . . . than most countries . . . and also . . . the other thing is that Americans in addition to having the right *to* vote also have the right *not* to vote which in many countries . . . people do not have that right . . . where people are afraid for their lives if they don't vote . . . here we have the right both to vote and not to vote . . . so that makes the picture a little more optimistic . . . even though on the whole . . . I think it's pretty sad that so few people take the responsibility . . . now in terms of the future . . . I think that the institutional causes of nonvoting will be easier to change than the political reasons . . . the political reasons are deep in the system . . . the institutional reasons can be changed just by changing laws . . . but perhaps because of the increased incidence of women and minorities running for office . . . some of the disillusionment that a lot of minorities . . . a lot of under or unrepresented groups feel . . . may change.

Answers, page 142:
1. voting rights   **2.** low voter turnout   **3.** reasons for not voting; institutional; political   **4.** people didn't vote   **5.** poor; uneducated; members of racial minorities   **6.** United States has more elections than many countries; Americans have the right not to vote

Defining Vocabulary Audioscript, pages 142–143

1. <u>time-consuming</u>: I spent twenty-five minutes filling out papers at the voting booth. It turned out to be quite a time-consuming task.
2. <u>obstacle</u>: She had to overcome a number of obstacles in order to reach her goal of being an engineer. She was poor and didn't have money for books or school. Also, she was a woman in a field traditionally dominated by men.
3. <u>explicit</u>: He gave me explicit directions regarding how to fill out the ballot because he wanted to make sure I did it correctly.
4. <u>respondent</u>: I sent out hundreds of questionnaires but only received twenty-five replies. However, those twenty-five respondents gave me the information that I needed.
5. <u>regardless (of something)</u>: Equal opportunities should be given to all. All people, regardless of age, race, sex, or religion, should have the same chances.
6. <u>ethnicity</u>: To see how different groups voted, the newspapers did a survey trying to get a good representative sample of the population. They divided their sample according to sex, ethnicity—in particular black, white, Hispanic, and Asian—and age.
7. <u>status</u>: The position of mayor in small towns is often a job that has high status but low pay. People take the job because it commands respect.
8. <u>trend</u>: After examining statistics regarding voting habits, we can see one clear trend: Voter participation is decreasing rather than increasing.
9. <u>bleak</u>: The president of the country painted a bleak picture for the future, saying that costs and taxes were going to increase, and unemployment was unavoidable.

Possible Answers:
1. requiring a lot of time   **2.** something that stands in the way and prevents action or success   **3.** clear, direct, and fully expressed   **4.** one who responds (to a survey or questionnaire)   **5.** without worrying about; without considering   **6.** racial, national, or tribal group   **7.** recognition and respect by others; position in relation to others   **8.** general direction; tendency   **9.** cheerless, uninviting, depressing

Note-Taking Practice, pages 143–144
See pages 216–217 of Appendix C in the textbook for example notes.

Post-Lecture Reading and Discussion, pages 144–145

Answers:
1. Answers will vary.   **2. a.** Four types are mentioned: (1) the plurality system (winner takes all); (2) approval voting (everyone casts one vote per candidate, and the candidate that most voters approve of wins); (3) cumulative voting ("each voter has as many votes as candidates and can distribute those votes among the candidates or give them all to one candidate"); and (4) preference voting, also known as the transferable ballot ("each voter ranks each candidate first, second, third, and so forth [b]ut if after an initial count, someone's first-place choice seems doomed to defeat, then that voter's second-place vote is counted instead").   **b.** The plurality system is generally used in the United States. The article says that it "can encourage extremism, reward name-calling, alienate voters, and fail to reflect the wishes of most of the people much of the time."   **c.** Answers will vary.

Using Your Notes, page 146

Answers:
1. a. As education goes up, the likelihood to vote goes up regardless of race or ethnicity.   **b.** Generally, those with higher incomes and with higher-status careers are more likely to vote than those with lower-status jobs.   **c.** Generally, the older (until about age seventy-eight) you are, the more likely you are to vote.   **d.** Women are slightly more likely to vote than men.   **e.** Generally, whites go to the polls more frequently than blacks, who go more frequently than Hispanics.   **2. a.** 38%   **b.** 14%   **3.** See Lecture Outline sections I.B.1 and I.C.3.   **4.** See Lecture Outline sections I.B.2 and I.C.2.   **5. a.** T   **b.** F   **c.** T   **d.** F   **e.** F   **f.** F

Using Vocabulary Audioscript, page 147

1. He was nominated as a candidate, but he decided not to run.
2. People were upset because the candidate was speaking against ideas expressed in the party platform.
3. Her campaign was one of the most expensive campaigns in history.
4. He chose to drop out of the race because he found it too time-consuming to continue running for office.
5. People went to the polls in order to cast a ballot.
6. She believed married life would be ideal, but she was disillusioned.
7. He feels alienated from his friends and can't understand why there are obstacles to communication.
8. Education, regardless of race or ethnicity, seems to be the most important influence on voter turnout.

Answers:
1. c   **2.** a   **3.** b   **4.** c   **5.** b   **6.** c   **7.** b   **8.** b

Lecture 14: How to Look at Art

Lecture Outline for Listening for the Larger Picture, page 151
Use this outline if you'd like to deliver the lecture yourself.

> **INTRODUCTION:** At the beginning of this class, I asked you to give me your reactions to six different pieces of art, and many of you gave your reactions in ways that I would describe as "intuitive." You told me whether you liked the art or not, how you felt when you looked at it. This is a great starting point for looking at art because art should evoke a response in you.
>
> Intuitive appreciation is fine in many situations; however, in this class, I'd like to give you a language that will allow you to look at art more carefully and analytically, to talk about art more systematically, and, perhaps, to understand what is behind some of your intuitions about art. Let's call this "directed looking."
>
> **I.** A way to look at art: "directed looking"
>
> > **A.** Directed looking involves seeing what can be learned from examining works of art directly (not reading or getting historical information about the work).
> >
> > **B.** Additional information about art movements and historical settings often add to one's appreciation of an art piece, but today the focus is simply on how to *look* at the work.
>
> **II.** The components of a "directed looking" approach to art appreciation: five categories of observation—physical properties, subject-matter exploration, illusionary properties, formal properties, and viewer perspective.
>
> > **A.** Each category is an "avenue into an artwork, a way to begin looking for meaning."
> >
> > **B.** Though these categories can be examined separately, in real life, when looking at a piece of artwork, the categories overlap.

Lecture Comprehension and Note-Taking Practice   **65**

1. Observing physical properties requires paying attention to the physical properties of the artwork. Examples:
    a. How big is it and how does its height relate to its width? (Imagine if I told you that Kline's painting was the size of this book. Would you be surprised? What if I told you it was the size of this room? Would that change your view of it?)
    b. What mediums (paint, charcoal, metal, pencil) were used? (Imagine if I told you that Kline's work had been done with a pencil. Think how surprised you were to learn that the Callahan work was a photograph.)
    c. How were the mediums applied (by hand, with brushes, by machine)?
    d. What textures result from the application? Is Kline's painting smooth and shiny? Or is it rough and heavy?
    e. Is the work 2-D (flat) or 3-D (multidimensional)?
2. Exploring the subject matter requires examining what a work is about.
    a. Sometimes the artwork is a representation of something: a figure, a portrait, a landscape, a still life. You can certainly see that in Van Gogh's painting and Lange's photograph and Hopper's painting.
    b. However, recognizing objects and people does not necessarily tell us all there is to know about the artwork and its subject matter.
        (1) Take a look at Van Gogh's *Hospital Corridor at Saint-Remy*.
        (2) This is a picture of a hall in a hospital. However, the subject matter is not simply a hall.
        (3) The viewer immediately feels the darkness and endlessness of the hall, perhaps a sense of foreboding. Perhaps the subject matter is fear or confusion.
        (4) What about Lange's photo? Is the subject matter mothers and children? [Encourage student responses.]
        (5) So Lange's subject matter is more than women and children. Perhaps it is about poverty, or about the strength of women, the strength and dignity required to survive poverty.
    c. When dealing with abstract work, the subject matter is much less apparent.
        (1) Look at Callahan's *Weeds in Snow*. This is a photograph. Although it looks abstract at first, once we realize it is a photograph, we can see that it is not abstract. However, the photographer's choice to develop the photograph emphasizing the black-and-white and eliminating any shades in between has made it abstract. What's the subject matter? [Encourage student responses.]
        (2) Look at Franz Kline's *Painting Number 2*. This is truly abstract. Even the title is no help. What is the subject matter here? [Encourage student responses.] Black often recedes, but here the black lines seem to sit securely on the painting surface and suggest structure. The white could be empty space, but this is not pure white—not as pure as the Callahan photo; there seem to be shades within the white spaces. Instead of suggesting emptiness, there is a feeling of substance, like fog that fills the space between the black lines.
        (3) Perhaps strength or power is the subject matter of this painting? Could this painting be about architectural structures and the concept of growth and progress?
    d. Overall, when dealing with subject matter, we need to examine both the representational (or recognizable) elements along with the abstract (or unrecognizable) elements.
3. Observing the illusionary properties of an artwork requires us to look at how the artist made us believe something that is not literally possible.
    a. How does the artist make the viewer see something in three dimensions when drawing on a two-dimensional space? How does the artist make the viewer believe that some objects are in front of each other and some are in the distance?
        (1) Shading and highlighting can create illusions of three dimensions; on the contrary, when it is gone—as in the Callahan photo—the photo seems flat, two-dimensional.
    b. What techniques do you know of for creating the illusion of distance? [Encourage student responses.] Examples:
        (1) Making an object smaller can create the illusion of distance—you can see this in Van Gogh's watercolor—the door at the end seems far in the distance.
        (2) Contrasting distinct objects with objects that are out of focus can give the illusion of distance.
4. Examining formal elements of an artwork requires attention to line, color, and shape and to how these elements are arranged to create composition.
    a. Are the lines or strokes short and choppy? Are they heavy or light? Notice the difference between the Kline and the Callahan. One is heavy, substantive, powerful; the other is delicate, ephemeral.
    b. Some lines are explicit and others are implied.
        (1) In the Hopper painting, there are strong, explicit horizontal and vertical lines. (The shadows on the street parallel the lines on the building; the barber pole parallels the vertical lines of the entrances and windows.)
        (2) In the Van Gogh painting, the horizontal tops of the columns line up with the little

door all the way at the end. This line is not drawn, but it is implied and has the effect of taking our eyes to the door.
- (3) In the Lange photo, there is a strong implied diagonal line leading along the woman's arm up to her face—and this is emphasized by the lighting that seems to shine along this path. This implied line brings the focus to the woman and her expression.
- c. What shapes are in the artwork? How are they positioned in relation to one another? Do they touch? overlap?
  - (1) Lange's photo seems to contain a triangle of the woman overlapped by the shapes created by the children, perhaps to express the feeling of pressure weighing on her.
  - (2) Hopper's painting is full of rectangles and squares and is very regular, perhaps a symbol of the regularity of the life there.
- d. Composition is the organization of the work.
  - (1) Composition looks at explicit and implied lines to see how parts of the artwork relate to each other.
  - (2) It looks at how space and shapes interact.
  - (3) It looks at the focal points—where the eyes naturally go.
  - (4) When we talk about composition, we talk about shapes and lines, explicit and implied.
- e. What colors are used? Are they realistic? Colors have varied effects. Examples:
  - (1) In some cases, blacks can seem to create holes on the canvas
  - (2) In some cases, bright yellows may seem to jump out from the canvas, especially when in contrast with a dark color.
    - (a) In the Hopper painting, the light and bright yellow window shades stand out, especially in contrast to the heavily shadowed stores.
  - (3) An in-depth discussion of color is beyond the scope of this lecture.
5. Examining the viewer perspective requires that we determine where the artist positions us, the viewer, in relation to the artwork.
   - a. Are we looking at the object from below? from above? from an equal level? Do we have to be close to the artwork to see it? Do we need to walk around it? Do we need to stand at a distance?
   - b. Degas's work provides an example of an unusual perspective. Degas wanted to position us, the viewers, at the level of the orchestra pit, looking *up* at the stage.

CONCLUSION: Sometimes it's important to take the time to look. I hope this talk has given you a better sense of how to look at art. Now, let's put this all together and look at some artwork, some of your favorites.

Lecture Audioscript for Listening for the Larger Picture, page 151
This audioscript shows one speaker's delivery of the lecture, as recorded in the audio program. Use it as a resource.

TEACHER: at the beginning of this class, I asked you to give me your reactions to six different pieces of art . . . and many of you gave your reactions in ways that I would describe as "intuitive." You told me whether you liked the art or not . . . how you felt when you looked at it . . . whether you felt you understood it or not . . . and this is a great starting point for looking at art because art *should* evoke a response in you . . .

and intuitive appreciation is fine in many situations . . . however, in this class . . . I'd like to give you a bit more . . . to ask you to do more . . . to explore your intuitions a bit deeper . . . I'm going to give you suggestions that will encourage you to look at art more carefully . . . more analytically . . . to talk about art more systematically . . . and perhaps . . . to understand a bit more about what is behind some of your intuitions about art . . . so not only to say "I like it" but also to explain more accurately what it is about the artwork that you like . . . and I'm going to call this way of looking at art . . . of observing art . . . "directed looking" [written on board] . . . it's a technique of how to look at art . . . and we're talking about *looking* at art . . . we're not talking about learning the history of it . . . we're just talking about how you can stand in front of a piece of artwork and say something about it . . . what do you look at? . . . so directed looking involves seeing what you can learn by examining works of art directly . . . not necessarily reading about the work or getting historical information about it . . . I think that getting additional information about art movements . . . historical settings . . . a lot of times it adds to your appreciation of an art piece . . . but again . . . today . . . all I'm going to focus on is how do you *look* at a piece of work . . . just simply standing in front of that artwork . . . what can you look at and examine? . . .

now the components of a directed-looking approach to art appreciation . . . there are five components . . . five categories of observation that I'm going to focus on . . . the physical properties of the artwork . . . the subject matter of the artwork . . . the illusionary properties of the artwork . . . the formal properties of the artwork . . . and the viewer's perspective regarding the artwork . . . all of those different properties . . . and I'll go over each one of them in turn . . . and each of those categories is a way to get into an artwork . . . an avenue into the artwork . . . it's a way to begin looking for meaning . . . and I think this is especially important for modern art because the meaning may not be very apparent and you're going to need some way to help you look at the work . . . to help you understand it . . . this is a way perhaps to move and start exploring the meaning of the artwork itself . . . and I'm going to divide these into categories but really the categories in real life are not so separate . . . when we look at a piece of artwork these categories often overlap . . .

but let's start with a very basic one . . . the physical properties . . . observing the physical properties of the artwork . . . what are these? let me give some examples . . . how big is it and how does its height relate to its width . . . for example . . . take a look at the Kline painting . . . the black-and-white piece . . . what if I told you that this Kline piece was the size of a postage stamp? . . . would that affect your view of the work? . . . and what if I told you it was the size of a room? . . . how would that create a different effect? . . . so size . . . also what mediums were used? is it paint? is it oil or watercolor? is it charcoal? is it metal? is it pencil? what if I told you that that same Kline work was made with a pencil . . . *and* was the size of a room? or in another example . . . were you surprised when you found out that Callahan's work *Weeds in Snow* was a photograph? it looks like pencil lines . . . other physical properties . . . how were the mediums applied? by hand . . . with brushes . . . by machine for example? . . . another one . . . what textures result from the application . . . is Kline's paint-ing smooth and shiny? . . . or is it rough and heavy? is the work two-dimensional . . . flat . . . or is it three-dimensional . . . 3-D . . . multidimensional . . . if Kline's painting were made up of layers of paint and it actually stood out from the canvas . . . think how much more powerful it might seem . . . that might give you a very different feeling than if it were flat . . . so all these physical properties are important to observe . . .

the second part of observation . . . is exploring the subject matter . . . here we're looking at what is this work about . . . and sometimes if you look at an artwork . . . it's really easy . . . because it's very representative . . . we can say it clearly represents something . . . you can see a figure . . . you can see a portrait . . . you can see a landscape . . . you can see a still life . . . if you look at Van Gogh's painting there's no question that it's a hallway . . . if you look at Lange's photograph, it's a woman and children . . . Hopper's painting is a scene in a town . . . however . . . recognizing the objects and the people really doesn't tell us *all* that there is to know about the subject matter . . . let's look at Van Gogh's work . . . *Hospital Corridor at Saint-Remy* first . . . it's a picture of a hall in a hospital . . . we can all see that . . . but do you think the subject matter is simply a hall? . . . there's more to it . . . when you look at it you can feel a sense of the endlessness . . . the darkness of the hall . . . there's that little little door at the end . . . maybe there's a sense of foreboding . . . is there danger? despair? where is it leading? . . . perhaps the subject matter is more fear or confusion? . . . what about Lange's photo? is the subject matter mothers and children? well . . . what do you think? . . .

STUDENT: I think maybe the subject matter is poverty. She looks really poor . . .

TEACHER: and it's not maybe just poverty but also a mother's desire to protect her children . . . a mother's strength in the face of poverty . . . OK so Lange's subject matter then is more than women and children . . . so recognizing objects and people is not going to tell us all there is so we still need . . . when we look at subject matter . . . to look a little deeper than what might immediately be apparent . . .

but now let's look at works that are not so representational . . . more abstract work . . . take a look at Callahan's *Weeds in Snow* . . . now if I showed it to you . . . you might not realize at first that it's a photograph . . . you might think it's a pencil drawing . . . anyway it *is* a photograph and it looks very abstract at first and when we realize it's a photograph we realize that it's not abstract . . . it's *weeds* in *snow* . . . that it was the photographer's vision that made it the way it is . . . the photographer chose to develop the photograph in a way so that there are no shades . . . there are no shadows . . . it's all black or white . . . and that has made it kind of abstract . . . so what's the subject matter? . . .

STUDENT: weeds in snow . . .

TEACHER: that is one . . . sure . . . it's weeds in snow . . . but what is Callahan trying to say? . . .

STUDENT: well the weeds look fragile or dead . . . maybe he's saying something about life's passing or its fragility . . .

TEACHER: that's possible . . . yes . . . OK . . . let's go to something harder . . . look at Franz Kline's *Painting Number 2* . . . this is really abstract . . . even the title doesn't give you any help . . . at least Callahan *called* his *Weeds in Snow* . . . this one by Kline is called *Painting Number 2* . . . what's the subject matter here?

STUDENT: it kind of gives me the feeling of buildings . . . of buildings . . . maybe cities . . . maybe roads . . .

TEACHER: that's actually very insightful . . . because Kline is considered an "urban" artist . . . an artist of the cities . . . let's look at this one . . . *I* look at this one . . . and I think . . . black . . . even though it's a color that typically recedes . . . here the black lines seem to sit right on the painting surface . . . and I think you're right . . . they *do* suggest a kind of structure . . . now the white could be empty space . . . but it's not pure white . . . in fact it's not anything like the Callahan photo which is pure white . . . in this case there's shading within the white spaces . . . it almost feels as if you can *feel* the substance of the white . . . so there's some kind of substance between the black lines . . . I kind of think of it as architectural . . . structural as well . . . maybe something having to do with strength or power as the subject matter of the painting . . . maybe something about architectural structures and the idea of growth and progress . . . so anyway . . . the area of subject matter is certainly a big area of observation . . . an important area . . . and when you're dealing with subject matter you have to deal with both the representational . . . that is, the recognizable elements . . . along with the abstract . . . or unrecognizable elements . . .

OK the third category of observation is looking at the illusionary properties of an artwork . . . and illusion refers to the idea of making someone believe something that's not really there . . . magicians create illusions . . . so how does the artist make us believe something that is not really possible? . . . if an artist is painting on two dimensions . . . it's flat . . . how does the artist make us believe that there are *three* dimensions when we look at it? . . . we . . . we . . . believe . . . when we look at a painting that some things are closer . . . some things are farther . . . but it's really all on the same flat surface . . . how does the artist do that? . . . now there are different techniques for creating illusion . . . and we're not going to talk about all of them . . . but let's talk about some of them . . . what do *you* know about how artists make us *think* we're seeing three dimensions? . . .

STUDENT: uh shading . . .

TEACHER: right . . . shading and highlighting create the illusion of three dimensions . . . and actually on the contrary . . . when the shading and highlighting are gone . . . as we see in the Callahan photo . . . the artwork seems very flat . . . it's a very different feeling . . .
   what about the illusion of distance? . . . any ideas about how that can be created?

STUDENT: uh . . . size? . . .

TEACHER: yes . . . making the object smaller can create the illusion of distance . . . and you can see this in the Van Gogh . . . the door at the end seems really far in the distance . . . good point . . .

STUDENT: sometimes when objects are out of focus . . . then it seems as if they're farther away . . .

TEACHER: absolutely right . . . so something that is blurrier . . . that creates the illusion of distance as well . . . so these are just different techniques . . . and that's all part of this third category of observing the illusionary properties . . . considering how illusions are created . . .
   OK the fourth one is examining the formal elements of an artwork . . . and when we talk about formal elements of an artwork we're looking at *line* . . . we're looking at *color* . . . we're looking at *shapes* . . . and we're looking at how these lines and colors and shapes . . . are arranged . . . to create *composition* . . . some of the things you might look at regarding lines . . . are the strokes short? choppy? heavy? light? notice the difference between the Kline and the Callahan . . . one is heavy . . . substantive . . . powerful . . . one is delicate . . . ephemeral . . . when we talk about lines of a painting or an artwork . . . sometimes they're explicit . . . you can actually see the line in the painting . . . but many times they're implied . . . if you look at the Hopper painting . . . there are strong explicit horizontal and vertical lines . . . the shadows on the street are parallel to the horizontal lines on the building . . . the barber pole line is a vertical line and it parallels the lines on the entrances and the windows . . . these are all explicit lines . . . but what do I mean by implied lines? . . . if you look at the Van Gogh painting . . . the horizontal tops of the columns . . . they line up with that little door all the way at the end . . . but it's not a continuous line . . . but if you look . . . you see that they're lined up at the same level . . . this is an *implied* line . . . and the *effect* of it . . . is that it takes our eyes to the door . . . Van Gogh didn't need to draw a line across the page . . . however . . . the line is implied . . . another example is in the Lange photo . . . there's a strong implied diagonal line . . . leading along the woman's arm up to her face . . . do you notice that line? . . . and this is *emphasized* by the *light* that seems to shine along this path . . . what's the function of this implied line? . . . what it does is it brings the woman and her expression to our attention right away . . . it takes our eyes to the woman's face . . .
   another formal element is shape as I said . . . so what are the shapes in the artwork? . . . triangles . . . squares . . . and so on . . . and how are they positioned in relation to one another . . . do they touch each other . . . do they overlap? . . . and again if we look at Lange's photo . . . we can see almost a triangle of the woman . . . but the triangle is overlapped on all sides by the children . . . perhaps to give us a sense of this woman who is . . . on all sides hemmed in . . . by children . . . by poverty . . . Hopper's painting on the other hand is full of rectangles and squares and is very regular . . . perhaps to convey a sense of the regularity of the life lived there . . .
   composition . . . another formal element . . . is the organization of the work . . . it's the bringing together of all these elements . . . the lines . . . the shapes . . . the color . . . and looking at how they relate to one another . . . so when we talk about composition . . . we're going to talk about the explicit and implied lines and see how they relate to the artwork . . . we look at the space and how the shapes interact . . . we look at where our eyes travel and what they focus on . . . so when we talk about composition . . . we talk about all these things . . .
   also . . . included in formal properties . . . we talk about what colors are used . . . are they realistic? some artists choose not to use realistic colors and we need to question why . . . and an in-depth discussion of this is beyond the scope of this short talk . . . but colors have different effects . . . for example . . . a black in some cases can almost seem to create a hole in the canvas and a bright yellow in other cases can seem to jump out of the canvas . . . and you can see that in the Hopper painting . . . the window shades are a bright . . . and light yellow . . . and these yellow shades . . . where there might be a little sun . . . seem to jump out . . . especially in contrast to the heavily shadowed stores . . . anyway . . . there's a lot more to be said about color . . . but that's way outside the scope of this lecture . . .
   finally . . . the last category . . . is looking at the viewer's perspective . . . and what this means is we have to talk about where the artist is putting *us* . . . the *viewer* . . . in relation to the artwork . . . sometimes we're looking at the artwork and we're looking at it from directly in front of us . . . but sometimes the artist is forcing us into a different position . . . if you look at the Degas pastel . . . our position in regard to the dancers is not face to face . . . we wouldn't see the dancers this way if we were . . . our position is below the dancers . . . looking *up* at the stage . . . we're down in the pit with the orchestra . . . a very different perspective . . . so another way to look at artwork is to observe where we are placed as viewers . . . are we at an equal level? above . . . below? looking up? looking down? . . . some other questions to ask are whether

we need to stand at a distance from the artwork to appreciate it? or do we need to get close to it? so . . . overall . . . how do we have to relate to the artwork as a viewer? . . .

so what I've tried to do in this talk is . . . give you a sense of directed looking . . . it's so easy to say . . . "oh . . . I don't know anything about this kind of art . . . and therefore I can't understand this" . . . and I think that sometimes it is important to understand the history . . . the philosophy of certain schools of art . . . but on the other hand sometimes it's important to just take the time to *look* . . . but looking also requires attention to different things . . . and I hope this talk has given you a little bit of a sense of *how* to look at art . . . the many *different* ways that you can look at art . . . that you can talk about art . . . without being an expert . . .

so . . . let's put this all together and hear about your favorite pieces of artwork.

Answers, page 151:

1. a way of appreciating artwork through direct observation (not necessarily through reading about the work, understanding its philosophical roots, or getting historical information about the work)   **2. a.** physical properties   **b.** subject matter   **c.** illusionary properties   **d.** formal properties   **e.** viewer perspective

Defining Vocabulary Audioscript, page 152

1. appreciation: We wanted to show our appreciation for the wonderful dinner that he made for us, so we sent flowers and a thank-you card.
2. emotion: I find it very difficult to hide my emotions; I always cry at sad movies.
3. intuitive: She had an intuitive sense that she could trust him; she didn't know why she felt that since she knew very little about him.
4. illusion: The magician made a rabbit disappear. The children were amazed and tried to figure out where the rabbit had gone. The adults, of course, knew it was an illusion.
5. to overlap: I work from nine to five and my coworker works from four to twelve. Luckily, our hours overlap a little or I would never see her.
6. apparent: It's apparent to everyone that you love your daughter very much; we can see it immediately when we observe how you look at her.
7. progress: I just started driving lessons and I'm really making a lot of progress. I think I'll be ready to take my driver's test in a day or two.
8. technique: There are a number of techniques for learning vocabulary. One simple technique is to write new words down when you hear them.
9. to imply: My boss implied that he expected me to work overtime; however, he never said it directly. He just told me that his best workers always worked overtime.
10. explicit: He gave me explicit directions about how to take the medicine. He said it was very important that I follow them exactly.

Answers:
1. c   **2.** c   **3.** a   **4.** a   **5.** b   **6.** a   **7.** c   **8.** a   **9.** c   **10.** b

Note-Taking Practice, pages 153–154

See pages 218–219 of Appendix C in the textbook for example notes.

Post-Lecture Reading and Discussion, page 154

1. The chart on page 71 includes information from the lecturer and text about each piece of art. Students should add their own ideas based on their interpretation and discussions.   **2.** Answers will vary.   **3.** The writer's criteria for "good" art are stated in the second paragraph. Key points are that it makes the writer think new or different thoughts and feel new or different emotions. Also, it sustains the writer's interest over time.

Using Your Notes, pages 155–156

Answers:

1. a. F (It only requires observation.)   **b.** F (They do overlap.)   **c.** F (They can, even if they are not representational. For example, the lecturer suggests that Kline's painting relates to progress and building.)   **2. a.** physical properties   **b.** subject-matter exploration   **c.** illusionary properties   **d.** formal properties   **e.** viewer perspective. (See outline for explanations.)   **3.** any four of the following: size, medium, methods for applying the medium, texture, dimensionality (two-dimensional or three-dimensional)   **4. a.** making an object smaller can create the illusion of distance   **b.** contrasting distinct objects with objects that are out of focus   **5.** The subject matter is obviously something having to do with mothers and children, but also has to do with poverty and the strength to withstand it. The composition has a woman in the center surrounded on all sides by children. There is an implied line going from her arm to her face (which is also lit), having the effect of bringing attention to her face. There is a triangular shape created by the woman's head and body that is hemmed in by the children. Students might also comment on other aspects of the composition (such as how the woman's arm parallels the line of her sweater and the line of the child's arm). Finally, the viewer perspective is straightforward; we feel as if the woman is looking directly at us (though her focus seems inward). This can be interpreted as Lange's attempt to force the viewer to "read" the woman's emotions and "see" her as an equal.

Artwork Analysis

	Physical Properties	Subject Matter	Illusionary Properties	Formal Elements	Viewer Perspective
Kline, *Painting No. 2*	Oil on canvas 6′ 8½″ × 8′ 9″ (204.3 × 271.6 cm.)	perhaps strength and power? architectural structures? growth and progress?	feeling of substance between black lines	heavy, substantive, powerful lines	
Van Gogh, *Hospital Corridor at Saint-Remy*	Gouache and watercolor on paper; 24⅛″ × 18⅜″ (61.3 × 47.3 cm.)	representational: hall in hospital; perhaps subject matter is also fear and confusion	the door in the background is small, creating the illusion of distance	the horizontal line of the top of the columns lines up with the door (implied line resulting in taking our eyes to the door)	
Lange, *Migrant Mother, Nipomo, California*	Gelatin silver print (photo)	representational: woman and children; also subject matter may be poverty and the strength and dignity needed to survive		strong implied diagonal line leading along the woman's arm up to her face, bringing the focus to the woman and her expression; also, the photo seems to contain a triangle of the woman overlapped by the shapes created by the children, perhaps to express the feeling of pressure weighing on her	
Callahan, *Weeds in Snow*	Gelatin silver print (photo)	representational: weeds in snow; also subject matter may be the fragility of life	seems flat because no shadows	lines are fragile	
Degas, *The Orchestra of the Opera*	Oil on canvas				viewer is positioned in the pit with the orchestra, looking up at the stage
Hopper, *Early Sunday Morning*	Oil on canvas	representational: a town, quite early in the morning		strong explicit and implied horizontal and vertical lines (window, pole, etc.); also, the painting is full of rectangles and squares and is very regular, perhaps a symbol of the regularity of the life there; yellow of window shades jumps out	

Lecture Comprehension and Note-Taking Practice

Using Vocabulary Audioscript, page 156

Group A
1. My friend gave me information about some techniques for using my new camera.
2. The pictures I took were out of focus.
3. I tried to photograph a still life.
4. I wanted the focal point to be a red rose on the table.

Group B
1. My boss implied that he wasn't pleased with my progress at work.
2. He never shows any appreciation for things I do.
3. It's apparent to everyone that I'm not happy.

Group C
1. She has good intuition about people.

Answers:
Group A: 1. b   2. b   3. c   4. b   **Group B:** 1. b   2. b   3. b   **Group C:** 1. a

Lecture 15: Paging Robodoc: Robots in Medicine

Pre-Lecture Reading and Discussion, pages 158–159

Answers:
1. Answers will vary.   2. a. Richard Satava is a program manager for advanced medical technologies at the Defense Department's Advanced Research Projects Agency. His vision of medical treatment in the future involves computers creating a "virtual" environment for surgeons and other medical practitioners. That is, medical practitioners could work on patients even at a distance (for example, by using virtual reality helmets and guiding robotic instruments in battlefield mobile surgical units.)   b. Examples are given of technology being developed and tested at SRI International in Palo Alto, California, and Wayne State University Medical School. In addition, the article mentions endoscopic procedures.   c. The change is fundamental because instead of humans doing all medical work, robots and computers are involved. This might allow for greater precision as well as changes in the notion of "hands-on" medical work. It might change the appearance of the doctor's office and hospital. It might even change the doctor/patient relationship. Students might have different answers to the second part of the question. They might discuss the awareness of germs or research into genes as other fundamental changes, for example.   3. Answers will vary.

Lecture Outline for Listening for the Larger Picture, page 159
Use this outline if you'd like to deliver the lecture yourself.

> **INTRODUCTION:** Many of us, when we think of robots, still imagine mechanical, walking and talking tin men—the kinds we may have seen in cartoons or science-fiction movies. However, that is definitely not the case with most robots.

What I'm going to do in this lecture is talk a little bit about what a robot is and then talk specifically about how they are being used in our world today in one important place—the hospital operating room.

I. What is a robot?

  A. The word *robot* comes from a Czech word meaning "forced labor."

  B. The Robot Industries Association has come up with the following definition for *robot*: A robot is a reprogrammable, multifunctional, manipulator designed to move material, parts, tools, or specialized devices through variable programmed motions to perform a variety of tasks. [Repeat definition slowly to allow students to note it.]

   1. Key words in this definition are *reprogrammable* and *multifunctional.*
     a. *Reprogrammable* ensures that the robot can get new instructions without changing its basic structure.
       (1) e.g., A robot can be taught (by a new program) a new task or a new routine, such as changing the order of activities or changing the placement of materials.
     b. *Multifunctional* ensures that the robot can perform a variety of tasks.
       (1) e.g., A robot can be programmed to check its work, make a decision, and alter its performance as needed.

II. How do robots work?

  A. A microprocessor acts as the "brain," controlling a mechanical manipulating device.

   1. A microprocessor is a tiny chip, like those found in computers, which activates different movements by the robot.

72   Unit 6

B. Most robots are equipped with a single hand (called an "end effector") and a single arm with a total of five or six joints.

   1. Some robots have two-fingered hands, used like tongs to pick up objects.

   2. Some have no recognizable hand and just contain the tools necessary for the job it is to do.

III. How are robots being used in hospitals?—e.g., Robodoc

   A. "Robodoc" isn't very smart, but in the operating room it can display a surgical precision that the steadiest hand of the best surgeon couldn't match.

   B. Observers say that Robodoc is to medical robots what the first Apple computers were to microcomputing—first-generation technology likely to spawn increasingly sophisticated offspring.

   C. It is "showing its stuff," particularly in hip replacement surgery.

   1. Hip surgery was an obvious choice for medical researchers exploring the use of robots because of the physically laborious nature of the surgery and because of the high number of hip replacement surgery procedures done worldwide—over half a million.

   2. Previously, surgeons would manually carve a cavity in the patient's thighbone, a process that has been compared to carpentry. They would also need to bore holes in a patient's thighbone (or femur) manually, using a mallet and chisel. Like crude woodwork, the process results in a very rough fit. Surgeons usually get around this problem by using cement to hold the implant in place, but the cement loses its grip in five to ten years, forcing many patients to undergo one or more replacement surgeries.

   3. With Robodoc, the most suitable implant—and the exact size of the bone cavity needed to fit that implant—is predetermined with the aid of computer imaging. After Robodoc bores a hole in the bone, the implant fits to within a tenth of a millimeter.

   D. Here's how it works.

   1. The surgeon takes a 3-D CT scan of the patient's femur, the large bone running from the hip to the knee.

   2. The surgeon transfers the image to a computer workstation.

   3. While viewing the 3-D image, the physician chooses the correct hip implant for the patient from a variety of implants stored in the computer's memory.

   4. The digital information about the patient's hip and the implant is stored in the workstation.

   5. In the operating room, the surgeon exposes the patient's femur. The computer relays detailed instructions to the robot about the size, shape, and location of the implant cavity.

   6. Robodoc precisely drills a cavity into the patient's bone. The surgeon retains full control of the robot's operation, using a remote-control device with a "stop" button. When the robot is finished shaping the cavity about twenty minutes later, the surgeon fits the implant and completes the ninety-minute surgery.

   E. According to the computer scientist who helped develop Robodoc, "These machines will be very good at things the surgeon isn't so good at. . . . They'll combine a machine's precision with human judgment."

CONCLUSION

   A. There is some resistance to the use of robots in the operating room.

   1. Some surgeons express concerns that robots will replace them.

   2. Others fear that the robot could "go crazy" and drill a hole in the brain, for example, instead of the femur.

   B. Developers insist that robots are being developed to assist surgeons, not replace them—something that should comfort patients as well. In addition, they stress that numerous safety controls are built in to the design.

   C. As we move further into the 21st century, we can only begin to imagine the changes that computers and technology will bring to us. Robodoc gives us a glimpse into the future.

Lecture Audioscript for Listening for the Larger Picture, page 159
This audioscript shows one speaker's delivery of the lecture, as recorded in the audio program. Use it as a resource.

a lot of us . . . when we think about robots . . . we imagine these walking and talking mechanical men . . . you know, something that we might have seen on TV when we were children or read about in science-fiction stories or seen in movies . . . but that's not the case . . . robots are not designed to look human . . . and they're probably nothing like you imagined them in your mind . . .

now what I'm going to do in this lecture is talk a little bit about what a robot is . . . and then I'm going to talk specifically about how it's being used in our world today in one very important place . . . it's being used in many many different places of course . . . but . . . the place I'm going to focus on is the hospital operating room . . . uh . . . you might be surprised if you look up one of these days . . . and instead of seeing your doctor . . . well you may see a robot doing some of the work . . .

so let's just start with a definition . . . what is a robot? . . . it's interesting because the word *robot* comes from a Czech word . . . I think the word might be something like *robota* . . . and the word means "forced labor" . . . so the idea is that the robot is something that we can get to work for us . . . the robot isn't taking over . . . the robot is assisting us . . . we're forcing it to do work . . . and follow our orders . . .

now . . . the Robot Industries Association . . . came up . . . many years ago . . . with a definition for robots that was more specific . . . and I'd like you to take this definition down because . . . it gives you a . . . a good sense about what um . . . what . . . what the qualities of all robots are . . . what do *all* robots have in common . . . so here's the definition . . . a robot . . . is . . . a *re*programmable . . . multifunctional . . . manipulator . . . designed to move materials . . . parts . . . tools . . . *or* specialized devices . . . through variable programmed motions . . . to perform a *variety* . . . of tasks . . . it's a long definition but it's worth looking at . . . and let me repeat it . . . a robot is a reprogrammable . . . multifunctional . . . manipulator . . . designed to move materials . . . parts . . . tools . . . or specialized devices . . . through variable programmed motions . . . to perform a variety of tasks . . . now the key words in that definition are *reprogrammable* and *multifunctional* . . . *reprogrammable* lets us know that all robots can get new instructions and we don't have to change the basic structure . . . the structure will remain the same but we can keep giving it new instructions . . . we can program it to do different things . . . so it can be taught a new task or a new routine . . . so it can change the *order* of activities . . . it can change the placement of materials . . . so it's some kind of machine where the basic structure stays the same but we can program different activities and tasks for it to do . . . *multifunctional* the other key word here . . . tells us that the robot can perform a *variety* of tasks . . . so the robot is not only going to do the same movement over and over again . . . but it can do many *types* of tasks . . . it can check its work . . . it can make decisions . . . it can alter its performance as needed . . . uh as an example . . . there are robots that are being built today that can sense when there is something in its path . . . and they can then alter their direction or move around an object placed in the way . . . obviously they're not really seeing . . . but they're making decisions based on what is around them . . . and changing their performance accordingly . . .

now how do robots work? . . . OK all robots have some kind of microprocessor . . . like a computer chip . . . that acts as its . . . quote, brain . . . and this microprocessor activates different movements by the robot . . .

most robots are equipped with a single hand . . . we call that hand an "end . . . effector" . . . here let me write that on the board . . . an "end . . . effector" . . . and this end effector is at the end of a single arm . . . which has about five or six joints in it . . . OK so you have a single arm . . . with five or six joints . . . and a single hand at the end of that arm called the "end effector" . . . but don't imagine a human-looking hand here . . . some robots have two-fingered hands . . . which can be used like tongs to pick things up . . . but some robots have no recognizable hand at all . . . they just contain the tools that are necessary for the job . . . so maybe they contain something like scissors or a knife or something like that . . . but that . . . that hand part . . . is called the "end effector" . . . whether it's a two-fingered tong . . . or whether it's a tool . . . it's the end effector . . .

OK now as I said . . . I'm going to talk about one *use* of robots and that's their use in hospitals . . . and . . . robots can be seen in different parts of hospitals at this point . . . but one particular example that I'm going to discuss is the use in the operating room . . . of a robot called "Robodoc" . . . and Robodoc is not necessarily very smart . . . but what it *can* do . . . it does brilliantly . . . and what it *can* do is work with a precision and a steadiness that can't be matched by even the best of surgeons . . . the steadiness of its hand . . . its end effector . . . is something that the best surgeon can't match . . . and observers are looking at Robodoc and saying that it is um . . . it's to medical robots what the first Apple computers were to microcomputing . . . that is, it's still in the first stages . . . it's first-generation technology of medical robots . . . but the future holds more and more sophisticated offspring . . . developed from this first-generation technology . . .

and the area that Robodoc is particularly excelling in . . . it's really showing its stuff . . . is in the area of hip replacement surgery . . . now, most of you are too young to even think about hip replacement surgery . . . but for elderly people . . . or older people . . . it's actually a very *common* surgery . . . there have been more than a half a million hip replacement surgeries performed worldwide . . . and that was part of the reason this is an obvious choice for researchers when they were looking at how to use robots in the operating room . . . they looked at hip replacement surgery, one, because it's a very *common* surgery . . . and the other thing . . . the other reason it's especially appropriate for robots is because it's a very physically demanding . . . physically laborious surgery . . . it takes a lot of *physical* labor on the part of the surgeon . . . to perform this surgery . . . and I'll explain this more in a second . . .

OK . . . in the past . . . and still now when *not* using Robodoc . . . what surgeons had to do is . . . when they wanted to do hip replacement surgery is . . . they carved a cavity in the patient's thighbone . . . and this carving is actually what it sounds like . . . it's almost like carpentry . . . the surgeons need to cut a cavity into the bone . . . and this is why I say it's a very laborious operation . . . it's not an easy thing to do . . . and they also need to bore holes in the patient's thighbone . . . another word for that bone is *femur* . . . and they have to do this carving and drilling manually . . . so like carpenters, they're carving . . . they're drilling . . . and often they use tools like a mallet and a chisel . . . tools not exactly known for precision . . . and like crude woodwork, this process results in a very imprecise fit of the implant into the cavity . . . so here you've got an implant that you want to fit into the cavity . . . but . . . manually . . . surgeons just aren't able to achieve the precision that would be needed for a precise fit . . . and so the way surgeons get around this is they need to use a kind of cement to hold the implant in place . . . OK well that might work for a while . . . but the problem is that this cement loses its grip over time . . . between five to ten years or so later . . . and what happens then is that many patients have to undergo a second replacement surgery . . .

and so what Robodoc does . . . *it* does the boring of the holes . . . *it* does the carving of the cavity . . . and . . . in that process, it's able to fit the implant into the cavity within a *tenth* of a *millimeter* . . . which is precision that no surgeon . . . even the best surgeon . . . could possibly achieve . . .

let me give you a little detail about how this would work . . . now what happens is . . . a patient comes in for a hip replacement operation . . . and the surgeon first takes a CT scan of the patient's femur . . . the thighbone . . . the large bone running from the hip to the knee . . . and this CT scan provides a three-dimensional picture of the bone and surrounding area . . . and then the surgeon transfers that 3-D image to a computer workstation . . . now the surgeon sits down at the computer and he or she is viewing the 3-D image in order to choose the correct hip implant for the patient . . . and the implant is chosen from a variety of sizes stored in the computer's memory . . . so the computer has information about a range of implants . . . and the physician chooses the best implant for the patient . . . and all of this is stored in the computer . . . all this information about the patient's hip and the implant is in the computer's memory . . .

OK now we get to the operating room . . . so far we've been in an office . . . working with computers . . . CT scans . . . but in the operating room . . . the surgeon . . . does what doctors do in operating rooms . . . the surgeon makes the incision which exposes the patient's femur . . . but what happens next is different . . . the computer then relays detailed instructions to the robot about the size, shape, and location of the implant cavity . . . so the computer then is transmitting this information to the robot saying "Here's the size . . . here's the shape . . . and here's the location of the implant cavity" . . . and then the robot goes to work . . . the robot drills the cavity into the patient's bone . . . so the robot is doing the cutting . . . now of course the surgeon is retaining full control over the robot during the operation . . . it's not the surgeon's opportunity to take a quick nap . . . the surgeon retains full control over the robot using a remote-control device with a stop button . . . now . . . when the robot is *finished* shaping the cavity . . . about twenty minutes later . . . it takes about twenty minutes for the robot to actually drill the cavity and bore the holes . . . the surgeon fits the implant into the cavity and then completes the ninety-minute surgery . . . closing up the incision and all that . . .

according to the robot's inventors . . . Robodoc is good at the things that surgeons aren't so good at . . . they combine a machine's precision with the human judgment . . . we *need* the human's judgment but we also can benefit from the machine's precision . . .

but now this doesn't mean that there hasn't been resistance to the idea of robots in the operating room . . . some express concern that robots will replace surgeons . . . others fear that the robots could "go crazy" and drill a hole . . . a hole in the brain . . . instead of the thighbone, for example . . . these are both pretty irrational . . . *again* . . . as I said before . . . developers insist that the robots are being developed to *assist* surgeons . . . that human judgment is still *very* important . . . and the robots are designed to *assist* surgeons . . . not replace them . . . and . . . in addition . . . they stress that numerous safety controls are built into the robot design . . .

so here we are . . . on the edge of the 21st century . . . we can only begin to imagine the changes that computers and technology will bring to us . . . remember that people are saying that Robodoc is probably only first-generation operating room robot technology . . . but I think that Robodoc can give us a glimpse at what that future might be.

Answers, page 159:
1. a, c, d, g, h   2. a, c, d

Defining Vocabulary Audioscript, pages 160–161

1. labor: It took him two years to build a house for his family, but he didn't mind. He said it was a labor of love.
2. to manipulate: She had no problems manipulating the race car through the course and around the corners. She won the race easily.
3. task: Each child was responsible for completing one household task per day. The youngest took out the garbage, for example. The oldest washed the dishes.
4. to alter: After she lost weight, she needed to have a tailor alter her clothes so that they fit her.
5. precision: Some jobs require a great deal of precision. Architects and engineers, for example, must be exact when drawing their plans. A mistake of even a millimeter can ruin the plan.
6. steady: That waiter has a steady hand. He's carrying a tray of filled water glasses and he hasn't spilled a drop.
7. manual: I was surprised that she was still using a manual typewriter. Nowadays, most people have switched to electric typewriters or computers.
8. to carve: I watched the artist take a piece of wood and slowly carve it into the shape of a person.
9. to bore: The electric outlet was behind a bookcase full of books. Instead of emptying the bookcase and moving it, I bored a hole through the back to reach the outlet. As long as the books were in place, you couldn't see the hole I had made.
10. to lose one's grip: Mountain climbing is a challenge. It's important to find a solid rock to hold on to so you don't lose your grip and fall.
11. cavity: My dentist told me I had two cavities and suggested filling them right away. I don't know why I get so many cavities; I don't eat a lot of sugar and I brush my teeth regularly.
12. remote control: Sometimes I'm very lazy. I just lie in front of the TV and use the remote control to change the channel.
13. glimpse: I caught a glimpse of the movie star as he was leaving the theater. Of course, his bodyguard and driver rushed him out the door and into the car before anyone could ask for his autograph.

Answers:
1. b **2.** c **3.** c **4.** b **5.** c **6.** a **7.** c **8.** a **9.** b **10.** b **11.** c **12.** c **13.** a

Note-Taking Practice, pages 161–162
See pages 220–221 of Appendix C of the textbook for example notes.

Post-Lecture Reading and Discussion, pages 163–164
Answers:
1. Answers will vary. **2. a.** Laparoscopic surgery is surgery in which instruments are inserted through tiny incisions. **b.** It requires shorter hospital stays and heals faster than conventional surgery. **c.** It is hard because surgeons feel as if they are "operating with chopsticks"; only certain types of laparoscopic instruments are common (scissors, staplers, graspers), and these are only appropriate for some simpler tasks. **d.** They have developed laparoscopic tools that have robotic hands with great dexterity. The system consists of two joysticks, a computer, and a right-hand and left-hand end effector (which are presently hydraulically powered and consist of a single digit, three to four inches long, and less than ½ inch wide with four joints that rotate, swivel, and swing back and forth, and a grasper at the end). To operate it, the surgeon operates the joysticks. (A computer program translates the surgeon's motions into the movements of the end effectors.)

Using Your Notes, pages 164–165
Answers:
1. A robot is a reprogrammable, multifunctional manipulator designed to move material, parts, tools, or specialized devices through variable programmed motions to perform a variety of tasks. **2. a.** F (It means "forced labor.") **b.** F (It is reprogrammable.) **c.** F (It may not have a recognizable hand.) **d.** F (It is very common.) **e.** T **f.** F (Though the doctor retains control, Robodoc does the drilling.) **g.** F (The surgeon exposes the femur. Therefore, she or he is involved in making incisions.) **3.** Because the cavity and holes are fairly roughly made, there is not an absolutely perfect fit. Cement is used to hold the implant in place, but cement loses its grip in five to ten years, requiring additional surgeries. **4.** It can be more precise than traditional hip replacement surgery. Robodoc can carve a cavity and bore holes that hold the implant snugly (without cement). **5.** See Lecture Outline section III.D.

Using Vocabulary Audioscript, pages 164–165
Group A
1. Carpentry requires precision.
2. I know a carpenter who uses no power tools and prefers to do everything manually.
3. I caught a glimpse of him working in his workshop and was amazed at the amount of physical labor involved in his work.

Group B
1. My doctor said I needed to see a specialist so he recommended a neurosurgeon he knows.
2. The neurosurgeon told me that the operation would only require a one-inch incision.

Group C
1. Mountain climbing requires a steady hand.
2. Still, most mountain climbers use ropes to protect themselves in case they lose their grip.

Group D
1. I have a simple task for you to do.
2. Type this letter without altering anything.
3. When you finish, log off.

Answers:
Group A: **1.** b **2.** b **3.** c   Group B: **1.** a **2.** a   Group C: **1.** b **2.** a   Group D: **1.** b **2.** a **3.** a

Lecture 16: Earthquakes: Can They Be Predicted?

Pre-Lecture Reading and Discussion, page 168
Answers:
1. Answers will vary. **2.** Answers will vary. **3.** Galper believes he has discovered a way to predict earthquakes that could provide a warning as much as three hours in advance of major quakes. However, the subtitle of the news article says that U.S. experts remain doubtful.

Lecture Outline for Listening for the Larger Picture, page 169
Use this outline if you'd like to deliver the lecture yourself.

> **INTRODUCTION:** Over 30,000 earthquakes that are strong enough to be felt occur worldwide annually. Fortunately, most are minor tremors and do very little damage. Generally, only about seventy-five significant earthquakes take place each year, and many of these occur in remote regions. However, occasionally a large

earthquake occurs near a large population center; it is under these conditions that an earthquake is among the most destructive forces on earth.

The study of earthquakes is important not only because of the devastating effect that some earthquakes have on us, but also because they furnish clues about the structure of the earth's interior.

I. What is an earthquake?

    A. An earthquake is "the vibration of the earth produced by the rapid release of energy."

II. What causes earthquakes?

    A. Some are caused by atomic explosions or volcanic eruptions, but these events are relatively weak and infrequent.

    B. Most often earthquakes are caused by slippage along a fault in the earth's crust. The energy released radiates in all directions from its source (its focus) in the form of waves.

        1. Imagine a stone dropped in a calm pond. Just as the impact of the stone sets water waves in motion, an earthquake generates seismic waves that radiate throughout the earth.

        2. This is related to the plate-tectonics theory, which states that large slabs of the earth's crust are in continual slow motion. These mobile plates interact with neighboring plates, straining and deforming the rocks at their edges. To get a sense of how this works, look at Figure 1.

            a. In the first picture, you see an existing fault, or break, in the rock. Imagine it as a flexible stick.

            b. In the second picture, tectonic forces ever so slowly deform the crustal rocks on both sides of the fault, as demonstrated by the bent features. Under these conditions, rocks are bending and storing elastic energy, much like a wooden stick does if bent.

            c. Eventually, the frictional resistance holding the rocks together is overcome. As slippage occurs at the weakest point (the focus), displacement will exert stress farther along the fault, where additional slippage will occur until most of the built-up strain is released (the third picture). It is at this point that the stick breaks.

            d. This slippage allows the deformed rock to "snap back." The vibrations we know an as earthquake occur as the rock elastically returns to its original shape. The "springing back" of the rock is termed "elastic rebound" because the rock behaves elastically, much like a stretched rubber band does when it is released (the fourth picture in each column).

        3. In summary, most earthquakes are produced by the rapid release of elastic energy stored in rock that has been subjected to great stress. Once the strength of the rock is exceeded, it suddenly ruptures, causing the vibrations of an earthquake.

II. Have we made any advances in earthquake prediction?

    A. Substantial research to predict earthquakes is underway in Japan, the U.S., China, and Russia—countries where earthquake risk is high.

    B. There are two types of prediction strategies that seismologists are researching: short-range prediction tools and long-range prediction tools.

        1. Short-range prediction tools focus on identifying phenomena that precede major earthquakes.

            a. Some are studying peculiar animal behavior that may precede a quake.

            b. Some are looking at changes in seismic activity, such as a period of seismic quiescence (quiet or inactivity) followed by renewed activity or changes in the type of movements along a fault zone (such as uplift or subsidence of land).

            c. Others are examining changes in groundwater levels near fault zones.

            d. Others are examining decreased electrical resistivity and changes in radio waves near fault zones.

                (1) Some researchers have asserted that they can predict the location, time, and magnitude of a number of earthquakes by measuring anomalous electric currents in the ground. They say that changes in such currents indicate changes in the stress on rock just before an earthquake.

            e. Others are measuring the emission of the gas radon.

                (1) One notable success in foretelling a large earthquake near a major city was in 1975 in China.

                (2) Here, for the first time, seismologists forecast a large earthquake that was about to destroy a major city. They evacuated 3 million residents from their homes and saved tens of thousands of lives.

                (3) Though this action clearly saved lives, some researchers are skeptical about the prediction success claims. According to Lucille M. Jones, a seismologist at the U.S. Geological Survey in Pasadena, California, who studied the Haicheng prediction for five years, "If you ask whether they really evacuated them, the answer is clearly yes, . . . but if you ask, 'Did they do any better than random success? Could we do this by just guessing?' The answer

is, 'We don't know.' " "The circumstances surrounding the prediction were unusual," adds Jones. "There were 400 earthquakes in four days in an area that hardly ever had them. So they guessed that these were foreshocks and evacuated on that basis. Well, that's not a bad guess. But that doesn't mean it's a successful, repeatable earthquake prediction."

(4) In fact, tragically, only a year later, another devastating earthquake in China was *not* predicted and more than 200,000 people were killed. The following month, they predicted an earthquake in Guandong Province and evacuated people, but nothing happened.

2. Long-range prediction tools are based on the premise that earthquakes are repetitive or cyclical, like the weather. This has led seismologists to study the history of earthquakes for patterns, so that their occurrences might be predicted.

a. Though some patterns have been observed, they have not proven useful for predicting with any accuracy. For example, two American seismologists in the 1980s looked at a California faultline and noted that in one fifteen-mile stretch, six fairly large earthquakes had taken place at intervals of approximately twenty-two years. However, predictions that another earthquake would occur by the end of 1988 proved wrong.

CONCLUSION

A. So far, all of these physical clues have encountered complications when applied to a series of earthquake situations.

B. Virtually all seismologists now agree that short-term earthquake prediction is difficult, if not impossible. But some hold out hope for long-term prediction.

C. Continued application of these procedures to monitored fault zones should show which, if any, will prove to be reliable prediction techniques for the time of earthquake occurrence.

Lecture Audioscript for Listening for the Larger Picture, page 169
This audioscript shows one speaker's delivery of the lecture, as recorded in the audio program. Use it as a resource.

OK . . . um what I'd like to do is . . . tell you a bit about earthquakes . . . did you know that every year there are 30,000 earthquakes that are strong enough to feel? . . . every year there are 30,000 earthquakes that are strong enough to feel . . . but most of these are minor quakes . . . so we don't really need to worry about these . . . generally every year there are about seventy-five earthquakes in the world that are significant . . . that uh . . . that really are major earthquakes . . . and many of these occur in places that are far away . . . remote regions where there aren't many people . . . so again . . . we don't need to worry about the total number because they aren't affecting a lot of people . . . but as we know . . . occasionally there's a large earthquake in a population center and these are the ones that are the most devastating . . . the most destructive . . .

now the study of earthquakes is important not only because of the devastating effect that some earthquakes have on us . . . but it's also important because it provides us with clues about what's going on inside the earth . . . it provides us with clues about the structure of the earth's interior . . .

what I'm going to do in this lecture . . . this is a short lecture . . . and what I want to do is talk about earthquakes . . . what causes them . . . what is happening within the earth's interior to cause them . . . and then talk about earthquake-prediction possibilities . . . as long as we've had earthquakes people have been looking for ways to predict if an earthquake is coming . . . where it's going to hit . . . because if we can predict the earthquake . . . we have a better chance of saving people . . . evacuating people . . . and as you know up until now we really haven't found a perfect way to do this . . . still . . . what I'd like to do is tell you some of the things that scientists and researchers have looked at . . .

let me start with general earthquake information . . . what it is . . . why it happens . . . if I asked you to define an earthquake what would you say? . . . it's the shaking of the earth? . . . that's true . . . well here's a scientific definition . . . an *earthquake* is the *vibration* . . . of the earth . . . produced . . . by the *rapid release* of energy . . . let me repeat that . . . an earthquake . . . is . . . the vibration . . . the shaking of the earth . . . produced by the rapid release of energy . . . where does this energy come from? and why is it produced? . . . let's look at the sequence of steps that occurs when a typical earthquake happens . . . now there are earthquakes that occur due to atomic explosions or volcanic eruptions but these are not typical . . . these events occur but they're relatively weak and infrequent . . . I don't want to talk about those . . . but rather I want to look at a *typical* earthquake scenario . . .

typically . . . most earthquakes are caused by slippage along a crack or a break in the earth's crust . . . this crack or break is called a fault . . . so slippage along a fault in the earth's crust . . . and when this slippage occurs . . . there is energy that is released . . . and this energy radiates from the place where the slippage first occurred . . . radiating from this source in the form of waves . . . to give you a sense of how this happens . . . imagine a calm pond . . . no waves . . . and then all of a sudden someone throws a stone in that pond . . . what happens? . . . the impact of the stone sets water waves in motion . . . you'll see circular rings spreading from the source of impact . . . and it is in this way that an earthquake generates seismic waves that radiate throughout the earth . . .

but let's go back a step . . . what caused the slippage in the first place? . . . and here we need to talk about a theory called the "plate-tectonics" theory . . . let me write that for you . . . the plate-tectonics theory [on board] . . . and this theory suggests that large slabs of the earth's crust are in continual slow motion . . . really slow . . . nothing that we normally feel . . . so there are these mobile plates . . . and they're interacting with neighboring plates . . . and as they interact . . . as the plates move against each other . . . there's pressure on the rocks at the edges . . . so the movement is *straining* . . . and *deforming* those plate edges . . .

now take a look at the diagrams in your book . . . in the first picture . . . you see an existing fault or break in the rock . . . you can imagine this fault as a flexible stick . . . and like a stick, it has some degree of flexibility . . . but if you bend it too much . . . what happens? . . . look at the second picture . . . in the second picture . . . the tectonic forces slowly . . . very slowly . . . deform the crustal rocks on both sides of the fault . . . in a way it's, it's like bending the flexible stick . . . under these conditions the rocks are bending and storing elastic energy . . . but *then* . . . if the rocks continue to be strained and deformed . . . there comes a point when the resistance holding the rocks together is overcome . . . uh . . . again . . . just as with the flexible stick . . . you bend it . . . bend it . . . bend it . . . and while you're bending it elastic energy is continually building up . . . it might be flexible for a while . . . but eventually it breaks . . . releasing the built-up elastic energy . . . just like that . . . when the stress builds up along the fault line . . . eventually slippage occurs at the weakest point . . . and then displacement exerts stress even farther along the fault where additional slippage occurs . . . until eventually most of the built-up strain is released . . . this is the rapid release of energy we talked about in the definition of an earthquake . . . remember that definition . . . "the vibration of the earth produced by the rapid release of energy" . . . so here we are in the third picture . . . slippage has occurred at the weakest point . . . and when the slippage occurs there . . . this exerts stress farther along the fault . . . where more slippage occurs . . . all of this helping to release the built-up strain . . .

what happens when the energy is released? here . . . imagine a rubber band . . . keep stretching it but don't let it break . . . what happens if you let it go? . . . it will snap back to its original shape . . . in a similar way . . . the vibrations that we know of as an earthquake occur when the rock . . . just like the rubber band . . . elastically "snaps back" . . . to its original shape . . . more or less . . . the term used to describe this *springing back* is *elastic rebound* because . . . like a stretched rubber band . . . the rock rebounds back to its original shape . . .

so . . . in general . . . most earthquakes are produced by the rapid release of elastic energy . . . elastic energy that had been stored in the rock . . . and building up in the rock . . . because it had been subjected to great stress . . . and once the strength of the rock is exceeded . . . once the built-up energy goes beyond the strength of the rock . . . an earthquake results . . .

so now you have the general science of earthquakes . . . we're learning more about that each day . . . but there's another aspect of earthquake research that is interesting . . . not only interesting . . . but potentially life-saving . . . and that is the research into *earthquake prediction* . . .

the places where the most research is happening in terms of earthquake prediction research are in countries where there are earthquakes . . . Japan . . . the U.S. . . . China . . . Russia . . . it's in these areas that we're seeing a lot of research about this . . . these are countries where earthquake risk is high . . .

there are two types of prediction strategies that the seismologists are researching . . . they're exploring two different ways to look at earthquake prediction . . . they're looking at *short-range* prediction tools . . . and they're looking at *long-range* prediction tools . . . that is . . . they're looking at earthquakes and questioning whether there's any way they can predict them on a short-range basis . . . and then . . . is there any way they can predict them on a long-range basis . . .

let's look at the short-range prediction studies . . . what they look at in those studies is identifying *any phenomena* . . . that *precede* earthquakes . . . that is . . . what happens before an earthquake? . . . is there anything that you can look at that tells us that an earthquake is coming? . . . I don't know if anyone has heard about this but . . . they say for example that certain animals act strangely before an earthquake . . . so this is one type of short-range prediction tool that has been investigated . . . any peculiar animal behavior that might precede a quake . . .

another example of short-range prediction is looking at changes in seismic activity right before the earthquake happens . . . so for example . . . scientists may be watching the seismic activity in the area and note that all of a sudden there has been a great change in activity . . . either going from a highly active area to a quiet or inactive area . . . or vice versa . . . or maybe scientists are watching an area and suddenly notice that the type of movements along the fault have changed . . . so scientists have looked at changes in seismic activity as a possible short-range prediction tool . . .

another thing they might look at in terms of short-range prediction . . . is changes in groundwater levels . . . so the groundwater may usually be a certain level in the area . . . but maybe there's a sudden change in the groundwater level . . . maybe it's much higher or much lower . . . that could be a short-range prediction tool . . .

another short-range prediction tool . . . is . . . changes in electric currents . . . or radio waves . . . near the fault zones . . . so they can measure the radio waves . . . measure the electric currents . . . and if there's a change near the fault zone . . . they think maybe this can be an indication of a forthcoming earthquake . . .

one more area that scientists have looked at is the emission of a kind of gas . . . it's a gas called radon . . . R-A-D-O-N, radon . . . they've looked at this to see if perhaps there's more of this particular gas that's emitted . . . maybe that's a sign that an earthquake is coming . . . so the emission of radon is looked at as a possible short-term prediction tool . . .

now in the history of short-term earthquake prediction . . . there was one particular success . . . I don't know if anyone here has heard about it . . . but in 1975 . . . in 1975 in China . . . scientists were very successful in foretelling a large earthquake . . . the scientists had actually forecasted an earthquake that was about to destroy a major city . . . and they evacuated *all 3 million* residents . . . can you imagine . . . evacuating 3 million people because scientists felt that an earthquake was imminent . . . and in this particular case the earthquake *did* happen . . . and because they evacuated so many people . . . thousands and thousands and thousands of lives were saved . . .

now the controversy is . . . was this luck? . . . or was this real prediction? . . . a number of seismologists are very skeptical about the scientific value of the claimed prediction . . . they say that this particular area in China was an area that never had earthquakes before . . . it was . . . all of a sudden there were a lot of tremors . . . 400 smaller earthquakes in four days in an area that hardly ever had them . . . and they say . . . well that was pretty easy to forecast . . . there was never any earthquake activity and all of a sudden there are tremors . . . it's not hard to imagine that there is going to be something happening . . . and just because scientists were able to make a good guess based on those unusual occurrences . . . that doesn't mean that this type of earthquake prediction can be repeated successfully . . . so many seismologists are skeptical . . .

in fact . . . the *following* year . . . in China . . . there was another earthquake . . . and this was not predicted and in *that* case more than 200,000 people were killed . . . and a month later . . . the seismologists predicted *another* earthquake . . . and this time evacuated people . . . but *nothing* happened . . . though I can imagine blood pressure levels went up pretty high . . .

so again . . . the studies and history show that yes . . . there has been success . . . but scientists are very skeptical about whether there really were any predictions involved or whether they were just good guesses . . .

OK . . . what about long-range prediction? . . . all the short-range prediction tools look at what immediately precedes an earthquake . . . but the idea behind long-range prediction is that if you study the history of earthquakes . . . then you're going to see patterns . . . you're going to see cycles . . . you're going to see repetition . . . so they're saying that maybe earthquakes are like the weather . . . there are certain patterns that are going to repeat again and again . . . so they think . . . if they look at the history of earthquakes in certain areas . . . and look for patterns . . . maybe they can predict when the next earthquake will occur . . . so that's the idea behind *long*-range prediction . . .

has it been . . . uh has it worked? . . . in general scientists found some patterns but mostly they haven't proven useful for predicting with any accuracy . . . it's been very difficult for them to find patterns that have predictive value . . . let me give you an example in California . . . in the 1980s . . . two American seismologists looked at some California faultlines . . . and they noted that in one area . . . six earthquakes had occurred at about twenty-two years apart . . . and they thought "aha" . . . we have a pattern here . . . a big earthquake every twenty-two years . . . so they estimated that the next one would occur again . . . twenty-two years later . . . well that was supposed to have occurred in 1988 . . . and it still hasn't occurred . . . so you can see that *still* . . . with long-range predictions . . . they haven't really found the answer yet . . .

so the conclusion is that all of the physical clues have encountered complications . . . so we really haven't found the answer yet to earthquake prediction . . . and virtually all seismologists agree at this point that short-term earthquake prediction is difficult . . . if not impossible . . . so most seismologists think at this point that short-term prediction is nearly impossible . . . at best it's difficult . . . but more likely impossible . . . but some are still hoping that long-term prediction studies will produce results . . . that we can find patterns that might help us to predict earthquakes with reasonable accuracy over the long term . . . and over the years . . . we hope that as we continue monitoring fault zones . . . we will at some time understand earthquakes well enough to come up with *reliable* earthquake-prediction tools.

Listening for the Larger Picture, page 169

Encourage students to share what they remember; it is not necessary to have the full information at this point. Encourage students to listen for the information that is unclear or missing during the second listening.

Answers, page 169:
1. Answers will vary. **2.** peculiar animal behavior; changes in seismic activity; changes in groundwater levels near fault zones; decreased electrical resistivity and changes in radio waves near fault zones; emission of radon **3.** patterns in the occurrence of earthquakes **4.** Short-term earthquake prediction is difficult, if not impossible. Some seismologists hold out hope for long-term predictions. We still don't know what will prove to be reliable earthquake-prediction techniques.

Defining Vocabulary Audioscript, pages 170–171

1. <u>remote:</u> The village was so remote that people had to travel for days to reach it.
2. <u>rapid:</u> He reads so rapidly. Nobody can believe how quickly he can finish a book.
3. <u>to radiate:</u> The sun radiates so much heat in the desert that people try not to work outside during the afternoon.
4. <u>to deform:</u> Leaving a cassette tape in my car in the hot sun was a mistake. When I got back, the heat had deformed the plastic casing.
5. <u>flexible:</u> My plans for next weekend are flexible. Let me know what works for you, and I'll change mine accordingly.
6. <u>to exceed:</u> Don't exceed the speed limit on the roads or you'll get a ticket.
7. <u>phenomenon:</u> Lightning, thunder, and earthquakes are all examples of natural phenomena.
8. <u>to precede:</u> The years that preceded my school days are not very clear to me. I only remember things that happened after I was five years old.
9. <u>peculiar:</u> He has a peculiar habit of writing down everything that you say, but don't worry. He's not dangerous—just a bit unusual.
10. <u>to emit:</u> Open the windows when you use that paint. It emits some powerful smells and poisonous fumes.

11. <u>to foretell</u>: No one could have foretold our present economic problems. We all thought that the economy was healthy and there were no signs to make us believe differently.
12. <u>to evacuate</u>: The firefighters knew that the fire was spreading, so they evacuated the nearby buildings. In that way, they protected lives though they couldn't save the buildings.
13. <u>skeptical</u>: He says that people can lose ten pounds in two days if they follow his diet. I'm skeptical about his claims. That seems unreasonable, if not impossible.
14. <u>cyclical</u>: Some people love the cyclical nature of the seasons. They enjoy watching the leaves fall every autumn and return every spring, knowing that it will follow the same pattern every year.
15. <u>interval</u>: The nurses check the patient at half-hour intervals, so they stop by nearly fifty times a day.
16. <u>virtually</u>: Virtually the whole town was destroyed by the fire. The only building left standing was the bank.

Answers:
1. c 2. a 3. c 4. a 5. b 6. c 7. b 8. c 9. b 10. a 11. c 12. c 13. b 14. a 15. c 16. c

Note-Taking Practice, pages 171–172
See pages 222–223 of Appendix C in the textbook for example notes.

Post-Lecture Reading and Discussion, pages 173–174
Answers:
1. Several answers are possible. No major scientific papers have been published on Galper's earthquake-forecasting idea; his ideas have not been subjected to the scrutiny of peer review that is standard in the U.S.; some say that there is "little evidence to support it or any other prediction theory"; some feel they haven't seen enough multiple successes; some feel that it is only theoretical, but wouldn't necessarily work in practice; it has never actually predicted a quake.   **2.** His claims are based on data and paper calculations; however, his method hasn't ever been used to actually predict a quake.   **3.** See the last two paragraphs in the article.   **4.** The article does seem to present a lot about other scientists' doubts and deep skepticism. It quotes someone who says that the theory is "implausible," but that person also explains what he would need in order to take it seriously. He doesn't completely rule out the possibility. Therefore, the article's tone suggests that Galper's idea is not impossible but does require much more explanation and research.

Using Your Notes, page 174
Answers:
1. (v)ibration; (e)nergy   **2. a.** changes in seismic activity preceding a quake   **b.** peculiar animal behavior before a quake   **c.** changes in groundwater level near fault zones before a quake   **d.** changes in radio waves and electric currents near fault zones prior to a quake   **e.** changes in the emission of the gas radon before a quake   **3. a.** F **b.** T **c.** F **d.** T **e.** F **f.** T **g.** F   **4.** When a flexible stick is bent, it can be compared to what happens to rocks when they are deformed by tectonic forces. If a flexible stick is bent far enough, it will break. This can be compared to what happens when the deformation of the rocks is so great that slippage occurs at the weakest point and the strain is released. After the slippage, the rock vibrates as it "snaps back" to its original shape, which is similar to what happens to a stretched rubber band when it is released. An earthquake's energy is not just felt at its epicenter; rather, it is like a stone dropped in a calm pond. When the stone hits the water, it sets waves in motion; in a similar way, the slippage releases energy in all directions in the form of waves.

Using Vocabulary Audioscript, page 175
Group A
1. The train usually goes by at intervals of twenty minutes.
2. A whistle always precedes its passing.
3. It goes by rapidly, but it never exceeds the speed limit.
4. Occasionally, I notice that dishes and other loose objects vibrate when it passes.

Group B
1. The general told the residents of the village to evacuate immediately because the enemy was advancing.
2. The problem is that the village is very remote and the population exceeds 1,000.
3. Another problem is that the people are skeptical. They've had bad experiences with the general before.
4. No one can foretell the outcome of all this.

Answers:
Group A: 1. c **2.** b **3.** c **4.** b   **Group B: 1.** a **2.** c **3.** b **4.** b

Lecture 17: Hall's Classifications of Cultures

Pre-Lecture Discussion, pages 177–178

Answers:
1. **The Personal Space Test:** Answers will vary.   2. **Attitudes toward Time:** Answers will vary.   3. **Attitudes toward Interpersonal Relationships:** Answers will vary.   4. **Discussion: a.** This means that our culture controls the way we interpret what we see, the way we think.   **b.** Though we think that we each have our own "mind," in reality, our way of thinking is deeply affected by our culture, often without our realizing it.

Lecture Outline for Listening for the Larger Picture, page 179
Use this outline if you'd like to deliver the lecture yourself.

> **INTRODUCTION:** We deal with others as if they were members of our own culture. However, it is possible that people from different cultures have different ingrained assumptions about the world regarding such important and basic ideas such as interpersonal relations, time, and personal space.
>
> This is the view of Edward Hall, an anthropologist who has spent a large part of his life studying American Indian languages and cultures.
>
> Hall does not aim to study cultures in isolation but rather the relations between cultures.
>
> Hall believes that cultures can be classified by placing them on a continuum from high- to low-context (terms which will be defined in the lecture). This talk today will deal with these two opposites on the continuum—the high-context culture and the low-context culture.
>
> I. High-context cultures
>
>   A. A high-context culture is a culture in which the context of the message, action, or event carries a large part of its meaning and/or significance.
>
>   B. In other words, in a high-context culture, more attention is paid to what is happening in and around the message or event than to the message or event itself.
>   1. Examples in interpersonal relationships
>   a. There is a strong dependence on shared, built-in, and preprogrammed information concerning the message or event.
>   (1) e.g., High-context cultures can get by with less legal paperwork than a low-context culture because a person's word is his or her bond and people don't need to spell out the details to make someone behave.
>   (2) e.g., One depends more on the power and influence of established networks rather than on individual characteristics.
>   (a) e.g., A loan of money may be given simply because you belong to a certain known group.
>   b. There is a strong dependence on social rather than legal restraints on behavior.
>   (1) What the group or society thinks restrains people more than laws.
>   (a) e.g., A person will not break the law because it will dishonor his/her family more than because of a personal fear for him-/herself.
>   c. There are strong feelings of personal responsibility for the group.
>   (1) e.g., The top person in an organization shoulders the blame for something that goes wrong because he/she is responsible as the leader of the group.
>   2. Examples concerning personal space
>   a. High-context cultures (with greater dependence on group identity) tend toward heavy sensory involvement, greater physical closeness, and less respect for the individual's "bubble" of personal space.
>   (1) People tend to stand closer when talking, touch a lot, not feel violated when jostled in a crowd, etc.
>   (2) High-context cultures pay more attention to body language.
>   3. Examples concerning time
>   a. High-context cultures have a polychronic attitude toward time (i.e., people believe that people, things, and events each have their own time).
>   b. This polychronic attitude means that there is no one standard of time that applies to everything and dictates the course and order of everything.
>   (1) Thus, the culture doesn't emphasize punctuality.
>   (2) Thus, the culture pays little attention to clock time.

C. *Disadvantages* of high-context cultures are that reforms and change come slowly and that rigid class structures and family structures may bind people.

   D. One of the *advantages* of the high-context culture is that it provides a sense of social security through the family bonds and tradition that give one a secure sense of place in the world.

II. Low-context cultures

   A. A low-context culture is one in which the message, event, or action is seen as a separate entity having meaning unto itself.

   B. In other words, low-context cultures pay more attention to the event itself than to the context around the message or event.
      1. Examples in interpersonal relationships
         a. There is a reliance on legal means rather than social bonds.
            (1) e.g., A piece of paper (such as a contract) is more important than spoken words and everything is said in written negotiations; nothing is taken for granted.
         b. Responsibility is kicked down as far down in the system as possible ("pass the buck").
      2. Examples concerning personal space
         a. There is a concept of "personal space"—a minimal distance around one's body beyond which people should not overstep without permission or apology.
         b. There is a tendency to feel violated when this personal space is invaded.
         c. There is a respect and a desire for privacy.
         d. There is less awareness of body language; people touch less; people stand farther apart.
      3. Examples concerning time
         a. There is a *monochronic* attitude (i.e., a linear attitude toward time which assumes that everything follows the same standard of time).
            (1) Therefore, the culture emphasizes punctuality.
            (2) Therefore, the culture looks on time as a commodity, as seen in sayings such as "time is money," "have no time," "waste time," and "spend time."

   C. *Disadvantages* of the low-context culture are that there is less commitment to a system (a society, a family, etc.) and less human trust, with a more businesslike relationship.

   D. One of the *advantages* of the low-context culture is that there is greater individual independence and more allowances for creativity and differences.

III. Cultures on the continuum (these are examples given by Hall)

Low-context									High-context
German-Swiss	German	Scandinavian	U.S.	French	English	Italian	Spanish	Greek	Arab

CONCLUSION

   A. All people are unaware of their assumptions about reality.
      1. We unconsciously learn how to divide time and space, how to walk and talk and use our bodies, what to notice and what not to notice, how to behave as men and women, how to relate to others, how to handle responsibility, whether experience is seen as whole or fragmented.

   B. What we think of as mind is really internalized culture.

   C. In multicultural situations, context must be taken into account and all of these ingrained concepts must be dealt with in order to understand one another.

Lecture Audioscript for Listening for the Larger Picture, page 179
This audioscript shows one speaker's delivery of the lecture, as recorded in the audio program. Use it as a resource.

OK . . . usually when we deal with different people, we deal with them as if we were all members of the same culture . . . however, it's possible that people from different cultures have *different* . . . unconscious . . . ingrained assumptions . . . about the world . . . regarding such important and basic ideas as interpersonal relationships . . . time . . . personal space . . . and basically this is the view of Edward Hall . . . and that's more or less what I'll talk about later on in more detail . . . and Edward Hall is an anthropologist who spent a large part of his life studying American Indians . . . their culture . . . their language . . . but he was different from a lot of other anthropologists who just study one culture . . . *he* was interested rather . . . in the *relations* between cultures

. . . how cultures interact . . . and basically Hall believes that cultures can be placed . . . or classified . . . by placing them on a continuum . . . ranging from what he called *high-context* . . . to *low-context* . . . and I'll do . . . I'll define those terms later on . . . and so what this talk is going to deal with are the two opposites on the continuum . . . the high-context culture . . . and the low-context culture . . .

OK . . . a *high-context* culture is a culture in which the *context* of the message . . . and you all understand context . . . context meaning surroundings . . . the *context* of the message . . . or the action . . . or an event . . . carries a large part of its meaning and significance . . . so what this means is that in a high-context culture . . . more attention is paid to what's happening in and around the message . . . or event . . . than to the message itself . . . OK . . . so more attention is paid to what's going on *around* the words . . . or the event . . . than to the actual event or message . . . and you'll get a better idea of what this all means when I give you examples . . . OK?

first of all, let's look in terms of interpersonal relationships . . . and I said I'm going to look at three areas . . . interpersonal relationships . . . personal space . . . and time . . . OK . . . in a high-context culture . . . in terms of interpersonal relationships . . . one thing that you might find very clearly is that there's a strong dependence on shared . . . or built-in preprogrammed information concerning a message or event . . . so for example . . . in terms of legal paperwork . . . contracts, etc. . . . there's more dependence on the circumstances around it than just the words themselves . . . so you might care about who's doing the signing . . . where their family is from . . . how much um . . . how respectable the family is . . . rather than just the actual paperwork . . . the event itself . . . OK? . . . and you'd find in a high-context culture that people would trust someone's word rather than care so much about all the details being spelled out . . . because again . . . there's more reliance on external messages . . . such as the society's expectations, etc. . . . OK? . . . and *also* in a high-context culture . . . *again* with this idea that if you share these built-in messages . . . there's also a lot of expectations or . . . uh what what can I say? . . . focus placed on *who* you know . . . your networks . . . so uh for example . . . if I wanted to borrow money from you . . . if you went to a bank *here* in the States . . . they would just say "well, you've got to fill out all of these papers . . . tell me all about who you are" . . . whereas in another place where there's a high-context culture . . . they might only say "who is your family? . . . oh, that family! . . . I know them . . . you can have the loan" . . . so there's a . . . in the high-context culture, there's a lot of dependence on built-in . . . uh shared expectations or information about an event . . . outside of the event itself . . . OK? . . . *also* you might find that there's a strong dependence on *social* restrictions . . . rather than legal restrictions . . . so what I'm saying is that what the *group* thinks . . . the society thinks . . . restrains people . . . more than just the law . . . so for example . . . in a high-context culture . . . a person wouldn't break the law . . . well *why* wouldn't a person break the law in a high-context culture? . . . their reason would probably be "it would bring shame on my family . . . my family would be ashamed . . . society would be ashamed" . . . their reasons wouldn't be so much "oh, I'd have to go to jail . . . I'd have to pay a fine" but rather "my family or society would feel bad . . . or think less of me" . . . OK? . . . and *another* thing about interpersonal relationships is that there's strong feelings of responsibility for the group . . . they really care about what's going to happen to the group . . . and not as much what happens to the individual self . . . and that could also be demonstrated in business . . . because in a high-context culture . . . the *head* of an organization . . . if something goes wrong . . . the head of the organization will take responsibility for the whole group . . . rather than just keep passing the responsibility . . . on to someone else . . . OK? . . . so those are basically some of the characteristics of the high-context culture in terms of interpersonal relationships . . .

OK . . . what about personal space? . . . generally, in a high-context culture . . . because there's a greater dependency on group thinking . . . people lean toward heavier sensory involvement . . . or closeness . . . to people . . . and they have less respect for privacy . . . for personal space . . . or what we might call a "bubble" of personal space . . . and if you go into that culture . . . people might stand closer when they're talking to you . . . OK . . . they, they might touch more . . . and if they're jostled in a crowd or touched inadvertently . . . they won't feel as violated . . . as someone from a low-context culture . . . and *also* people from a high-context culture pay attention to body language . . . because remember what I said . . . the definition of a high-context culture is that *more* attention is paid to the *context* of the message than to the message itself . . . and part of the context is body language . . . so it's paying attention to *all* the *other* . . . things . . . *around* the message . . .

OK . . . what about time? . . . in high-context cultures . . . generally they're considered to have what is called a polychronic [on board] attitude toward time . . . and you can tell the word . . . *chron,* C-H-R-O-N, means "time" . . . *poly,* P-O-L-Y, means "many" . . . so that what they mean by a polychronic attitude toward time is that they believe that people . . . things . . . events . . . have their own time . . . that there can't be a standard system of time for everything . . . and what this leads them to believe is that you can't emphasize punctuality . . . things happen when they're supposed to happen . . . so there's a different attitude toward time . . . there's no set standard of time . . . or they don't see time in that way . . . that is . . . there's a sense that . . . you can't control time . . . everything has its own sense of time . . . OK so it's a culture that pays little attention to time . . . to clock time . . .

OK . . . what are the advantages or disadvantages of such a system? . . . in terms of disadvantages we see that change comes to the society pretty slowly . . . that class structure . . . the family structure . . . is pretty rigid . . . because they have . . . because the system is so strong . . . the group identification . . . the feeling of connection between all things . . . but it's hard to make changes . . . all right . . . and *another* disadvantage is that it often can make people feel *bound* . . . that they almost feel that they're restricted in what they can do . . . and one of the advantages of course is that people feel more connected to other people . . . there's a greater system of security . . . system of family connectedness . . . society connectedness . . . you don't have as much of a sense of alienation as you might have in . . . what I'll talk about later . . . uh a low-context culture . . . OK . . . so you've got all those things in a high-context culture . . . now when I talk about a low-context culture you'll *see* the differences . . . and remember that I'm talking about extremes . . . not in terms of . . . remember I said that most cultures will place on a continuum . . . not on the ends or the extremes . . .

OK . . . a low-context culture is just the opposite . . . a low-context culture . . . is one in which the message . . . the event . . . or the action . . . is a separate *entity* . . . having meaning unto itself . . . *regardless* of the surroundings . . . *regardless* of the context . . . that the message . . . the event . . . the action . . . has meaning in itself . . . OK so what this means in a low-context culture is that people pay more attention to the event itself . . . rather than to the context which surrounds the event . . . so . . . for example . . . interpersonal relationships . . . in a high- . . . in a low-context culture . . . there's going to be a lot of emphasis on getting things on paper . . . having a *legal* bond rather than just words . . . because . . . you don't trust anything except the event itself . . . you're not going to worry about the social context . . . you're not going to worry about the family . . . you just really want to have everything . . . contained . . . in the event . . . in the message . . . so we're going to rely . . . in a low-context culture . . . on a piece of paper more than someone's words . . . and if you're in business, you want everything spelled out . . . you want everything spelled out in negotiations . . . you don't take anything for granted . . . OK? . . . and *again* . . . just the opposite of the high-context culture . . . in terms of responsibility . . . because there's not as much group identification . . . there's more individual identification . . . if you're the president of a company . . . rather than taking responsibility for everyone in your company . . . basically you feel that individuals should take their own responsibility . . . OK so if something goes wrong in your company . . . then *that* person will take the blame . . . not necessarily the president . . . so it's possible to pass the buck . . . as they say . . .

OK what about personal space? . . . again that's the opposite of a high-context culture . . . remember in a low-context culture there's more emphasis on individuality . . . and so the concept of privacy is very very important . . . whereas before as I said . . . in a high-context culture . . . they might not even be concerned with privacy or personal space . . . but in a *low-context* culture . . . there's a feeling that we each have our own personal space . . . if you get too close . . . if you don't knock on doors before entering . . . that's an invasion of privacy . . . people feel violated . . . OK? . . . and as I said before . . . there's a respect and a desire *for* privacy . . . which is not found in a low- . . . I mean in a *high-context* culture . . . you'll see that people stand farther apart . . . and you'll also see that people might pay less attention to body language because as I said . . . the message is "the message is everything" . . . they're not going to worry about all the details around it . . . what you *say* is the important thing . . . or what you do is the important thing . . .

OK what about time? . . . in terms of time . . . I said before there was a polychronic sense of time in a high-context culture . . . what do you think there would be in a low-context culture? . . . *mono*chronic [on board] . . . a monochronic sense of time . . . and by that we mean that there's *one* time . . . and that concept means . . . that people in a low-context culture believe that there's one standard of time . . . and that should be for everything . . . and so I'm not willing to hear "oh . . . the traffic was heavy . . . that's why I'm late" . . . or "oh . . . I slept late" . . . people in a low-context culture will be much more upset with lateness . . . because they feel that everyone should follow the same time . . . OK? . . . there shouldn't be all this flexibility with time . . . they expect punctuality . . . and they look at time as almost a commodity . . . that they use expressions like "use time" . . . "to waste time" . . . "to spend time" . . . uh "time is money" . . . all of those expressions reinforce the concept that time is actually something you can hold onto . . .

what about the disadvantages and advantages? . . . OK . . . in terms of disadvantages . . . what you'll find is . . . that there's less commitment to a system . . . people often can feel alienated . . . separate . . . because people move a lot . . . they might not be as close to or as *tied* to a family . . . to a society . . . so there could be less connectedness . . . less commitment . . . less human trust . . . now the *advantages* . . . and remember . . . Ed Hall points out . . . that he doesn't make any value judgments about these cultures . . . he basically says that there are differences . . . he doesn't say that one is better than the other . . . so they all have advantages and disadvantages . . . but in terms of advantages for the low-context culture . . . he says a great advantage is that change happens . . . there's very . . . there's often a lot of flexibility in what people do . . . how they can be . . . there's a lot more individuality . . . people have freedom to change and be different . . .

and let me just give you an example of the continuum . . . of some cultures on the continuum between high-context and low-context . . . and you can see that chart in your book . . . Hall puts the German-Swiss down here at the extreme low-context end . . . the Germans . . . the Scandinavians . . . the Americans . . . the French . . . the English . . . the Italians . . . the Spanish . . . the Greeks . . . the Arabs . . . and notice he doesn't have all cultures here . . . obviously he doesn't have one single Asian culture here at all . . . so I'll let you look into that later . . . we'll talk about that another time . . . where you might place your own culture on this continuum . . .

so . . . basically what this is all about is that . . . Hall stresses that . . . people need to be aware of these different assumptions about reality . . . and he thinks that this has all kinds of relevance no matter what you're doing . . . if you're in business . . . negotiations . . . if you're in politics . . . interpersonal relations . . . if you're just dealing with people from different cultures in any way . . . it's going to affect every part of your life . . . because . . . these assumptions that we make . . . are so unconscious that we don't think about them . . . we automatically assume that everyone thinks about time . . . place . . . personal relationships . . . in the same way . . . but he says . . . these things that are so basic . . . are actually different . . . that we unconsciously learn these things . . . and they're based on culture . . . and he basically says that what we think of as mind . . . is really internalized culture . . . OK? . . . he's of the belief that mind is basically your culture . . . your culture's imposition . . . and he stresses the fact that in any multicultural situation . . . that these assumptions need to be taken into account . . . for successful interactions.

Answers, page 179:
1. low-context; high-context; interpersonal relationships, time; space   2. Encourage students to share what they remember and understand; it is not necessary to have the full information at this point.   **a.** See Lecture Outline sections I.A and I.B (high-context culture) and sections II.A and II.B (low-context culture).   **b.** See Lecture Outline section I.B.3 (high-context culture) and section II.B.3 (low-context culture).   **c.** See Lecture Outline section I.B.2 (high-context culture) and section II.B.2 (low-context culture).   **d.** See Lecture Outline section I.B.1 (high-context culture) and section II.B.1 (low-context culture).   **e.** Though individuals within a culture obviously vary, there is a greater likelihood that individuals from low-context cultures would agree with the statements in the questionnaire about time and disagree with the statements about interpersonal relationships. On the other hand, there is a greater likelihood that individuals from high-context cultures would disagree with the statements in the questionnaire about time and agree with the statements about interpersonal relationships.

Defining Vocabulary Audioscript, page 180

1. ingrained: The work ethic, the belief that work is morally good and necessary, was so deeply ingrained in him that when he became unemployed, he felt completely worthless.
2. assumption: She didn't wear a wedding ring, so he made the assumption that she wasn't married. Later, he found out that he was wrong.
3. unconscious: Although she claimed to like him, she kept her body turned away from him. I think this was unconscious, but it probably expressed her true feelings. I'm sure that if she had been aware of what her body was saying, she would have been more careful.
4. striking: The results of the experiments showed striking differences between the experimental group and the control group. The differences were so apparent that even untrained people were able to see them.
5. continuum: Hall claims that his classification system is not either/or. That is, a culture is not either high-context or low-context. Rather, he says, all cultures fall somewhere along a continuum between those two extremes.
6. entity: In a low-context culture, the message, event, or action is seen as a separate entity, distinct from the context that surrounds it. That is, it has meaning in itself.
7. negotiation: The management and workers had different needs. Therefore, their negotiations took a lot of time, with each side listening to what the other had to say, stating its own needs, and stating what it would be willing to compromise. The negotiations ended when the two sides reached an agreement that was acceptable to them both.
8. commodity: In a culture that considers time as a commodity, one hears expressions such as "time is money" and "don't waste time." Time, in these cultures, is almost looked on as something material that one can hold onto.
9. network: In the United States in the 1800s, there was a network of people who worked together to bring slaves from the South to safety in the North.
10. to restrain: In a high-context culture, society's opinions and judgments keep people in line. What the group thinks restrains people. In low-context cultures, that controlling function is taken care of through laws and threats of punishment such as jail sentences.
11. to feel violated: When people in a low-context culture get too physically close to one another, as, for example, on a crowded bus, people may feel violated. An individual may feel that his personal space has been invaded, entered without his permission.
12. reform: People are calling for reforms in our prison system. They believe that prisons are overcrowded and prisoners are not being trained so that they can go back to society. They suggest that more prison space be built and that more training programs be instituted. They say that if these reforms are not made, the prison system will only get worse.
13. rigid: In some countries, class structure is very rigid. If one is born into a particular class, one is generally assured of dying within that class.

Answers:
1. b   **2.** c   **3.** c   **4.** b   **5.** c   **6.** b   **7.** b   **8.** a   **9.** c   **10.** b   **11.** a   **12.** c   **13.** a

Defining Idioms and Sayings Audioscript, page 181

1. to shoulder the blame: Although the whole group was at fault, one person shouldered the blame for everyone. That person ended up being kicked out of school while the others never got into any trouble.
2. Her word is her bond.: If she says that she will pay you back immediately, you can believe her. Her word is her bond.
3. to pass the buck: Someone made a mistake in the construction of the building. When I went to see the construction company, everyone kept passing the buck. No one would accept responsibility.
4. The buck stops here.: This statement was originally made in reaction to the saying "to pass the buck." When a person says that "the buck stops here," he is saying that he will accept responsibility and not pass it on to anyone else.
5. Time is money.: She is always rushing people in and out of her office. She hates to even waste one minute. She sees time in terms of dollar signs, the money needed to keep the office running, the money that she believes her time is worth. "Time is money," she always says.

Answers:
1. b 2. b 3. b 4. b 5. a

Note-Taking Practice, pages 181–183
See pages 224–225 of Appendix C in the textbook for example notes.

Post-Lecture Reading and Discussion, pages 183–184
Answers:
1. a. There might be different cultural expectations about how business relationships are built. The executives from Turkmenistan seem to be taking a great deal of time with ritual welcomes while the executive from India seems more concerned with professionally and briefly ("in about ten minutes") introducing his company and products. The executive from India gets irritated at what he probably sees as a waste of time and opportunity; even though the executives from Turkmenistan had specific business issues to discuss, they couldn't do that before going through the ritual welcomes and speeches to establish a context and relationship. In addition, they seem to be trying to place the Indian businessman in the context of his Indian history (commenting on key historical figures and places) rather than immediately treating him as an individual.   **b.** From the excerpt given here, it seems that the businessman from India is showing more low-context culture characteristics. He is extremely concerned about the time and wants to get "down to business." The executives from Turkmenistan, on the other hand, are showing more high-context culture characteristics. They seem more intent on establishing a context for their relationship. (This excerpt might raise interesting points of discussion. Are the Indian businessman's attitude and behavior typical of Indian culture? Or is it typical of Indian international businessmen of a certain class? Or are this individual's behavior and expectations unique in Indian culture?)   **2.** Answers will vary.   **3.** Answers will vary.   **4.** Answers will vary.

Using Your Notes, pages 184–185
Answers:
1. a. A high-context culture is a culture in which the context of the message, action, or event carries a large part of its meaning and/or significance.   **b.** A low-context culture is one in which the message, event, or action is seen as a separate entity having meaning unto itself.   **2. a.** F (They're on a continuum from high to low.)   **b.** F (People are unaware.)   **c.** F (high)   **d.** F (high)   **e.** F (high)   **f.** F (low)   **g.** T   **3.** See Lecture Outline sections I.B.3 and II.B.3. Examples will vary.   **4.** See Lecture Outline sections I.C, I.D, II.C, and II.D.   **5.** Many answers are possible. For example, members of a high-context culture may be insulted by someone from a low-context culture wanting everything in writing, or a businessman from a low-context culture may be insulted by a colleague from a high-context culture who is always late. Someone from a high-context culture may feel insulted when insufficient attention is paid to expected protocol, or individuals from low-context cultures may miss important messages sent through body language.

Using Vocabulary Audioscript, page 186

1. He refuses to shoulder the blame for anything.
2. No one likes to work with her because she always passes the buck whenever something goes wrong.
3. There are striking differences in their negotiating styles.
4. The members of the audience restrained themselves during the meeting.
5. She unconsciously picked up her neighbor's purse when she left the restaurant.
6. Expectations about sex roles—that is, standards of behavior for men and women—are sometimes quite rigid and deeply ingrained.
7. She feels that her privacy is violated when people visit without calling first.
8. The voters called for reforms in the education system, but the leaders didn't listen.
9. Knowledge and information are distinct entities.
10. The researcher rated the participants on a continuum labeled "sad" at one end and "happy" at the other end.

Answers:
1. a 2. b 3. b 4. b 5. b 6. b 7. b 8. a 9. b 10. b

UNIT 7 POST-COURSEWORK EVALUATION

Unit Summary: Unit 7 provides students with an opportunity to synthesize note-taking skills learned in previous units. To help teachers evaluate students' progress (and to help students evaluate their own progress), there is less listening and note-taking guidance in this unit. Instead, students listen and take notes to prepare for quizzes. These quizzes (found in this section of the manual) consist of True/False, multiple-choice, and short-answer questions; they are designed to simulate situations in which students use their notes in an academic setting. Lastly, students apply information gained through their listening and note-taking and use critical thinking skills to respond to essay questions.

Lecture 18: The Pyramids of Egypt: An Engineering Feat

Pre-Lecture Reading and Discussion, pages 188–189

Answers:

1. different pyramids located in Egypt   2. a. an eight-mile road and rock-cutting saws   b. At the time of its construction, the road ended at a quay on the shore of a lake. This lake was at one time connected to the Nile. The road was used to transport stone blocks from the quarry to barges that waited at the lake, eventually going down the Nile (to the monument sites, including the pyramids).   c. The road is a major engineering achievement. The road is earlier than researchers thought possible. The discovery of the rock-cutting saws and the road challenges previous views that the Egyptians lacked them.

Lecture Outline for Listening for the Larger Picture, page 190
Use this outline if you'd like to deliver the lecture yourself.

INTRODUCTION: The pyramids of ancient Egypt never cease to ignite the human imagination. Is it their age? Is it their power—standing tall in the harsh desert? Is it the mysteries surrounding them—the mysteries of the people who built them, who were buried in them? Is it the awe we feel when we see this feat of human engineering—structures built when we didn't have cranes, bulldozers, and other machinery?

The focus of this lecture is the design and engineering of the pyramids.

I. Background on pyramids of Egypt

   A. Between 2700 and 1640 B.C., more than eighty pyramids were built along the Nile.

   B. Pyramids were built as tombs for kings.
      1. According to the religious beliefs of the ancient Egyptians, when the king died, he joined the gods.
      2. By preserving the king's body and keeping it safe, his spirit would be able to return to it and his power would preserve Egypt.
      3. The pyramids were designed to keep the king's body safe forever in a burial chamber deep inside the monument.

II. Pyramid design and engineering

   A. No one really knows why the ancient Egyptians chose the pyramid shape.

   B. There are some possible reasons.
      1. It is a very stable, strong shape.
      2. It is a practical shape in that the majority of the stone is in the bottom half; the higher one goes, the fewer stones that are needed.
      3. It developed in a gradual and natural progression from earlier burial practices.

   C. There are three main types of Egyptian pyramid: the step pyramid, the bent pyramid (only one exists of this type), and the straight-sided pyramid.
      1. See picture of "step pyramid"—these were the oldest pyramids and are basically a series of supporting walls surrounding a central core, with the walls varying in height, thus creating the step appearance.
         a. The step pyramid may have been a symbolic stairway to the stars.
      2. See picture of "bent pyramid." This began as a straight-sided pyramid, but halfway up the engineers may have panicked and thought the angle was too steep, so they changed to a more gentle slope.
         a. There is only one in existence.
      3. See picture of "straight-sided pyramid"; this is the smooth-sided pyramid that most of us associate with Egyptian pyramids.
         a. Some experts believe that it represents the rays of the sun, upon which the king can climb to join the gods.
         b. The core of the straight-sided pyramid is essentially a step pyramid. Additional blocks filled the "steps" to create the straight sides. Often, a better and whiter stone was added as a casing stone, surrounding the initial blocks.

D. The building process
1. A site was chosen along the west bank of the Nile, above the flood level, and on a solid rock base.
2. The position of the pyramid was important, and the priest studied the stars to calculate true north.
3. The work force included priests, architects, surveyors, metalworkers, stonemasons, carpenters, painters, sculptors, scribes (to keep records), and laborers.
4. Workers made a level base for the pyramid.
    a. Since modern surveying instruments didn't exist, leveling was a procedure in which a wall was built around the proposed site and flooded with water.
    b. By cutting holes and trenches into the ground and measuring and equalizing the level of the water, builders were able to level the site.
5. Stone was quarried.
    a. To break the stone into rough blocks, laborers used wooden wedges that were soaked with water. As the wood swelled, the stone would break away. Recent research has also suggested the possibility of rock saws.
    b. Each block weighed nearly three tons.
    c. The blocks were roughly squared by stonemasons with a copper chisel (iron had not yet been made) and wooden mallet.
    d. The blocks were transported from the quarries by ship. Each year, the Nile River flooded, so if the workers dragged the blocks to the edge of the flood zone and waited until the flood season, the stones could be floated right up to the edge of the desert by ship.
6. A path was built leading from the water to the pyramid site.
    a. Blocks were dragged using ropes, sledges, and a great deal of human labor.
    b. Although the Egyptians had the concept of the wheel (and used it for several purposes), they did not use wheeled vehicles or wheels for transporting material.
7. A room was constructed in the center of the pyramid to contain the stone coffin, the sarcophagus.
    a. A number of burial chambers contained descriptions of the changes the king would go through until he became a god.
    b. On the walls of the chamber were false doors, through which it was believed the king's spirit could pass.
    c. Surrounding rooms and chambers often contained food and objects for the king's eternal comfort.
8. The sides were built one layer at a time, using ramps.
    a. Once the blocks had been hauled up the ramp, ropes and levers were used to maneuver the huge blocks into position.
    b. When the pyramid reached its planned height, a casing stone was put on the rough stone. This casing stone was made of a white limestone. The top may have been capped with gold.
9. Once the stones were in place, workers would remove the ramp, polishing the sides of the pyramid as they went so that the white limestone shone in the sun.
    a. Sadly, over the years, most of the casing blocks have been stolen.
10. The path leading to the pyramid was broken up and destroyed.

III. The Great Pyramid of Khufu (Greek name—Cheops)

A. It was the burial tomb for Khufu, who ruled from 2551 to 2528 B.C.

B. This is the largest pyramid and the largest stone building in the world.
1. It was originally 481 feet (146.5 m) tall but now is only 449 feet (137 m) due to the loss of the white limestone casing.
2. It was built with about 2,300,000 blocks, with an average block weight of two and a half tons.

C. It is located at Giza, near Cairo.

D. It is a straight-sided pyramid. The blocks fit so perfectly that you cannot get a knife blade between them.

E. It probably took more than twenty years to build and a labor force of 20,000 or so (though estimates vary).
1. Who were these 20,000 and what was their life like? Another lecture.

CONCLUSION: The pyramids of ancient Egypt allow us glimpses into a long-ago world. It makes me wonder—what legacy will we pass down to our descendants? What will remain of us and our technological achievements 5,000 years in the future? These are questions worth pondering.

Lecture Audioscript for Listening for the Larger Picture, page 190

This audioscript shows one speaker's delivery of the lecture, as recorded in the audio program. Use it as a resource.

the pyramids of ancient Egypt just never cease to ignite the human imagination . . . people just continue to look at them in awe . . . people dream about going to Egypt to see them . . . what do you think it is? . . . is it their age? . . . is it their power . . . just standing so tall in the harsh desert? . . . is it the mystery surrounding them . . . the mysteries about the people who built them . . . the people who are buried there and the culture they had? . . . is it the awe we feel when we see this feat of human engineering . . . structures that were built when we didn't have cranes and bulldozers and other machinery that we have today? . . .

what I'm going to do in this lecture is talk about the design . . . and engineering . . . of the pyramids . . . to give you a sense of what went into the building of these incredible structures . . . first let me give you some background on the pyramids . . .

the pyramids were built . . . and they're . . . when we see pictures, we usually see pictures of the same group of three or four pyramids . . . but actually there are more than *eighty* pyramids that were built along the Nile River . . . and those were built over a . . . almost a thousand-year period primarily . . . between 2700 . . . and 1640 B.C. . . . 2700 and 1640 B.C. . . . and they were built as the tombs . . . for kings . . . they were royal tombs . . . burial places . . . that was their function . . . and the idea behind it was that . . . according to the religious beliefs of the ancient Egyptians . . . when the king died, he was going to join the gods . . . and by preserving the king's body and keeping it safe . . . they believed that his spirit would be able to return to the body . . . and in this way his power would continue to safeguard . . . to preserve Egypt . . . so in general we have to remember that the pyramids are tombs first and foremost . . . they're royal tombs . . . and they were designed to keep the king's body safe forever . . . and so the burial chambers are deep deep deep within the monuments . . . very often they're at the center of the monuments . . . to protect the king's body . . .

now actually the design and engineering . . . no one is really sure exactly why the ancient Egyptians chose the shape of the pyramid . . . there is speculation . . . for one thing . . . a pyramid is a very stable strong shape . . . so . . . the idea, remember, is to protect the body forever . . . so they have a design that is very very stable . . . it's also a very *practical* shape . . . when you have . . . when you don't have cranes and bulldozers and other machinery . . . it's a practical shape because the majority of the stone that's needed is in the bottom half . . . and the higher you go . . . the fewer stones that you need . . . and of course it's the higher part that would require that much more labor to go up . . . so there's less work involved in building a pyramid than perhaps other structures . . . and *also* . . . if we look at the progression of burial structures in ancient Egypt . . . we can see that there was a gradual and natural progression from earlier practices . . . and I'm not going to go into exactly what those practices were . . . but over time . . . you can see how a pyramid would have developed from earlier styles of burial structures . . .

if you look in your book . . . you can see that there are three main types of Egyptian pyramids . . . we have what's called a *step* pyramid . . . the *bent* pyramid . . . and the *straight-sided* pyramid . . . and the straight-sided pyramid is the one we usually think of when we think of a pyramid . . . but these other two pyramids are also types that you can actually see if you go to Egypt . . . the step pyramid is the oldest pyramid . . . or they're among the oldest pyramids . . . and they're actually basically a series of walls surrounding a central core . . . and the walls vary in height . . . each wall is progressively smaller than the last one . . . so it creates the step appearance that you see in the picture . . . and people have speculated that this might have been a symbolic stairway to the stars . . . OK so these are the oldest pyramids . . . *another* pyramid is the *bent* pyramid . . . and you can see that picture as well . . . and this might have actually been a mistake . . . it began as a straight-sided pyramid . . . but halfway up it changes . . . and it changes into a more gentle slope . . . and the idea behind it is . . . we wonder if maybe the engineers who created it started getting a little nervous . . . maybe they panicked . . . and they thought that the angle was just *too* steep . . . and so they changed to a more gentle slope midway . . . and there's only one of these in existence . . .

most of the pyramids you see today in Egypt are what we call *straight-sided* pyramids . . . they're the smooth-sided pyramids . . . that most of us imagine when we think of Egyptian pyramids . . . again . . . there is speculation as to what the shape means . . . just as I said the step pyramid may have been a symbolic stairway to the stars . . . some experts believe that the straight-sided pyramid . . . the smooth-sided pyramid represents the rays of the sun upon which the king can climb to join the gods . . . the connection between the sun and the king . . . the king joining the gods after death . . . now regarding the engineering . . . the *core* of the straight-sided pyramid is basically a step pyramid . . . and what the later designers did is they added additional blocks to *fill* the steps to create these straight sides . . . and as we'll talk about later . . . often a better and a whiter stone was added on top . . . as a layer on top . . . as a *casing* stone . . . to surround the initial blocks and it gave an even smoother and brighter appearance . . .

OK the building process . . . what was the process that was involved in building these incredible structures? . . . the first thing that would happen is that a site needed to be chosen . . . along the west bank . . . always the west bank of the Nile River . . . and it had to be above the flood level . . . and on a solid rock base . . . and this idea of the Nile River flooding . . . it flooded regularly . . . and this flooding actually played a very important role in the building of the pyramids . . . but the site had to be *above* the flood zone . . . or else once a year the pyramid would be surrounded by water and they didn't want that . . . and they also calculated . . . they spent time calculating the position of the pyramid . . . because the directions that the pyramid faced were very important . . . so the priest would study the stars to calculate true north . . . and then position the pyramid accordingly . . .

the work force was huge . . . it included priests . . . architects . . . surveyors . . . metalworkers . . . uh stonemasons . . . carpenters . . . painters . . . sculptors . . . scribes . . . who are the ones that kept the records

. . . and thousands and thousands of laborers . . .

what would happen is the workers would first make a level base for the pyramid . . . they have to look at the ground and figure out a way to make it level for this huge structure . . . and since at that time they didn't have our modern surveying instruments . . . they had a special procedure for leveling the ground . . . what they did first was build a wall around the proposed site . . . and then they flooded the site with water . . . and then what they'd do is they'd cut holes and trenches into the ground . . . and they'd measure the level of the water . . . and mark off the same water height in each hole and trench . . . and this mark would give them guidance in leveling the ground . . .

the next thing they would have to do is quarry the stones . . . now they had to have a method for breaking the stone into rough blocks . . . and the method they would generally use required wooden wedges . . . and the laborers would take pieces of wood . . . and put them . . . into . . . cracks in the rock . . . and they would soak the wooden wedges with water . . . which would make them swell . . . and as the wood swelled the stone would break . . . and . . . only most recently . . . as you read . . . there have also been suggestions that they might have had *rock saws* as well, a saw that would have helped them cut the rock . . . but on the whole . . . they used this technique of soaking wood with water . . . and having the wood expand enough to force the rock to break along a crack . . . now we're not talking about little blocks here . . . we're talking about rocks that weighed nearly three tons . . . so once the blocks were quarried . . . they were roughly squared by stonemasons . . . and the tools they used for this were copper chisels . . . they didn't have any iron yet . . . they'd use a chisel . . . a copper chisel . . . and a mallet . . . a wooden hammerlike instrument . . . and they would roughly square these stones . . .

then they had to figure out how do we transport these blocks from the quarry . . . to the pyramid site . . . and this is where the ingenuity of the ancient Egyptians really becomes apparent . . . they knew that every year the Nile River flooded . . . so if the workers dragged the rocks to the edge of the flood zone . . . and then they waited until the flood season . . . the stones then could be floated right up to the edge of the desert . . . by ship . . . OK? . . . so when they were cutting the blocks from the quarry, it was the dry season . . . but if they managed to move those rocks to the point where they'd be within the flood zone . . . they could eventually then kind of float it right onto the boats . . . down to the pyramid sites . . .

so . . . imagine that they've gotten the rocks onto the boats . . . down the river . . . then they need to build a path from the water to the site of the pyramid . . . and this is where you might have seen pictures of laborers dragging these huge huge blocks . . . using ropes . . . uh sledges . . . and a great deal of human labor . . . you know the Egyptians had the concept of the wheel . . . but interestingly enough . . . they didn't use wheeled vehicles or wheels for transporting materials . . . so really . . . these blocks . . . these three-ton blocks . . . were dragged . . . using ropes . . . sledges . . . like sleds . . . but mainly a lot of human labor . . .

OK . . . then they would first construct a room in the center of the pyramid which would contain the coffin of the king . . . the word used for this stone coffin is *sarcophagus* [on board] S-A-R-C-O-P-H-A-G-U-S . . . sarcophagus . . . what was inside of the burial chamber . . . in addition to the sarcophagus? . . . many of the chambers had on the walls . . . descriptions of the changes the king would go through until he became a god . . . there are also some false doors in the room . . . people believed that the king's spirit could pass through these doors . . . and surrounding the burial chamber there were often some other rooms . . . which contained food and other objects for the king's eternal comfort . . . and it is these rooms . . . with the food . . . and objects . . . which have provided an incredible amount of information about the lifestyles of ancient Egypt . . .

now the sides of the pyramid were built one layer at a time . . . and they would use ramps . . . remember again . . . no cranes . . . no machines to lift the rocks . . . but they would build ramps . . . going up . . . and they'd haul the rocks up the ramps using ropes and levers . . . to maneuver the huge blocks into position . . . and finally when the pyramid reached the planned height . . . they would put a casing stone . . . as I said earlier . . . the casing stone was put over the rough stone . . . and this casing stone was made of a very white limestone . . .

now once the stones were in place . . . workers would remove the ramp . . . and polish the sides of the pyramid as they went down . . . so that the white limestone shone in the sun . . . and it's too bad . . . because over the years most of the casing blocks have been stolen or used for other projects . . . and so what we see nowadays in the desert is not what the ancient Egyptians saw . . . what the ancient Egyptians saw was a structure that had the same shape but was much smoother and covered with a very bright white . . . and the top may even have been capped with gold . . . we don't see this now . . .

the last step . . . finally the path leading to the pyramid from the river . . . would be broken up or destroyed . . .

OK . . . before I end this talk I'd like to tell you about one of the pyramids . . . just a little bit of detail about one of the more researched pyramids . . . and this is called the Great Pyramid of Khufu . . . K-H-U-F-U . . . Khufu . . . and uh Khufu was a king who ruled from 2551 B.C. to 2528 B.C. . . . 2551 to 2528 B.C. . . . he's also called Cheops . . . that was his Greek name . . . Cheops . . . C-H-E-O-P-S . . . and the Great Pyramid is one of the pyramids that you often see in pictures . . . it's right near Cairo . . . in an area called Giza . . . G-I-Z-A . . . and it's the largest of all pyramids . . . in fact, it's the largest stone *building* in the world . . . it was originally 481 feet tall . . . and for those of you who use the metric system . . . 146.5 meters tall . . . but actually now it's much smaller . . . it's only 449 feet tall . . . or 137 meters . . . and as I said before . . . the reason for this is that we've lost that white limestone casing . . . that bright white casing . . . so it's lost almost forty feet in height due to this . . .

it was built with almost two and a half million blocks . . . to be more exact . . . 2,300,000 blocks . . . and remember I said these blocks are not small . . . an average block in this pyramid weighs 2½ tons . . . 5,000 pounds . . . so imagine 2,300,000 blocks and the average block weighs 2½ tons . . . think of the human labor that went into this . . .

and I said it's located in Giza . . . which is near Cairo . . . very near Cairo . . . in fact . . . it's amazing to go there because you're in Cairo . . . you're in a major city . . . and you're driving . . . or taking a taxi, a bus . . . and all of a sudden . . . behind the houses . . . behind the buildings . . . you see the tops of the pyramids . . . it's that close to the city . . .

anyway . . . the Great Pyramid is a straight-sided pyramid . . . and . . . the blocks fit together so perfectly that you can't even get a knife blade in between them . . . so when we talk about feats of engineering . . . this is an amazing feat . . . that not only is it made with these huge stones . . . but also . . . that they're put together so perfectly . . . that you can't even get a knife blade between the stones . . .

estimates for how long it took to build are about twenty years . . . researchers are thinking that it took about twenty years to build and required a labor force of 20,000 or thereabouts . . . although estimates vary . . . who were these 20,000 people and what was their life like? well . . . that's going to be another lecture . . .

for today . . . I'd just like you to think about . . . reflect on these pyramids . . . these pyramids of ancient Egypt allow us glimpses into worlds of long ago . . . and it makes *me* wonder when I think about them what is *our* legacy to the future? . . . what legacy are *we* going to pass down to *our* descendants? . . . what's going to remain of *us* and *our* technological achievements 5,000 years in the future? I think that these are questions that are worth pondering . . . what do you think?

Answers, page 190:
1. c, e, f, g 2. They were built as tombs for the kings, to preserve the body and keep it safe, thus ensuring that his spirit would be able to return to it and his power would preserve Egypt.

Defining Vocabulary Audioscript, pages 190–191

1. feat: The Olympic games provide the world with an opportunity to watch athletes perform amazing feats of strength and endurance.
2. tomb: In the national cemetery, there is a tomb called the "Tomb of the Unknown Soldier." This structure was built over the remains of a soldier whose body had not been identified and was created in memory of all soldiers whose bodies were never found or identified.
3. spirit: Many religions believe that the body dies but the spirit lives on.
4. to preserve: Many cultures hope to preserve the traditions of the past. However, often the younger generation is more interested in modern ideas.
5. stable: This table is not very stable. Don't put anything heavy on it because it'll probably break.
6. steep slope: The hill had such a steep slope that she couldn't bicycle up it. She had to walk with the bicycle until they came to a part of the trail that was flatter.
7. huge: Their house is huge; it's so big that you almost need a map to find your way around.
8. to swell: He hit his head on the ground when he fell. Though he wasn't bleeding a lot, a bump appeared and the injury started to swell. He put an ice pack on the injury to stop the swelling.
9. to drag: The bag full of concrete was too heavy to lift, so he dragged it along the ground until he found someone to help him carry it.
10. coffin: In some religions, people are buried in coffins. In other religions, dead bodies are wrapped in white sheets and placed directly in the ground.
11. ramp: Many buildings have ramps alongside stairs to accommodate the needs of those in wheelchairs who cannot use the stairs.
12. to speculate: Many people speculated about the reasons for the divorce; however, no one was sure.
13. to ponder: I pondered the offer for hours. Even after all that consideration, I still didn't have an answer.

Answers:
1. b 2. b 3. a 4. c 5. b 6. c 7. c 8. a 9. c 10. a 11. c 12. a 13. c

Note-Taking Practice and Quiz, page 192

Give students this quiz about one week after they listen to the lecture. Allow them to use their notes to answer the questions.

Questions:
1. True or False? If false, correct the sentence.
    ___ a. The pyramids were all built during the same century.
    ___ b. More than eighty pyramids were built along the Nile River.
    ___ c. The pyramids were built in the flood zone of the Nile River.
    ___ d. Although the ancient Egyptians had the concept of the wheel, they didn't use wheeled vehicles to transport material.
    ___ e. The *sarcophagus* is the name of the boat that transported the rocks from the quarry.
2. State at least three possible reasons why the ancient Egyptians chose the pyramid shape.
3. Contrast the types of Egyptian pyramids in terms of appearance. What speculations have researchers made regarding the reasons for each design?
4. Why was it so important for the ancient Egyptians to preserve the king's body?
5. How do the pyramids that we see in Egypt today differ from those that ancient Egyptians saw?
6. Name five features of the Great Pyramid of Khufu.
7. In a paragraph, describe the process used by the ancient Egyptians to build the pyramids.

Answers:
1. a. F (They were built over a period of more than 1,000 years (2700–1640 B.C.).) **b.** T **c.** F (They were outside of the flood zone.) **d.** T **e.** F (The sarcophagus is the stone coffin.) **2.** Any three of the following answers are appropriate: **a.** It is a very stable shape. **b.** It is a practical shape in that more stone is required in the bottom and fewer stones are required at the top (where it would be harder to build and reach). **c.** It was a natural and gradual development from previous burial practice. **d.** It represented their beliefs about the king's relation to the gods (e.g., the steps that the king would ascend to reach the stars or the rays of the sun upon which the king could climb to join the gods). **3.** See Lecture Outline section II.C. **4.** The religious beliefs of the time included the idea that the king's spirit could return to the body (if preserved) and its power would preserve Egypt. **5.** The pyramids of today do not have the outside white limestone casing. Therefore, the stones are rougher (unpolished) and a different color. Also, because of the loss of this casing, the pyramids we see today are smaller. The top of the original pyramids may have been capped with gold. **6.** See Lecture Outline section III. Any five features are appropriate. **7.** See Lecture Outline section II.D.

Writing Activity, page 192
These questions are open-ended. Therefore, a variety of responses are possible. Essays may include the following information.

Answers:
1. Students may talk about the significance of the pyramids from a perspective of the knowledge that we have gained about ancient religions (based on the design of the pyramids, the location of the sarcophagus, the drawings in the inner rooms, etc.), the social structure of an ancient society (e.g., who was buried in the pyramids, who did the work), or ancient technology (e.g., how stone blocks were moved and manipulated, how a pyramid was built). In addition, students may talk about how this knowledge has significance to our present lives by, as examples, allowing us to gain insight about our own human history of civilization, the rise and fall of civilizations, our own mortality, or human potential and ingenuity. **2. a.** Students may use information from the lecture to talk about life in Egypt 5,000 years ago relating to the role of kings and workers, religious leaders, and beliefs. **b.** Students' responses must take into account what elements in our civilization are likely to last into the future and what kind of message they will leave about our age. Will our buildings last? Which ones? The temples? The office buildings? The malls? If it is the bank vaults that last, what does that say about our society? Or will radioactive waste last? Or will the remains of satellites or rockets last? What would that say about our society? **3. a.** Students may use information from the lecture to speculate about why the pyramids were built the way they were (e.g., the religious reasons for using a pyramid design, the practical reasons). In addition, students may write about the environment of ancient Egypt and the use of nature and the seasonal flooding of the Nile to allow huge boulders to be transported without machinery or wheeled vehicles. **b.** Students' responses must focus on one location and the buildings in that location. Students should consider the materials used (e.g., brick, adobe), the typical architectural choices (e.g., skyscrapers, single-story designs, buildings with few windows), the typical layout, the typical building process. For example, do families get together and build a structure together? Do companies build communities with look-alike houses? Finally, students should consider how these choices relate to the culture and the environment. For example, in an area where there is snow, windows may be smaller. In an area where there is a high risk of fire, wood may rarely be used. More socially significant examples relate to the layout of houses. For example, an area in which a large number of bedrooms are the norm may indicate a priority on privacy. The design of a community around a central marketplace may indicate that the marketplace is the common meeting place and center of activity.

Lecture 19: Perfectionism

Lecture Outline for Listening for the Larger Picture, page 195
Use this outline if you'd like to deliver the lecture yourself.

> **INTRODUCTION:** Many people today live by the maxim "No pain, no gain," reflecting their conviction that significant gains are only made when one is pushed beyond one's natural limits. (e.g., Athletes, coaches, students might have this attitude.)
>
> We justify this attitude by the idea that perfectionism brings rewards. But are the rewards real? Or is the promise false? What are the costs and benefits of perfectionism? Why do some people have such strong perfectionist attitudes? Who is better off—the perfectionist or the nonperfectionist?
>
> In this lecture, I will define perfectionism and then discuss some of the costs and benefits of perfectionism in terms of business success, athletic success, educational success, and in terms of emotional and health costs. After that, I will briefly discuss some of the sources of perfectionism and some of the ways psychologists have devised to deal with perfectionism.

I. Perfectionism—definition

   A. Not the healthy pursuit of excellence

   B. Perfectionists, here, are those whose standards are high beyond reason or reach, people who strain compulsively toward impossible goals, and people who measure their own worth entirely in terms of productivity.

II. Costs versus benefits of perfectionism

   A. In terms of business success
      1. Test given to thirty-four highly successful insurance agents
      2. Test included two questionnaires—one to measure perfectionist attitudes, the other to assess tendency to measure personal worth and self-esteem by success and productivity
      3. Results showed that eighteen had perfectionistic cognitive styles; sixteen, nonperfectionistic.
      4. Results showed average earnings of perfectionists not significantly greater than those of nonperfectionists.
         a. In fact, the opposite was true—perfectionists who linked self-worth and achievement earned on the average $15,000 a year less than nonperfectionists.

   B. In terms of athletic success
      1. Study described attitudinal characteristics that differentiated Olympic-level male gymnasts from less successful athletes who failed to qualify for the Olympics.
      2. Results showed that Olympic athletes tended to underemphasize importance of past performance failures.
      3. Results showed that athletes who failed to qualify were more likely to get into near panic states during competition through mental images of self-doubt and fear of tragedy.

   C. In terms of education
      1. Study done of law students who sought counseling because of a high degree of stress. Many expressed urge to leave school, and most were suffering from depression or anxiety.
      2. Results noted an entrenched, perfectionistic thinking pattern in this group.
      3. Their problems in law school stemmed from the following:
         a. Prior to law school, these students were always the best.
         b. In graduate school, these students were no longer the "cream of the crop" because they were competing against equally intelligent people.
         c. Because their previous experiences left them psychologically unprepared for an "average" role, they are prone to perceive themselves unrealistically as second-rate losers.
         d. Their self-respect drops and they experience a strong desire to withdraw from painful circumstances.

   D. The conclusion of these studies is that perfectionists are not benefited in terms of productivity from their perfectionism. In fact, productivity may be lower because of perfectionism.

   E. Emotional costs of perfectionism
      1. The perfectionist may be plagued by loneliness and disturbances in personal relationships.
         a. Because perfectionists fear and anticipate rejection when judged as imperfect, they tend to react defensively to criticism, resulting in frustrating and alienating others.
         b. Because of a fear of appearing foolish or inadequate, perfectionists fear disclosure, which causes them to resist sharing inner thoughts and feelings.
         c. If perfectionists apply excessively high standards to others, they are inevitably disappointed.
      2. The perfectionist may be characterized by a number of mental distortions.
         a. All-or-nothing thinking (evaluating all experience in a dichotomous manner)
         b. Overgeneralizing (jumping to conclusions that a negative event will be repeated endlessly)
         c. Indulging in "should" statements ("I shouldn't have done that," "I should have known better," etc.)
         d. Perceiving the self as inefficient (Because of the perfectionist's compulsive drive to achieve a flawless product, he/she has trouble sensing when the point of diminishing returns has been reached and when a task should be considered complete.)
         e. Imagining that successful people achieve personal goals effortlessly and that he/she is the only one who ever fails or struggles
      3. These distortions cause perfectionists to adopt self-defeating strategies such as self-punishment and depression.

F. Health costs of perfectionism
   1. Risk of impaired health
      a. During the mid-1970s, reports correlated coronary disease with Type A behavior (behavior that is highly competitive, excessively achievement-oriented, impatient, easily frustrated and angered, time-pressured, preoccupied with deadlines).
      b. Perfectionism shares a number of traits with Type A behavior and may have the same risks.

III. Sources of perfectionism

   A. Perfectionism may have been learned partly from a child's interaction with perfectionistic parents.
      1. The child is regularly rewarded with love and approval for outstanding performances.
      2. When parents react to the child's mistakes and failures with anxiety and disappointment, the child is likely to interpret this as punishment or rejection.
         a. Parents personalize child's difficulties.
         b. Parents put pressure on child to avoid failure.
      3. Child anticipates that mistakes will lead to a loss of acceptance.
      4. Because child bases a sense of self-esteem on parents' approval, child begins to fear mistakes.
      5. This leads to fear of any experience or adventure in which the outcome is not guaranteed.
      6. As child grows up, the ratio of reward to punishment begins to shift in an unfavorable direction because children find it increasingly difficult to live up to unrealistic standards.
         a. Gap widens between expectation and performance.
         b. Child experiences stress and aversion to learning.
         c. Child becomes vulnerable to mood swings and loss of self-esteem.

   B. Culture as a source of perfectionism
      1. Perfectionist traits emphasized in religious doctrine, advertising, literature, schools, etc.

IV. Treatment for perfectionism

   A. Realize that perfectionism is not beneficial.

   B. Be aware that everything is not black or white.

   C. Be aware of and question the validity of self-critical thoughts.

   D. Test people to see if they really think less of you if you are not perfect.

   E. Set lower goals; allow yourself to be more average in some things.

   CONCLUSION: People don't normally think of a word with *perfect* in it as being negative, yet it can be a very dangerous and self-defeating problem.

Lecture Audioscript for Listening for the Larger Picture, page 195
This audioscript shows one speaker's delivery of the lecture, as recorded in the audio program. Use it as a resource.

OK . . . we've been talking about perfectionism . . . and . . . as is obvious from your answers . . . many people live by the maxim "no pain . . . no gain" . . . that means that if you don't have any pain . . . you're not going to make it . . . any profits . . . you're not going to succeed . . . and . . . this occurs in all kinds of areas . . . with athletes . . . coaches . . . students . . . etc. . . . and people believe that this attitude is good . . . because they believe that perfectionism . . . or perfectionist ideas . . . brings rewards . . . but the question remains . . . whether these rewards are real . . . or maybe the promise is false . . . and what *are* the costs and benefits of perfectionism? . . . why are some people so perfectionistic? . . . why are some people not? . . . and who's better off? . . . the perfectionist? . . . or the nonperfectionist? . . . now what I'm going to do in this lecture is define perfectionism . . . and then . . . I'm going to discuss some of the costs and benefits of perfectionism in terms of business success . . . in terms of athletic success . . . in terms of educational success . . . and in terms of the costs . . . both emotional and . . . health . . . physical . . . and after that I'm going to briefly discuss some of the sources of perfectionism . . . and some of the ways psychologists have devised to deal with perfectionism . . .

OK . . . first a definition . . . in this lecture I'm going to use the term *perfectionism* to mean . . . *not* the healthy pursuit of excellence . . . OK so not the healthy pursuit of excellence . . . but rather a perfectionist will be someone whose standards will be high . . . beyond reach . . . beyond reason . . . or people who continuously or compulsively strain . . . toward impossible goals . . . or people who measure their own worth entirely in terms of productivity . . . so let me repeat that again . . . a perfectionist in my use here . . . is *not* someone who pursues . . . who in a healthy way is pursuing excellence . . . but rather . . . someone whose standards are high *beyond* reach . . . or beyond reason . . . a person who strains continuously or compulsively toward an impossible goal . . . and people who measure their self-worth entirely in terms of productivity . . . how much they produce . . . they believe that what they're worth . . . is comparable to what they produce . . .

OK . . . let me talk about three different areas in which people have studied the differences between perfectionists . . . and nonperfectionists . . . how they compare . . . and first . . . let me talk about the business world . . . what are the costs versus benefits of perfectionism there? . . . OK what they did in this study is they gave a test to thirty-four highly successful insurance agents . . . so thirty-four successful businesspeople . . . and there were two questionnaires in this study . . . the first questionnaire measured their perfectionist attitudes . . . they wanted to see what kinds of attitudes they had . . . how much of a perfectionist they were . . . and the *other* questionnaire . . . measured their tendency to measure their personal worth and self-esteem . . . by their success and productivity . . . so the second questionnaire measured how much they rated their own value . . . their own self-esteem . . . by how much they produced . . . how much they made . . . if they were successful at their jobs . . . was this a requirement for them to feel good about themselves? . . . and what they found is that of the group . . . *eighteen* had perfectionist cognitive styles . . . sixteen . . . nonperfectionist . . . and what *do* you think they found? . . . actually what they found? . . . actually what they found is that the results . . . the results showed that average earnings of perfectionists were *not* greater than nonperfectionists . . . and in fact . . . the opposite was true . . . the perfectionists . . . who linked self-worth and achievement . . . earned on the average . . . $15,000 a year *less* . . . than nonperfectionists . . . so the perfectionists who connected their own self-worth with their achievements . . . actually earned less . . . than the nonperfectionists . . . OK . . . there's a case where it seemed to show that having a very strong perfectionist feeling . . . does *not* help a person succeed . . .

OK . . . now what about athletes? . . . and that's another area where people think it's really important to have a perfectionist attitude . . . well there was a study which looked at the different personality characteristics . . . the different attitudes . . . that differentiated Olympic-level male gymnasts . . . from the less successful athletes . . . who failed to qualify for the Olympics . . . so they compared two sets of men . . . one group who actually qualified for the Olympics . . . and one group who didn't . . . and they compared them in terms of their attitudes . . . what they found is that the Olympic athletes . . . tended to *under*emphasize the importance of their past performance failures . . . so . . . if they failed in the past . . . they didn't emphasize it . . . they basically took it in stride . . . and they kept looking ahead . . . rather than getting overly involved with their past failures . . . on the *other* hand . . . the athletes who did not qualify for the Olympics . . . were more likely to get into a panic state . . . during competition . . . and start having images of self-doubt . . . or fears of tragedy . . . they started getting really scared about their success . . . they got overly preoccupied with their success . . . whereas . . . as I said before . . . the Olympic athletes . . . tended to *under*emphasize the importance of past failures . . .

OK . . . let me look last in terms of education . . . this is important for all of you here . . . and how do perfectionist attitudes work in education? . . . is it a cost? . . . or a benefit? . . . now a study was done of law students . . . and . . . and . . . the group they studied . . . the subjects . . . were law students who sought counseling . . . because of a high degree of stress . . . and in this group . . . many expressed the urge to leave school . . . and most were . . . anxious and depressed . . . and what the psychologists noted . . . was that there was an entrenched . . . perfectionist . . . thinking pattern in this group . . . OK? . . . and their problems in law school stemmed from the following . . . so what happened was in law school . . . these students were no longer the cream of the crop . . . you know that if you get into law school you have to be a very good student to begin with . . . and these students were probably *always* the best students in all the other schools . . . in primary school . . . in college . . . but . . . when they got to law school . . . they were . . . compared, they were competing . . . with people who were *all* excellent students . . . OK? . . . and . . . before they got to law school . . . their experiences had not prepared them to be just average . . . their experience had only prepared them to be better . . . they had a hard time dealing with themselves when they couldn't be the best . . . and therefore they perceived themselves unrealistically . . . as second-rate losers . . . even though just getting into law school was demonstration of above-average intelligence . . . and ability. . . .

now . . . what these studies show . . . so the *conclusion* of these studies . . . is that perfectionists are *not* benefited in terms of productivity . . . from their perfectionism . . . and in *fact* . . . their productivity may be lower . . . because of their perfectionism . . . it actually may hurt them . . . more than help them . . .

so . . . we've looked at it in terms of productivity . . . but what about emotional costs? . . . which . . . which can't be measured as *clearly* as productivity . . . so you can't say . . . here $15,000 less . . . etc. . . . but what *are* the emotional costs? . . . well what counselors have found is that perfectionists may be *plagued* by problems in their personal relationships sometimes . . . again there are a number of reasons for this . . . first of all . . . because a perfectionist fears and anticipates rejection when they're considered imperfect . . . they're often defensive when faced with criticism . . . and people might get frustrated . . . or alienated . . . and what I mean by this is . . . for example . . . if you're a very very severe . . . a very strong perfectionist . . . you'll be afraid to let people think . . . that you're not doing something perfectly . . . and so you'll tend to . . . withdraw from criticism . . . or not accept criticism . . . *and* . . . people might get frustrated . . . OK . . . also because you're afraid of appearing foolish . . . or inadequate . . . you're afraid to open up to people . . . you're afraid to let people see the real person inside of you . . . your inner thoughts . . . because . . . well they might find out that you are not . . . perfect . . . and also . . . because a perfectionist applies high standards to everyone else . . . they're also often disappointed in other people . . . and . . . as I gave an example . . . as a teacher if my standards are too high . . . instead of encouraging my students . . . I might be disappointed . . . so it's not necessarily good in terms of personal relations . . .

OK . . . *another* emotional cost . . . is that the perfectionist may have . . . certain kinds of mental . . . distortions . . . by that I mean . . . distortions in their thinking . . . or perceptions of the world . . . let me give you some examples of this . . . one particular kind of mental distortion that most perfectionists experience . . . is what we call "*all-* . . . or-nothing thinking" . . . and that is they evaluate *all* experience . . . in a *dichotomous* manner . . . it's either good or it's bad . . . it's black or it's white . . . it's never gray . . . it's never in the middle . . . it's always all or nothing . . . I either did well . . . or I did badly . . . I did poorly . . . so . . . that's *one* mental distortion . . . a perfectionist's thinking is never in the middle . . . it's never gray . . . it's always "either . . . or" . . . thinking in a dichotomous manner . . .

another mental distortion is *over*generalizing . . . so . . . perfectionists jump to conclusions . . . so if they do something badly once they'll *always* do it badly . . . if they fail a test once . . . they'll *always* fail tests . . . if they can't learn English in one place they'll *never* learn English . . . they overgeneralize their mistakes . . .

OK . . . another problem is indulging in "should" statements . . . "I shouldn't have done that" . . . "I should have known better" . . . perfectionists always tell themselves what they should have done . . . or should do . . .

another mental distortion is perceiving themselves as inefficient . . . so because of their compulsive drive to achieve a perfect product, a flawless product . . . they have trouble sensing when the point of diminishing returns has been reached . . . and when something should be considered complete . . . and so they always think that they're *in*efficient . . . rather than human . . . so for example . . . they might spend eighty hours on something . . . and really only improve it a little bit . . . and they could have stopped at twenty hours . . . this may cause them to *feel* inefficient . . .

all right . . . the last mental distortion is imagining that successful people . . . achieve personal goals . . . effortlessly . . . and that *they* . . . the perfectionists . . . are the *only* ones that ever struggle . . . this is a *very* common one . . . I read a lot of times in students' journals . . . for my writing classes . . . and they talk about how it seems that everyone else has such an easy time . . . and they're the only ones who are suffering . . . and *I* end up reading the same thing in everyone's journals . . . but the students . . . the individual students . . . think that they are the only ones . . . that feel that way . . .

all right . . . now all of these distortions . . . all of these feelings . . . will lead to self-defeating strategies . . . self-punishment . . . and depression . . . or lack of motivation . . . so there are real problems . . . that are caused emotionally . . . by excessive . . . perfectionist . . . attitudes . . .

OK . . . now what about the health costs? . . . what about the health costs? . . . again . . . as mentioned before . . . there's a risk of . . . impaired health . . . or damaged health . . . way back in the 1970s . . . scientists first talked about a behavior that they named "Type A" behavior . . . I don't know if any of you have heard of it but . . . Type A behavior was characterized by competitiveness . . . achievement-oriented people . . . impatient people . . . people who are easily frustrated or angered . . . people who are always pressured by time . . . preoccupied by deadlines . . . and this was called "Type A" behavior . . . and they found that this Type A behavior was correlated . . . with high rates of heart disease . . . people who had heart attacks . . . often had these Type A characteristics . . . *and* . . . what people are suspecting . . . is that Type A behavior shares a number of traits . . . with perfectionist behavior . . . so there's no . . . there haven't been clear tests . . . but it is possible . . . that perfectionists are often Type A kind of people . . . and therefore . . . have a similar risk of heart disease . . .

OK . . . now where do perfectionists come from? . . . and again . . . we talked about that a little bit . . . what are the sources of perfectionism? . . . and we've mentioned basically that there are two sources . . . your childhood . . . your family . . . *and* . . . your culture . . . what happens in a family? . . . partly a child may be raised by perfectionist parents who might pass this trait down to them . . . OK . . . let me give you an idea of how this occurs . . . a child is very young . . . and whenever she succeeds . . . whenever she does something outstanding . . . she gets rewarded by the parents with love and with approval . . . well that happens all the time . . . but what happens . . . if the parents react to all the child's mistakes and failures with disappointment . . . with anxiety? . . . in that case . . . the child starts recognizing that when she succeeds . . . her parents are happy . . . and love her . . . and when she fails, her parents are disappointed and . . . maybe nervous . . . or reject her . . . so the child then . . . starts anticipating . . . that mistakes . . . making mistakes . . . will lead to a loss of acceptance . . . so if the child does something wrong . . . if the child fails . . . the child starts thinking that she won't be loved anymore . . . and so the child starts feeling that this . . . excuse me . . . the child's self-esteem is based then . . . on the parent's approval . . . it's not on his or her *own* sense . . . of *self-worth* . . . rather, it's on what *they* . . . the parents . . . think . . . are the parents happy? . . . or not? . . . "if I succeed, my parents love me" . . . "if I don't succeed, they don't love me" . . . and so what happens to the child . . . is that the child starts being afraid . . . afraid to experience things . . . in which the outcome is not guaranteed . . . if the child knows that he can't succeed . . . if the child knows that he can't be excellent . . . the child starts to avoid . . . that type of activity . . . and as the child grows up . . . the ratio of reward to punishment begins to *shift* . . . in an unfavorable direction . . . because . . . well . . . it's impossible to live up to continually higher and higher standards . . . OK so the *gap* . . . the distance between expectation . . . and performance . . . gets bigger . . . and the *child* experiences stress . . . and aversion to learning . . . so you can see the pattern . . . as the child is growing up, the parents associate success and achievement with love . . . and the child associates the two as well . . . and the child becomes afraid of failure . . . and then stops doing things *unless* he can be sure he can succeed at it . . . I think that's a very very *common* sequence of activities . . .

the *other* source . . . *culture* as a source of perfectionism . . . is a little more difficult to pinpoint . . . but for example in culture . . . *religious beliefs* can emphasize perfection . . . in many religions, people are *supposed* to be good people . . . they're *supposed* to *always* be unselfish . . . worthy . . . and that instills a form of perfectionism in people because they're always trying to live up to a standard that may be impossible . . .

advertising is *another* source of perfectionist beliefs . . . we're all supposed to be . . . beautiful, we're all supposed to be happy . . . we're all supposed to succeed . . .

schools encourage perfectionism . . . you want to be the top of the class . . . that's what you should strive for . . .

OK . . . so culture *definitely* is a source of perfectionism . . .

OK . . . now what can be done to treat perfectionism? . . . I'm going to list five ways that you might want to consider about . . . how *you* can deal with perfectionism . . . how you can reduce your perfectionist qualities . . . *one* thing is to realize that perfectionism is *not* beneficial . . . and that takes a lot of thinking . . . *and* . . . rethinking . . . *but* . . . start looking at perfectionism as *not* something that *really* helps you succeed . . . but actually . . . something that might *hinder* your success . . .

a *second* thing you might want to do is . . . be aware that everything is *not* black and white . . . everything is *not* "either . . . or" . . . there's a *middle* ground . . . so it's not either that you fail . . . or you pass . . . it's . . . well there's a middle ground . . . so everything is not black and white . . .

OK . . . and a *third* thing . . . if you start feeling self-critical thoughts . . . if you start thinking critical things about yourself . . . if you start criticizing yourself . . . *question* that . . . are they really true? . . . if you start saying to yourself "oh I'm so stupid I can't do anything right" . . . *question* whether that is really true . . . don't just take those self-critical thoughts for granted . . . question them . . . and be aware of them . . .

OK . . . *another* thing would be . . . to check with people to see if they *really* think less of you . . . if you're not perfect . . . many perfectionists feel that if they make a mistake . . . people will think less of them . . . *check that out* . . . don't just trust your own feelings but check it out . . . find out if they are *really* thinking less of you . . . most of the time . . . you'll probably find that people know that we're all human . . . and that we all make mistakes . . . so check that out . . . confirm it . . .

and the *last* way . . . to treat this . . . is to set *lower* goals for ourselves . . . all of us have to be average in *some* things . . . it's *impossible* to excel at everything . . . so *set lower goals* . . . allow yourself to be more average in some things . . .

so those are *five* ways you might want to deal with perfectionist tendencies . . .

in conclusion . . . people don't normally think of a word with *perfect* as being negative . . . *yet* . . . it can be a very dangerous and self-defeating problem.

Preparing for the Lecture, pages 194–195

First, have students write their own ideas (before listening to the lecture) in the column marked "My Ideas." Then have them share their ideas in groups and/or with the whole class. After this, have students listen to the lecture (without taking notes) to hear what the lecturer has to say about each of the questions they had just answered and discussed. Have students share what they remember after listening to the lecture without suggesting or expecting that they retain the full information at this point. Encourage students to listen for the information that is unclear or missing during the second listening (while they are taking notes).

Defining Vocabulary Audioscript, pages 195–196

1. maxim: The maxim "It's better to be safe than sorry" means that it is better to be careful than to rush into something and make a mistake.
2. No pain, no gain.: Many bodybuilders believe the saying "No pain, no gain." In other words, they don't feel that they are making progress unless they hurt a little.
3. pursuit of excellence: Competitions such as the Olympic games demonstrate human pursuit of excellence, a constant reaching for the highest limits of our possibilities.
4. to strain compulsively: She strains compulsively to reach impossible goals. She is constantly trying, but I doubt that she'll achieve what she wants because her goals are unrealistic.
5. to be prone (to something): That person is prone to getting into fights. In a crowd, if someone is going to be bothered, it's going to be him.
6. turmoil: The professor went through a lot of emotional turmoil while making a decision about whether to stay with her secure job and family or leave for exciting overseas opportunities.
7. to be plagued by self-doubt: Even though John tried to have more confidence in himself, he was always plagued by self-doubt and feared that he would fail.
8. to anticipate (something): Psychologists have studied the "self-fulfilling prophecy," the concept that if you expect something to happen, it often happens just because of the strong expectation. For example, if a teacher anticipates a student's failure, she may treat her differently, and thus bring about her failure.
9. defensive: When the man was questioned by the police, he was very defensive and appeared to be hiding something. This led the police to believe that he might be guilty.
10. to frustrate: Puzzles always frustrate me. If I can't get the answer right away, I get very impatient.
11. to alienate (someone): Jane thinks she's better than other people. This attitude alienates people and makes them feel distant from her.
12. inevitable: It's inevitable that it will rain during my vacation. If I plan a week off from work, you can be sure it'll rain!
13. cream of the crop: Every country chooses the cream of the crop of all its athletes to take part in the Olympics. Each country has to choose the best of the best.
14. dichotomy: Dichotomies exist in many parts of our lives: good and evil, communism and capitalism, truth and falsehood. However, in reality, everything is not black or white.
15. to reach the point of diminishing returns: I'm not sure I should spend another two days working on my pa-

per. I think I've reached the point of diminishing returns. It's quite good right now and two more days' work really won't make it much better.
16. <u>to distort</u>: If a mirror is not good, it may distort one's image.
17. <u>impaired</u>: The doctors say his impaired health is due to too much smoking and not enough exercise.
18. <u>to be preoccupied with deadlines</u>: June is the last month of the school year in many areas. At this time, all coursework is due. These deadlines cause a lot of tension for students. Many students become quite preoccupied with these deadlines and can think of little else.
19. <u>incidence</u>: There was a high incidence of birth defects among children whose mothers took a drug called thalidomide during pregnancy. Therefore, the drug was taken off the market.
20. <u>trait</u>: Certain traits characterize good readers. One of the most important traits is that they enjoy reading. Another one is that they read for overall meaning before focusing on details.

Possible Answers:
1. a rule or saying for good, sensible behavior   2. One won't progress without experiencing some discomfort.   3. to continue steadily, aiming for the best   4. to keep trying to do something because of a strong, perhaps unreasonable, desire   5. to have a tendency toward something   6. a state of confusion and excitement   7. to be repeatedly bothered by a lack of self-confidence   8. to expect something to happen   9. taking an attitude of protecting oneself against attack or danger   10. to cause someone to feel annoyed, disappointed, or dissatisfied, usually because one can't achieve what one is trying to achieve   11. to make someone feel distant from a person or group   12. describing something that cannot be prevented from happening   13. the best of a group   14. a division into two parts   15. to reach a point at which extra work brings less benefit than effort expended   16. to twist out of a usual or an original shape   17. harmed, weakened   18. to have one's mind fixed on certain due dates   19. the rate of something happening   20. qualities, characteristics

Note-Taking Practice and Quiz, page 196

Give students this quiz about one week after they listen to the lecture. Allow them to use their notes to answer the questions.

Questions:
1. According to the lecture, perfectionists are people who measure their self-worth in terms of _____.
2. According to the lecture, perfectionists are people whose standards are _____.
3. Two sources of perfectionism in adults are _____ and _____.
4. True or False? If false, correct the statement.
    ___ a. Results of the test comparing businessmen with perfectionist attitudes and businessmen without perfectionist attitudes showed that the average earnings of the perfectionist group were significantly higher.
    ___ b. Results of studies of Olympic male gymnasts showed that the most successful were those who emphasized the importance of their past performance failures and, thus, learned from them.
    ___ c. Studies show that students who have rarely fit into the "average" role are likely to consider themselves unrealistically as "losers" when competing with people of equal skills.
    ___ d. According to the lecturer, a perfectionist attitude is a positive trait.
5. Describe the study that was done to test the effects of perfectionist attitudes in the business world.
6. Describe the study that was done to investigate differences of attitude among successful and less successful athletes.
7. What reasons does the lecturer give as to why perfectionists may be lonely in their personal relationships?
8. What examples of mental distortions does the lecturer give that are due to perfectionist thinking?
9. State five ways to deal with perfectionist attitudes.
10. Essay Questions:
    a. The lecturer discusses how perfectionism may be learned partly from a child's interaction with perfectionistic parents. Discuss the sequence of steps that brings about this occurrence. How might a parent encourage excellence in a child without encouraging perfectionism?
    b. Describe an educational system that you think this lecturer would support. Describe the ideas in the lecture that led you to make your statements.

Answers:
1. productivity   2. beyond reason or reach   3. culture; childhood   4. a. F (nonperfectionist group was higher)   b. F (underemphasized)   c. T   d. F (negative)   5. See Lecture Outline section II.A.   6. See Lecture Outline section II.B.   7. See Lecture Outline section II.E.1.   8. See Lecture Outline section II.E.2.   9. See Lecture Outline section IV.A–E.   10. a. See Lecture Outline section III.3A for the sequence of steps. In response to the question about how parents might encourage excellence in a child without encouraging perfectionism, students might respond by suggesting that parents encourage and model the healthy striving characteristics and "what to do about perfectionism" ideas mentioned in the Post-Lecture Reading and Discussion. They might also include any of the five suggestions in Lecture Outline section IV. Alternatively, students might suggest that parents interrupt the typical sequence mentioned in Lecture Outline section III.A by, for example, rewarding the child for good attempts (not just outstanding performances), not reacting to the child's mistakes and failures with anxiety

and disappointment, or not personalizing the child's difficulties, etc. (Other answers are possible.) **b.** Responses should suggest that the educational system encourage excellence in children without encouraging perfectionism. Students might suggest that educators model and encourage the healthy striving characteristics mentioned in the Post-Lecture Reading and Discussion. In addition, students might suggest that teachers be aware of perfectionist traits in students and encourage those students to adopt some or all of the "what to do about perfectionism" ideas in the Post-Lecture Reading and Discussion or any of the five suggestions made in Lecture Outline section IV. Specific activities might involve encouraging a wide range of activities in the class, drawing on different types of intelligence and skills, and helping students recognize that it's OK to be average in some things and better at others. Teachers might also assist students in setting realistic goals. (Other answers are possible.)

Post-Lecture Reading and Discussion, pages 196–197

Answers:

1. A possible completed chart follows.

Healthy Strivers	Perfectionists
Set goals based on their own wants and desires	Set goals in response to external expectations
Set goals that are usually just one step beyond what they have already accomplished	Set goals that are way beyond what they have already accomplished (implied)
Set goals that are realistic and potentially attainable	Set unrealistic and potentially unattainable goals
Take pleasure in the process of pursuing the task at hand	Focus on the end result (rather than the pleasure of the process)
Their reactions, when they experience disapproval or failure, are generally limited to specific situations.	Their reactions, when they experience disapproval or failure, are generalized to their entire self-worth.

2. Answers will vary.   **3.** Answers will vary.

Writing Activity, page 198

These topics are open-ended. Therefore, a variety of responses are possible. Some considerations in evaluating students' responses to each topic follow.

Answers:

1. Students should describe aspects of a particular educational system and specific ways that system encourages or discourages perfectionism and healthy striving. They might use details from the readings and lecture about sources of perfectionism (see Lecture Outline section III, for example) or about perfectionist mindsets (e.g., from Lecture Outline section II.E.2) and examine how elements of the educational system relate to these factors.   **2.** Students need to describe aspects of a particular culture and specific ways that culture encourages or discourages perfectionism and healthy striving. They might use details from the readings and lecture about sources of perfectionism (e.g., from Lecture Outline section III) or about perfectionist mindsets (e.g., from Lecture Outline section II.E.2) and examine how elements of the culture relate to these factors.   **3.** In the letter from the school administrator, students might use examples from the lecture pertaining to the costs versus benefits of perfectionism and the results of studies showing that perfectionist attitudes did not result in greater benefits. In addition, the letter might warn parents that perfectionist thinking may not help students and discuss the study of the depressed and anxious law students. The letter might discuss the emotional and health costs of perfectionism. The letter should also include information about the difference between perfectionism and healthy striving and information about what parents can do to encourage healthy striving.   **4.** A response paper should demonstrate that the student has understood the concepts in the lecture and has, in some way, moved beyond a repetition of the ideas to a critical evaluation of the information (based on his/her own knowledge, experience, other readings, etc.).